CULTIVATING SENT COMMUNITIES

Missional Church Series

The missional church conversation continues to grow in importance in providing for many fresh ways to rethink what it means to be church in our rapidly changing context. The Missional Church Series, published by the Wm. B. Eerdmans Publishing Co., is designed to contribute original research to this critical conversation. This series will make available monographs as well as edited volumes produced from specially designed consultations.

Cultivating Sent Communities

Missional Spiritual Formation

Edited by

Dwight J. Zscheile

WILLIAM B. EERDMANS PUBLISHING COMPANY

GRAND RAPIDS, MICHIGAN / CAMBRIDGE, U.K.

Published 2012 by
Wm. B. Eerdmans Publishing Co.
2140 Oak Industrial Drive N.E., Grand Rapids, Michigan 49505 /
P.O. Box 163, Cambridge CB3 9PU U.K.

Printed in the United States of America

18 17 16 15   7 6 5 4 3

Library of Congress Cataloging-in-Publication Data

Missional Church Consultation (6th: 2010: Luther Seminary)
    Cultivating sent communities: missional spiritual formation /
    edited by Dwight J. Zscheile.
          p.   cm.   — (Missional church series)
    ISBN 978-0-8028-6727-8 (pbk.: alk. paper)
    1. Discipling (Christianity) — Congresses.   2. Spiritual
    formation — Congresses.   3. Mission of the church —
    Congresses.   4. Missional church movement —
    Congresses.   I. Zscheile, Dwight J., 1973-   II. Title.

    BV4520.M5545   2010
    266 — dc23

                                    2011041670

www.eerdmans.com

Contents

Contents

Preface

The missional church conversation is continuing to expand within the church today. Scores of books have come into print in the past decade that use the word "missional" as a key concept for discussing the identity, purpose, and ministry of the church. At Luther Seminary we are especially committed to contributing to this conversation through the graduate programs we offer — M.A., M.Div., D.Min., Ph.D. — as well as through special events. Our focus is primarily on trying to frame the ongoing missional discussion in light of biblical and theological perspectives, believing that central to this conversation is reclaiming the identity of the church as being basic to informing its purpose and ministry.

The church's identity has to do with its very nature: what the church *is* in light of its being created by the Spirit. So much of the missional church literature tends to assume this territory as being self-evident and moves all too quickly to focusing on what the church is to *do* on behalf of God in the world. But that approach can be hazardous to the missional discussion in terms of shifting the focus too quickly away from the agency of the Spirit in the midst of the church and redirecting it to the primacy of human agency and responsibility.

Being clear about the agency of the triune God through the Spirit with respect to God's mission in the world and the church's participation in that mission was central when the concept of "missional" was first introduced in the 1998 publication of the book entitled *Missional Church*. Since that time, maintaining the importance of this perspective has grown in importance as the Trinitarian conversation has become more nuanced as it incorporates more fully the perspectives of the social Trinity in relationship to the sending Trinity. This is the biblical and theological approach that Luther Seminary has sought to contribute to the missional conversation over the past decade: framing the role of human agency within divine agency with respect to the ministry of the Spirit.

One key event sponsored by Luther Seminary each year in contributing to this focus is our annual Missional Church Consultation. This consultation began in 2005 by addressing the dynamics of the missional church in context. Each succeeding year has picked up another theme regarding the missional church: the missional church and denominations (2006); the missional church and leadership formation (2007); the missional church and global civil society (2008); and planting missional congregations (2009). Each consultation consisted of the presentation of prepared essays by several established scholars as well as by a number of emerging scholars, many of whom were students in Luther Seminary's PhD program in Congregational Mission and Leadership.

One of the primary goals of Luther Seminary has been to contribute published works that provide biblical and theological frameworks for the growing missional church literature. To help us accomplish this, the Wm. B. Eerdmans Publishing Company has graciously agreed to publish as a series a number of the volumes of essays growing out of these annual consultations. The present volume represents the fourth such volume in print within the Missional Church Series.

The 2010 consultation was our sixth annual and was entitled *Cultivating Sent Communities: Missional Spiritual Formation*. This book of essays is the fruit of that consultation. We believe that the focus on spiritual formation is a crucial theme in the church today, and the work of this consultation sought to bring historical clarity as well as biblical and theological substance to this dimension of church life. It is our hope that readers will find this volume helpful in understanding more fully the complex character of spiritual formation, and that it will serve to deepen their perspective regarding the process and dynamics of spiritual formation.

CRAIG VAN GELDER
Series Editor

Contributors

Dinku Bato is an ordained minister in the Ethiopian Evangelical Church Mekane Yesus (EECMY), where he served as national coordinator of university student ministry for over a decade. Currently he is a PhD student in congregational mission and leadership at Luther Seminary.

Nancy S. Going serves as director of distributed learning for Luther Seminary's Center for Children, Youth and Family Ministry. A PhD graduate of Luther Seminary, she is a twenty-three-year veteran of congregational youth ministry, and she has spent four years teaching and leading the Youth and Family Ministry major at Augsburg College in Minneapolis.

Scott J. Hagley received a PhD from Luther Seminary in congregational mission and leadership in 2010. He is a teaching pastor at Southside Community Church in Vancouver, British Columbia, and serves on the national leadership team for Forge Canada.

David C. Hahn is a PhD student in congregational mission and leadership at Luther Seminary. As a pastor in the Evangelical Lutheran Church in America, he spent twelve years in ministry in Arizona, including serving a suburban congregation, leading a campus ministry, and cultivating an emerging church community.

Allen Hilton is minister of faith and learning at Wayzata Community Church, UCC, in Wayzata, Minnesota. He holds a PhD in New Testament from Yale Divinity School, where he also taught on the faculty before serving congregations in Seattle, Washington, and New Canaan, Connecticut.

Dirk G. Lange is associate professor of worship at Luther Seminary. He received his PhD in theology from Emory University after spending nineteen years as a brother of the Taizé Community. He is an ordained pastor in the Evangelical Lutheran Church in America.

Richard R. Osmer is Thomas Synott Professor of Christian Education at Princeton Theological Seminary in Princeton, New Jersey. An ordained minister in the Presbyterian Church (USA), he holds a PhD from Emory University and chairs the Committee to Write New Catechisms for the PCUSA.

Christian Scharen is assistant professor of worship at Luther Seminary. Ordained in the Evangelical Lutheran Church in America, he holds a PhD from Emory University. He previously served as a pastor in Atlanta and New Britain, Connecticut, and as director of the Faith as a Way of Life Program at the Yale Center for Faith and Culture.

Dwight J. Zscheile is assistant professor of congregational mission and leadership at Luther Seminary, where he received his PhD. An Episcopal priest, he has served congregations in Ashburn, Virginia, and St. Paul, Minnesota.

Introduction

> [E]arly on I start working with the leadership core in more of a
> teaching mode, studying the Bible and asking, "What is the
> missional church?" And in each case, the congregation has said,
> "You know, I think we want to do this." Then, after a while, they
> always say, "Now wait a minute, this thing is going to cost us our
> life." Right. That's the point.
>
> Missional pastor interviewed by Richard Osmer[1]

Across the United States and other Western societies in which the Christian church once held a privileged position, there is a growing awareness of a changed missionary situation. The erosion of various forms of cultural and social establishment that long propped up the church has raised deep and provocative questions about the church's identity in a strange new world. At the same time, renewed understandings have emerged of the church as missionary (or missional) in its very being — grounded in the triune God's mission in all creation. What does it mean to *form faithful disciples of Jesus Christ* in a missional church in light of *God's mission in the world*?

This question was the focus of the sixth annual Missional Church Consultation at Luther Seminary in St. Paul, Minnesota, on November 12-13, 2010. This book is a product of the presentations and conversations at

---

1. See page 39 for the full quotation.

that event, a consultation that brought together scholars, pastors, judicatory leaders, students, and other church leaders from around the world. The various voices converged around a series of central themes: (1) the church's new context has profound implications for spiritual formation; (2) God is actively engaged in formation and mission in the world, and God's mission proceeds in, through, and beyond us, even in the midst of our weakness and failings; and (3) missional spiritual formation involves a reordering of identity and communal life, a pushing out into the world that strips us of privileges and opens our hearts and hands to others on the way to renewal.

The Missional Church Conversation

The term "missional" has gained prominence in the past decade across churches around the globe. Its popularity was catalyzed by the seminal publication of the Gospel and Our Culture Network (GOCN) in 1998, *Missional Church: A Vision for the Sending of the Church in North America.*[2] That book, along with the other publications of the Gospel and Our Culture Network in the 1990s and early 2000s, comes out of an earlier conversation sparked by Bishop Lesslie Newbigin. Newbigin was a career missionary from England to India, a bishop of the Church of South India, who became one of the leading missiologists of the twentieth century. Upon returning to England at his retirement, he found that the "Christian" England he had left as a young man had lost its Christian identity. Newbigin initiated a serious discussion around what a missionary encounter of the gospel with Western culture might mean. The Gospel and Our Culture Programme, which he launched, inspired the North American equivalent, the GOCN.

Missional Church and the other publications of the GOCN recognized and analyzed the church's dramatically altered situation in the United States and Canada. No longer is Christianity at the center of society. Instead, the church finds itself on the edges, and Christianity is one religious option among many for individuals to choose from or appropriate as they will. Deep assumptions under which the church in Western contexts operated for centuries bear fresh examination and revision.

2. Darrell Guder, ed., *Missional Church: A Vision for the Sending of the Church in North America* (Grand Rapids: Eerdmans, 1998).

The missiologists in the GOCN made a pointed argument about what kind of response this new situation called for. Mere reversion to new strategies or techniques for attracting members or reclaiming lost ground will not suffice. Instead, the church's crisis calls for a deep theological and spiritual reenvisioning that begins with understanding God as a missionary God. It is in the triune God's sending movement that the church finds its identity. Mission isn't just something the church does on the side. It is its very lifeblood.

Since the publication of *Missional Church,* the term "missional" has exploded in popularity.[3] Some strains of usage of the term adhere to the original emphasis on renewing theological identity through discerning the church's participation in God's mission. Others use "missional" to describe yet another attempt by the church to be culturally relevant or strategic in reaching people in society, often with little attention to the theological questions at stake.

What is clear in the conversation that continues to unfold around the concept of "missional" is that the same old ways of doing and understanding church no longer suffice in many cases. Leaders are finding that old habits and patterns yield diminishing returns. There is a widespread sense of frustration, decline, crisis — and yet, in the midst of this, new hope. For missional church is an opportunity to rediscover what it means to be people of the way of Jesus in a dynamic and challenging apostolic environment. New energy is being unleashed through the missional conversation, and new generations of leaders are innovating exciting and fresh ways of being church through the power of the Spirit. Being a missional disciple or leader is nothing short of an adventure through uncharted territory, where the old maps no longer guide us but God goes with and before us, like the biblical journey through the wilderness.

Missional Spiritual Formation

Each of the authors in this book takes up this challenge uniquely, sharing particular perspectives and concentrating on specific dimensions of spiritual formation. Yet common themes are identifiable. For churches accus-

3. For an exploration and mapping of this development and the subsequent literature, see Craig Van Gelder and Dwight Zscheile, *The Missional Church in Perspective: Mapping Trends and Shaping the Conversation* (Grand Rapids: Baker Academic, 2011).

tomed to social privilege and institutional strength, missional spiritual formation involves a dispossession of all that would keep us from loving our neighbors in vulnerability and humility, as Christ comes to us. It is a movement outward, into the streets, public places, and neighborhoods where God may be found — at times in unlikely places — among the children, the strangers, those in need. Our own sinful humanity does not preclude us from participating. There are no quick programs or models to follow; instead, missional formation calls us to recover and deepen the core ancient practices that define us as Christians, yet within the context of cultural adaptation and innovation.

Dwight Zscheile begins the discussion by developing a missional theology of spiritual formation grounded in the Trinity. He traces a historical turn in construing spiritual formation as withdrawal from the world, which paralleled the emergence of Christendom. Exploring God's missionary engagement with the world as the Trinity opens up new ways of reenvisioning how our spiritual growth and discipleship are shaped by participation in the triune God's ongoing communal, creative, reconciling movement.

Richard Osmer shares research conducted among church leaders operating with an intentionally missional posture to trace distinctive practices, attitudes, and habits toward cultivating communities of missional engagement. He uses a variety of key theological and theoretical lenses to interpret this data and make sense out of the relationship between ministries of upbuilding and sending within the church's life.

Scott Hagley tackles short-term missions, one of the most popular ways in which churches engage in mission today, in light of research on their formative impact. While deconstructing some of the less helpful assumptions the church often brings to short-term missions, he proceeds to reframe them in light of the biblical theme of exile. Reconceived as exilic experiences, short-term missions offer significant promise for reinterpreting Christian identity in today's world.

Allen Hilton takes up the question of the role of Scripture in missional spiritual formation, first by demonstrating how *unintentional* people's participation in God's mission often seems to be in the Bible. In contrast to those who would find a clear line of eager missionaries in the biblical narrative, from Abraham to the church, Hilton explores how fallible, resistant, and uncomprehending God's key missionaries often are. This translates into a powerful message of hope for ordinary church members as they consider their own involvement in God's mission. Hilton shares some specific ways in which church members can be engaged in exploring God's biblical story within congregational life.

Christian Scharen works the key Christological theme of dispossession (Philippians 2) in three case studies of churches in the European and American contexts. For churches struggling with the legacy of Christendom, unlocking and opening their doors and lives to strangers is a vital way of adopting a new posture toward the world.

Nancy Going reflects on the missional formation of people in the first third of life, with a focus on adolescents. She contrasts the common ways of understanding faith development in psychological terms with a theological approach that asserts the missionary impact of young disciples' encounters with God and relationships with their neighbors in the church and world.

David Hahn unpacks the issue of congregational discernment — a central theme in missional discourse — both historically and theologically. He offers a compelling proposal for understanding congregational discernment as the triune God's action through engagement with the other in community.

Dinku Bato shares the remarkable story of missional spiritual formation in the world's fastest-growing Lutheran church, the Ethiopian Evangelical Church Mekane Yesus. Through a series of persecutions and challenges, this church has grown exponentially (from 20,000 to over 5 million members in fifty years) while offering a vital, holistic witness to the gospel.

Dirk Lange focuses on worship and communal prayer with respect to missional spiritual formation, drawing key lessons from the quiet but powerful impact of shared prayer among Christians in East Germany leading up to the collapse of the communist regime and the fall of the Berlin Wall. Lange finds in the theology of Luther and Bonhoeffer rich resources for envisioning the role of communal prayer in making missional Christians.

CHAPTER 1

A Missional Theology of Spiritual Formation

Dwight J. Zscheile

At the heart of the missional church conversation lies a challenge: to recover and deepen the church's Christian identity in a post-Christendom world in light of the triune God's mission in all of creation. This essay explores how the commitments of missional theology might inform the church's practice of forming disciples of Christ. In societies in which the surrounding culture can no longer be assumed to produce Christians, the church must engage the shaping of disciples with fresh intention. A missional view of God offers rich resources for reenvisioning how disciples might be formed in the power of the Spirit for faithful participation in the triune God's communal, creative, and reconciling movement in the world.

A Christendom Hangover?

As has often been noted, churches in Western societies whose cultures were once deeply influenced by various forms of Christendom (the formal or informal cultural, social, or political establishment of Christianity) are facing a crisis today. State churches — or former state churches — in Europe claim minuscule rates of Sunday attendance and participation relative to their populations.[1] In the United States so-called "mainline" Protes-

---

1. According to the European Social Survey, in 2004, weekly attendance at church services in Denmark was 3 percent, Sweden and Finland 5 percent, and France and Germany below 10 percent. Robert Manchin, "Religion in Europe: Trust Not Filling the Pews," Sep-

tant churches, whose identities were most directly linked to establishment, have experienced acute decline: membership, participation, and influence within their contexts have steadily eroded over the past several decades.[2] A resurgent evangelicalism has countered this trend in some respects, but evangelical growth is mixed.[3] Willow Creek's *Reveal* study demonstrated that even highly "successful" evangelical churches struggle with deepening the faith of their members.[4] Churches of all traditions face challenging questions of discipleship formation in a post-Christian culture.

In the United States, the percentage of persons claiming adherence to Christianity has stayed relatively robust.[5] Yet only a small minority of people actually attend weekend worship (17.5 percent on an average Sunday in 2005).[6] Moreover, the depth of the Christian identity of those who claim to be Christian warrants further scrutiny and concern. With the disintegration of cultural Christianity in the United States, what kinds of beliefs, practices, and identities are functioning among those who profess Christian adherence?

Perhaps the most provocative answer to this question comes from recent research conducted among young people. In *Soul Searching*, Christian Smith describes a predominant faith that surfaced in extensive interviews with teenagers from a variety of religious backgrounds, the great majority of whom were Christian. Smith calls it "Moralistic Therapeutic Deism" and defines its central tenets as follows:

---

tember 21, 2004: www.gallup.com/poll/13117/religion-europe-trust-filling-pews.aspx (accessed June 23, 2010).

2. See, for instance, Roger Finke and Rodney Stark, *The Churching of America, 1776-2005: Winners and Losers in Our Religious Economy,* 2nd ed. (New Brunswick, NJ: Rutgers University Press, 2005), 37; David T. Olson, *The American Church in Crisis* (Grand Rapids: Zondervan, 2008); Robert Wuthnow, *After Heaven: Spirituality in America since the 1950s* (Berkeley: University of California Press, 1998).

3. Olson, *American Church in Crisis,* 38. From 2000 through 2005, for instance, the evangelical church grew in twenty-eight states and declined in twenty-two states, including its traditional heartland in the South.

4. Greg Hawkins and Cally Parkinson, *Reveal* (South Barrington, IL: Willow Creek Association, 2007).

5. According to the 2008 General Social Survey, 75 percent of Americans identify themselves as Christian. Source: Association of Religion Data Archives, www.thearda.com (accessed June 24, 2010).

6. Olson, *American Church in Crisis,* 29. Only 3 percent were mainline Protestant. It should be noted that the percentage of Americans who *claim* to attend church weekly has hovered around 40 percent for several decades.

1. A God exists who created and orders the world and watches over human life on earth.
2. God wants people to be good, nice, and fair to each other, as taught in the Bible and by most world religions.
3. The central goal of life is to be happy and to feel good about oneself.
4. God does not need to be particularly involved in one's life except when God is needed to resolve a problem.
5. Good people go to heaven when they die.[7]

In Moralistic Therapeutic Deism, religion operates somewhere in the background of life, largely invisible.[8] It is instrumental, aimed at making one feel good about oneself and at resolving personal problems. Religion is a matter of individual, subjective choice; substantive differences between faiths are assumed not to exist. God is disengaged from everyday life in the world, unless a problem arises: "God is something like a combination Divine Butler and Cosmic Therapist: he is always on call, takes care of any problems that arise, professionally helps his people to feel better about themselves, and does not become too personally involved in the process."[9] The individual is at the center of the universe. Alan Wolfe draws similar conclusions in his book *The Transformation of American Religion*, pointing out how American religion has become co-opted by American culture, including the prevalence of therapeutic individualism. He writes: "American religion survives and even flourishes not so much because it instructs people in the right ways to honor God but because people have taken so many aspects of religion into their own hands."[10]

Given that young people's views are deeply shaped by older adults, there is good reason to believe that Moralistic Therapeutic Deism is also widely present among American adults.[11] Smith argues that Moralistic Therapeutic Deism has essentially colonized Christianity, as well as other major religious traditions, in the United States. A frightening indicator of this is the stunning inability of most young people in Smith's study to articulate their faith in the categories or language of their religious tradi-

---

7. Christian Smith and Melinda Lundquist Denton, *Soul Searching: The Religious and Spiritual Lives of American Teenagers* (New York: Oxford University Press, 2005).

8. Smith and Denton, *Soul Searching*, 129.

9. Smith and Denton, *Soul Searching*, 165.

10. Alan Wolfe, *The Transformation of American Religion: How We Actually Live Our Faith* (New York: Free Press, 2003), 36.

11. Smith and Denton, *Soul Searching*, 56.

tions, including Christianity. While highly articulate on many other matters, "the vast majority simply could not express themselves on matters of
God, faith, religion, or spiritual life." Smith concludes that these young
people could not express matters of faith because they have been insuffi-
ciently educated in their religious traditions and not given opportunities
for talking about their faith.[12] This echoes Wolfe's finding: "[I]n [Ameri-
can] religion, whatever the Lord requires, knowledge of his teachings is not
among them. . . ."[13]

Moralistic Therapeutic Deism must be understood against a larger
cultural backdrop of what Charles Taylor calls "a secular age" in modern
Western societies. Taylor traces the development from the Reformation
through the twentieth century of particular sets of assumptions, attitudes,
and perspectives that constitute the modern secular worldviews shared by
members of contemporary Western societies. He charts the shift from an
earlier "enchanted" universe characterized by a self that is relatively open
and porous to others and to the presence of God, to a sharply bounded,
"buffered" self disengaged from everything outside the mind. Whereas
once life proceeded in a rhythm of sacred or heightened moments (feast
days and festivals) interposed with "ordinary time," in the modern era
time was regularized to the ticking of mechanical clocks. In a process of
"excarnation," religion became disembodied from communal ritual, emo-
tion, and practice and focused in the mind, until humans were left alone,
concentrating on their own individual flourishing, which could be accomplished more or less without God.

The power of grace was replaced in this transition with striving to
attain moral norms available to all (not just spiritual elites, as in medieval
Europe). Taylor notes that "the plan of God for human beings was reduced to their coming to realize the order in their lives which he had
planned for their happiness and well-being." God's agency is largely
eclipsed in this modern worldview: "There is a drift away from orthodox
Christian conceptions of God as an agent interacting with humans and
intervening in human history; and towards God as architect of a universe
operating by unchanging laws, which humans have to conform to or suffer the consequences."[14]

12. Smith and Denton, *Soul Searching,* 133.
13. Wolfe, *The Transformation of American Religion,* 247.
14. Charles Taylor, *A Secular Age* (Cambridge, MA: Belknap Press of Harvard University Press, 2007), 38, 288, 242, 270.

The legacy of this secularism, despite various historical and contemporary counterstreams, is still pervasive in both the church and culture in Western societies today.[15] Many church members struggle to name God's presence or activity in their daily lives or in the world, particularly in categories, images, metaphors, or narratives from the Christian tradition. While nominal observance among Christians has been a recurrent problem since Christianity's establishment after Constantine, the contemporary situation seems particularly acute. In Christendom, churches could assume that the surrounding culture or families would make Christians; all the church had to do was make them members.[16] Today that is no longer the case. Without the scaffolding of cultural Christianity to support the church, fewer and fewer church members benefit from immersion in an integrated set of communal Christian practices, beliefs, and norms. Instead, many assemble beliefs, perspectives, and practices fluidly out of a variety of sources, some of which may be antithetical to core Christian commitments (see Moralistic Therapeutic Deism above). Taylor calls this the "nova effect" of an ever-widening variety of moral and spiritual options in late-modern societies whereby individuals seek to find their own way, express their true selves, or discover fulfillment.[17] By and large, the church has failed to take this reality seriously, preferring instead to operate as if nothing has changed, as if the old formative patterns of cultural Christianity still prevail. In this chapter I offer my attempt to address these realities in light of missional theology, a theology that offers a very different picture of God, the world, and human flourishing.

What Is "Missional" Anyway? Defining Some Terms

The missional church conversation started with a recognition that the church's relationship to its surrounding culture in the West had changed: the era of functional Christendom or a churched culture was over, and the

15. Among these are various forms of pietism, evangelicalism, revivalistic Christianity, nineteenth-century Romanticism, and Pentecostalism, which have sought to reassert an active spiritual presence in the cosmos or a sense of mystery and the numinous. It should be noted that this secularism has been strongest in the dominant white culture, while many oppressed groups and ethnic immigrant cultures have been more resistant to it.

16. Patrick R. Keifert, *We Are Here Now: A New Missional Era* (Eagle, ID: Allelon, 2006), 34.

17. Taylor, *Secular Age*, 299.

primary source of the church's identity and vocation could no longer rest on social centrality. In the years since its popularization in the 1998 book *Missional Church*[18] (from the Gospel and Our Culture Network), the term "missional" has taken on a life of its own.[19] Given the elasticity in its usage, the concept "missional" warrants closer definition.

Missional Church

By "missional church" I mean a church whose identity lies in its *participation in the triune God's mission* in all of creation. In the view of missional ecclesiology, it is God's mission that has a church, not the church that has a mission.[20] Much of the church's discussion of mission (even some of what is found under the "missional" term) still operates via the previous functionally Christendom paradigm of church-with-a-mission. In this paradigm, mission is something the church does on God's behalf. Mission is ancillary to the church's life (thus "mission" budgets, committees, and so on) rather than constitutive of the church's core identity. Mission takes place "over there" somewhere by specialist "missionaries." Local churches are only tangentially involved in mission in the church-with-a-mission view.

In contrast, missional church views mission as definitive of what the church is because the church is a *product of* and *participant in* God's mission. It exists to share meaningfully in the triune God's creative, reconciling, healing, restoring movement in the world. All its members are missionaries through baptism, not just a select few. Local churches are central to God's mission as they discern God's movement in their particular times and places and join up with it.

---

18. Darrell L. Guder, ed., *Missional Church: A Vision for the Sending of the Church in North America* (Grand Rapids: Eerdmans, 1998).

19. For a detailed exploration of the term and its usage, see Craig Van Gelder and Dwight Zscheile, *The Missional Church in Perspective: Mapping Trends and Shaping the Conversation* (Grand Rapids: Baker Academic, 2011).

20. Tim Dearborn, cited in The Archbishops' Council 2004, *Mission-Shaped Church: Church Planting and Fresh Expressions of Church in a Changing Context* (London: Church House, 2004), 85.

Missional Theology

This missional view of church is rooted in a missional view of God — thus "missional theology." Missional theology describes and interprets the mission of God *(missio Dei),* and the biblical story witnesses to this mission. The God we know in the biblical narrative creates humanity for a life of faithful and just community (Hebrew *shalom*) with God, each other, and the whole of the created order. When humans turn away, fail to trust God, and break relationships with God, one another, and the earth, God works tirelessly to restore them. God establishes a universal covenant with Noah, then chooses a particular family, Abraham and Sarah. This family grows first into a clan and later into a nation (Israel), called to bless all nations. God breaks the powers of empire to free God's people from slavery and gives them the Law to show to the world life in faithful covenant community. When they turn inward and fall prey to their own imperial patterns of idolatry and oppression, God raises up prophets to call them back to faithfulness. Finally, God sends his own Son, Jesus the messiah, to participate fully in human life, even to the point of suffering, torture, and death, so that humanity might be restored to community with God and all of creation. Jesus is raised from the dead as the first fruits of a new human future. The community of Jesus created and sent by the Spirit (the church) exists as a tangible sign and witness to God's reign over all creation, of a promised future already present that will be consummated on the last day.

Spiritual Formation

By way of defining "spiritual formation," I offer a slightly appended version of James Wilhoit's helpful definition: Christian spiritual formation refers to the "intentional communal process of growing in our relationship with God and becoming conformed to Christ through the power of the Holy Spirit," for the sake of the world.[21] Spiritual formation must be understood first and foremost as a work of the Holy Spirit. It is a communal process that unfolds over time, uniquely for each Christian and often in nonlinear patterns. Christ is the new Adam into whose image we are being formed,

---

21. James Wilhoit, *Spiritual Formation As If the Church Mattered: Growing in Christ through Community* (Grand Rapids: Baker Academic, 2008), 23. I have added "for the sake of the world."

but Christ must be understood in light of Trinitarian relationships. Spiritual formation is not just for our own individual growth; it is for love of God and neighbor. I will explore all these themes in more detail below; but first we must revisit spiritual formation in Christian history, for our present predicament is the product of a long line of contextual developments.

How Did We Get Here? Revisiting the Tradition

Christianity includes a rich complexity of traditions of spirituality and spiritual formation, far more than can be unpacked in any great detail here.[22] Christian spiritual formation takes place between multiple polarities: inner and outer; active and contemplative; individual and communal. For the purposes of this chapter, I want to highlight a particular development in the history of Christian spirituality, a turn in construing Christian spiritual formation that coincides roughly with the advent of Christendom and reflects the influence of Greek philosophy. It is a tendency to comprehend the Christian spiritual life as one of *withdrawal* from the world that continues to exercise significant influence on Christianity today, especially in its individualized, privatized, and modern Western forms.

The New Testament contains a multiplicity of voices and emphases regarding spiritual formation, from the synoptic Gospels' emphasis on the inception of the reign of God to Paul's teaching on participation in Christ through the Spirit.[23] What is striking throughout is the missionary framework within which spiritual formation takes place, always in relationship to Christ's ministry, the work of the Spirit, and witness to the world.[24] Just as, for Israel, the vocation of living a holy life was not an end in itself but to be a light to the nations, so the unfolding drama of Jesus' ministry and the formation of a community of believers play out on a public stage, in contact with multiple cultures, beliefs, powers, and ways of life. Spiritual transformation occurs within the emerging Christian community *and* in relationship with nonbelieving others. Often the apostles' own spiritual

---

22. For a helpful compendium, see Cheslyn Jones, Geoffrey Wainwright, and Edward Yarnold, SJ, eds., *The Study of Spirituality* (New York: Oxford University Press, 1986).

23. See C. P. M. Jones, "The New Testament," in Jones, Wainwright, and Yarnold, eds., *Study of Spirituality*, 58-89; Louis Bouyer, *History of Christian Spirituality*, vol. 1 (London: Burns and Oates, 1963).

24. On the missionary character of the New Testament, see David J. Bosch, *Transforming Mission: Paradigm Shifts in Theology of Mission* (Maryknoll, NY: Orbis, 1991), 15-178.

growth takes place as the Spirit sends them across social, cultural, and religious lines, such as Peter's encounter with Cornelius in Acts 10. The New Testament church is a church participating in God's mission — the first missional church.

During the centuries between the New Testament apostles and the conversion of Constantine, mission and spiritual formation unfolded in the context of costly public witness within a hostile Roman society: the spirituality of the martyrs.[25] Martyrdom (literally, "witness") was a way of life for the small but growing Christian communities who faced misunderstanding, resistance, and persecution. They attracted notoriety for their compassion, their egalitarianism, and the high standards of their moral conduct.[26] Spiritual formation had a decidedly ethical — as well as an eschatological — character. The dramatic faith of the Christian martyrs who died painful public deaths called into question the norms and values of pagan Roman society, attracted notice, interest, and commitment from nonbelievers, and deepened the faith of other Christians. Entry into the Christian community involved a long and intensive catechetical process that shaped new believers into a baptismal identity that stood in contrast to the norms and values of the surrounding pagan imperial culture.

A shift began to take place, however, with the toleration and eventual triumph of Christianity within the Roman Empire. Rather than being a community whose spiritual identity was shaped primarily through witness and service to non-Christian neighbors, the church found itself increasingly focused on influencing culture and consolidating its own institutional presence. The leading spiritual figures at this time and for the next few centuries found their identity in fleeing *from society* into the desert as monastics and hermits in order to grow into Christlikeness. Desert monasticism — as well as the later forms of early medieval monasticism that followed — represented a significant turn in the history of Christian spiritual formation that corresponds to this change in the church's missionary context.

For the desert fathers and mothers and the budding monastic tradition, leaving life in the ordinary world allowed a purity of focus on cultivating holiness through prayer, spiritual exercises, work, and communal

---

25. See Gerald Lawson Sittser, *Water from a Deep Well: Christian Spirituality from Early Martyrs to Modern Missionaries* (Downers Grove, IL: InterVarsity, 2007), 27-48.

26. Sittser, *Water from a Deep Well*, 54-71. See also Rodney Stark, *The Rise of Christianity* (Princeton, NJ: Princeton University Press, 1996).

formation. What was once a very tangible struggle by the church against external social and political opposition became interiorized into a fight against the spiritual powers of the devil, the passions, and the human will. The ideals were *ascesis* (discipline, training, or deprivation) and *apatheia* (freedom from the passions). The goal was *agape* (unconditional love), the highest virtue, reached only through a long process of self-discipline and renunciation.[27]

One of the major influences shaping this spirituality was Neo-Platonism, mediated into the Christian church through a variety of key thinkers, including Origen, Clement of Alexandria, Augustine, Evagrius of Pontus, Pseudo-Dionysius, and John Cassian.[28] While Platonic influence took different shapes in the thought of various patristic theologians, a number of common threads do appear. These include an abstract, transcendent view of God as pure truth and beauty, beyond the suffering and changeability of this world; a negative view of bodily passions; a focus on spirituality as interior attentiveness of the mind to God; and spiritual growth as a process of ascent out of the world, from the many to the One, from the material to the immaterial, and from temporality to eternity, often as a kind of return of the soul to its true home.

The reformulation of Christian spirituality in the terms of Neo-Platonism and Greek philosophy was a move of contextualization that fit the church's environment in the late-Roman Mediterranean world in many ways. The church must always be incarnationally translated (contextualized) into the cultural forms of its time and place; the danger lies in overcontextualization or undercontextualization. In this case, something important was lost. To begin with, spiritual growth increasingly became seen as an elitist enterprise accessible primarily to those who renounced ordinary life in the world. Jesus does call for a reordering of relationships, family, and community to follow him. Yet, what was once a spiritual call available to people of all social classes and walks of life became focused on those few who walked away from their homes, cities, villages, and vocations for the desert and the monasteries.

Second, the role of missionary witness with those outside the Christian community diminished as the church came to occupy a central place in society. The church's spirituality was less defined and heightened by its contrast with the prevailing norms of its context than its embrace and at-

27. Sittser, *Water from a Deep Well*, 85-93.
28. See Jones, Wainwright, and Yarnold, eds., *The Study of Spirituality*, 90-189.

tempted transformation of those norms. Along the way, the intentional, disciplined, and rigorous process of making Christians developed by the early church gave way to a cultural Christianity, and with it, the problem of nominality. Finally, Christian spirituality was interiorized and immaterialized by this embrace of Greek philosophy, with its tendencies to denigrate the material world and construe the spiritual path as an escape from it. The resurrection of the body was replaced by the immortality of the soul. David Bosch notes: "The church established itself in the world as an institute of almost exclusively other-worldly salvation."[29] Therein lies the paradox of an increasingly worldly, institutionalized church aimed at getting people out of this world to heaven.

The later medieval period saw the flourishing of monasticism as a primary locus for Christian spirituality. The missionary role of monastic communities in the Middle Ages, especially in spreading the gospel through northern Europe, derived in part from the depth of Christian spirituality that these communities fostered.[30] However, the spiritual formation of members of local parish communities typically received less rigor and intentionality. Benedictine monasticism brought a rich new spirituality of work and hospitality in which ordinary tasks were seen as spiritually formative; but the dualism of spiritual and temporal estates perpetuated spiritual elitism and escapism from the world.

Medieval mysticism brought the Neo-Platonic stream of Christian spirituality to the fore. In such seminal texts as Bonaventure's *The Journey of the Mind to God,* the material world is primarily an early stage to be contemplated on the way to the mind's mystical union with God. While the world is in some ways instructive, it is instrumental and to be left as quickly as possible on the spiritual ascent toward higher realms.[31] Often, spiritual formation in society beyond monastic relationships receives little attention.

Martin Luther's recovery of the priesthood of all believers and his reframing of the doctrine of vocation represent a key turning point in this narrative. Luther rejected the spiritual elitism of the monastic tradition and asserted the integrity and vitality of spiritual formation in ordinary life for all manner of people. He did so by recasting Christian freedom from escap-

29. Bosch, *Transforming Mission,* 213.

30. See Stephen B. Bevans and Roger Schroeder, *Constants in Context: A Theology of Mission for Today* (Maryknoll, NY: Orbis, 2004), 99-136.

31. Bonaventure, *The Journey of the Mind to God,* trans. Philotheus Boehner (Indianapolis: Hackett, 1993).

ing the material world to loving the neighbor.[32] Luther thereby retrieved the public and ethical dimensions of spiritual formation for all people, while retaining a strongly sacramental focus. The Reformation was in large part a project of deepening the Christian faith and identity of the church in Europe; yet it was essentially a Christendom Europe, and the church's mission remained primarily the maintenance of Western culture.[33]

The pietistic movements that arose during the late seventeenth century in Europe similarly sought to address lax Christian spirituality by a renewed emphasis on personal spiritual experience, conversion, and moral holiness. The evangelicalism that grew out of these movements continued the Western tradition's long-standing focus on individualized spiritual growth. Yet salvation came to be envisioned primarily as an escape from this world to heaven, the assurance of which is marked by disciplines of personal sanctification in the meantime. Pietism fueled the modern missionary movement, as well as major social reform efforts (such as the abolition of slavery). However, in many streams it fostered a view of God as uncontaminated by this world and a view of the church as separate from society.

Deism and liberal Protestantism took the long-standing tradition of Christian formation as moral discipline in a new direction by eclipsing God from a universe from which God was already understood to be largely removed. Humanity was now on its own to realize moral and social perfection. Thus we end up, in the late modern period, with Moralistic Therapeutic Deism and other distortions of Christian belief that diverge profoundly from the biblical narrative's emphasis on an active, participatory God engaged with human affairs — in other words, a missional God. The eschatological horizon of the New Testament and orthodox Christian thought is replaced with only the immediate present, a present that we construct by ourselves in the face of what seems increasingly an ambiguous future.

This brief narrative is, admittedly, an oversimplification of a very complex history. Nonetheless, the pattern of a turn away from the world that corresponded with the shift to Christendom bears critical reflection as we consider spiritual formation in the church's new missionary context today. The church now finds itself in a missionary environment that in many

---

32. See Luther's *The Freedom of a Christian* (1520), in Timothy Lull, ed., *Martin Luther's Basic Theological Writings* (Minneapolis: Fortress, 1989), 585-629.

33. Keifert, *We Are Here Now*, 30.

Beer. Monasticism Spiritual Formation Merton
Forest DO Not Depend on the Hope of Results

respects resembles more the first few centuries than the subsequent Christendom era. The recovery of a missional view of God, grounded in Trinitarian theology, offers fresh resources for reimagining spiritual formation in mission as participation in the triune God's communal sending movement in the world that God so loves (John 3:16).

Spiritual Formation within God's Ecstatic Communal Life

The development of missional theology in the West is rooted in the rediscovery of Trinitarian theology, with Karl Barth exercising particularly significant influence. In mid-twentieth-century ecumenical missiological circles, particularly at the 1952 International Missionary Council conference in Willingen, Germany, the theological basis for mission shifted from Great Commission obedience to the Trinity: "The classical doctrine on the *missio Dei* as God the Father sending the Son, and God the Father and Son sending the Spirit was expanded to include yet another 'movement': Father, Son, and Holy Spirit sending the church into the world."[34] This view of mission as the church's participation in the sending movement of God has come to be embraced across ecumenical lines, including by Vatican II.[35] But it has taken hold more slowly at the grass-roots level.

The Trinity is integral to a missional theology of spiritual formation. The God we know in salvation history, in Jesus Christ, and in the community of the church is a communal, relational God *for* and *with* us.[36] Such a theology must take into view not only the *sending* concept of the Trinity so characteristic of Western theology but also the *social* doctrine of the Trinity that has been so richly developed in Eastern theology and, more recently, by contemporary Western theologians.[37] To conceive of God, in

34. Bosch, *Transforming Mission*, 373, 89-90.

35. See *Ad Gentes Divinitus* I.2., in Austin P. Flannery, ed., *Documents of Vatican II* (Grand Rapids: Eerdmans, 1975), 814.

36. Catherine Mowry LaCugna, *God for Us: The Trinity and Christian Life* (San Francisco: HarperSanFrancisco, 1991). Jürgen Moltmann links the secularization of modernity with the loss of the Trinity. See Jürgen Moltmann, *God in Creation: A New Theology of Creation and the Spirit of God* (Minneapolis: Fortress, 1993), 1.

37. See LaCugna, *God for Us*; Jürgen Moltmann, *The Trinity and the Kingdom: The Doctrine of God* (Minneapolis: Fortress, 1993); John D. Zizioulas, *Being as Communion: Studies in Personhood and the Church* (Crestwood, NY: St. Vladimir's Seminary Press, 1985). For a helpful summary of the Trinitarian renaissance, see Stanley J. Grenz, *Rediscovering the Triune God: The Trinity in Contemporary Theology* (Minneapolis: Fortress, 2004).

whose image we are created and who is the primary agent of mission, not as a monad but rather as a relational community of three persons who share a common, interdependent life, has significant implications for how we envision spiritual formation.

In John 17:21, Jesus prays, "As you, Father, are in me and I am in you, may they also be in us, so that the world may believe that you have sent me." The deeply relational identity of Jesus, the Father, and the Spirit in the Gospels came to be described in later centuries in terms of *perichoresis,* or the mutual indwelling of the three divine persons. *Perichoresis* literally means "whirl," "rotation," "circulating or walking around."[38] With regard to the Trinity, it describes a relationship of dynamic mutuality, equality, openness, and shared participation among Father, Son, and Spirit. This divine community is composed of the relationship of genuine others; otherness is constitutive of God's Trinitarian life.[39] To be a person (whether human or divine) is to be in relationship, as John Zizioulas says: "The being of God is a relational being: without the concept of communion it would not be possible to speak of the being of God."[40] The triune community is composed of distinct persons united in a life of loving communion (*koinonia,* fellowship, sharing, belonging, or participation) precisely because of their otherness and difference. Difference makes communion possible.

Creation

At its Trinitarian heart, God's mission begins with the generation of others to share in loving communion: the Father's begetting of the Son and Spirit, and the creation of the cosmos itself out of nothing (ex nihilo). The Trinitarian life is not closed in on itself, but rather it is open, generative, and

38. Jürgen Moltmann, "Perichoresis: An Old Magic Word for a New Trinitarian Theology," in M. Douglas Meeks, ed., *Trinity, Community and Power: Mapping Trajectories in Wesleyan Theology* (Nashville: Kingswood, 2000).

39. "[A] study of the Trinity reveals that otherness is absolute. The Father, the Son, and the Spirit are absolutely different *(diaphora),* none of them being subject to confusion with the other two." John D. Zizioulas, *Communion and Otherness: Further Studies in Personhood and the Church* (New York: T & T Clark, 2007), 5.

40. Zizioulas, *Being as Communion,* 17. See also Stanley J. Grenz, *The Social God and the Relational Self: A Trinitarian Theology of the Imago Dei* (Louisville: Westminster John Knox Press, 2001).

outward-reaching. The classical term for this is *ekstasis* (literally "standing outside"). Creation is God's self-limitation in love and freedom so that created others might exist in relationship with God, not as equals but as created beings with their own creaturely integrity and otherness. Humanity is created in the image of God *(imago Dei)* for relational community. Creation is continuing and looks forward to the new creation — the promised new heaven and earth.[41]

This Trinitarian vision of a God of communion who creates humanity for community with God, one another, and the rest of creation offers a fruitful starting point for reconceiving spiritual formation. As we can see all too readily around us, the present human condition is marked by the fracturing of community, disordered and unjust relationships, and division. Adam's response to his freedom was to break communion, to turn from a loving, reconciled relationship with God, Eve, and the earth inward upon himself. "By claiming to be God," says Zizioulas, "Adam rejected the Other as constitutive of his being and declared himself to be the ultimate explanation of his existence." This is the tragedy of the human situation. It is only in Christ, the one in whom the human and divine natures coexist without division or confusion (in the Chalcedonian formulation) — in other words, where otherness and communion coinhere — that this condition is healed. Drawing from Irenaeus of Lyons and Maximus the Confessor, Zizioulas writes:

> The call has a specific content: the human being is called to bring creation into communion with God so that it may survive and participate in the life of the Holy Trinity. To this call, Adam in his freedom answered with a "no." It was Christ who fulfilled it, thus revealing and realizing in himself what it means to be truly human.[42]

God's mission is about the restoration of community, and our formation in Christ means our being redeemed, healed, and caught up in God's communal life by grace through faith.

Understanding the world as created by God in genuine otherness, with a dazzling array of difference in human cultures, ethnicities, perspectives, and ways of life that need not be cause for division, is critical for a postcolonial missiology. Christian mission involves building and restoring community in Christ through the power of the Spirit. Any attempts to

41. See Moltmann, *God in Creation.*
42. Zizioulas, *Communion and Otherness,* 43.

suppress, erase, or coercively denigrate genuine creaturely differences in the name of mission must be rejected. Seen in this Trinitarian light, the world is by no means godforsaken but rather imbued with deep integrity, richness, and vitality. Missional theology and spiritual formation must work from a robust and positive doctrine of creation that is also willing to name and address candidly and prophetically the distortions of human community brought about by human sin. Christian mission must point to Christ as the one in whom God's judgment and promise for humanity are most clearly revealed.

Life in the Spirit

Central to God's mission and presence within creation is the Holy Spirit, a key Christian way of talking about God's ongoing involvement in the world. The Spirit is the one who relates humanity with the Father and Christ, creates communion, restores relationships, and is a primary agent in mission. Jürgen Moltmann writes: "If the Creator is himself present in his creation by virtue of the Spirit, then his relationship to creation must rather be viewed as an intricate web of unilateral, reciprocal, and many-sided relationships."[43] Biblically, the Spirit makes God's power knowable through public works of communal restoration, justice, and mercy. It is in the Spirit that Jesus announces the jubilee promises from Isaiah of release to the captives, recovery of sight to the blind, and emancipation for the oppressed (Luke 4). The reconciliation of difference lies at the heart of the Spirit's communal work, as Michael Welker notes: "The Spirit of God gives rise to a multi-place force field that is sensitive to differences. In this force field, enjoyment of creaturely, invigorating differences can be cultivated while unjust, debilitating differences can be removed in love, mercy, and gentleness."[44]

Therefore, it is crucial that we understand Christian spiritual formation as *Spirit*ual formation — formation in and by the power of the Holy Spirit.[45] The spiritual life should not be understood as the nonmaterial dimension of human existence, but rather the new identity we have through

43. Moltmann, *God in Creation*, 14.

44. Michael Welker, *God the Spirit* (Minneapolis: Fortress, 1994), 2-3, 22.

45. See Gordon Fee, "On Getting the Spirit Back into Spirituality," in Jeffrey P. Greenman and George Kalantzis, eds., *Life in the Spirit: Spiritual Formation in Theological Perspective* (Downers Grove, IL: InterVarsity, 2010).

baptism when we dwell in the power and community of the Holy Spirit. Gordon Fee points out that there has been an unfortunate tendency to turn Paul's adjective *pneumatikos* ("life in the Spirit") into a more generic and bland English term ("spiritual") that misses the very powerful agency of the Holy Spirit so central to Paul.[46] The Spirit is the prime actor in Christian spiritual formation, and that action is *relational.* Our identities are reshaped and restored as we are brought by the Spirit into right relationship with God through Christ, as we experience the restoration of community in the church, and as we engage our neighbors and non-Christian others in mission in which the Spirit works between us.

Life in Christ

Paul talks not only about life "in the Spirit," but also life "in Christ"(see Rom. 8:1; 1 Cor. 1:30; and 2 Cor. 5:17, among the many uses of this phrase). Christology gives the Christian spiritual life definition, for Christ is the one in whom the image of God is restored and through whom, in the power of the Spirit, we are brought into community with God by grace through faith. The justification of the ungodly is at the fulcrum of God's mission. The incarnation signifies God's full participation in human life, even in its worst circumstances, so that humanity might once again participate by grace in the triune God's communal life.

Athanasius famously said, with regard to the incarnation of Christ: "He was made man so that we might be made God [literally, "he was humanized so that we might be deified"]."[47] The theme of participation in God (*theosis,* or divinization), derived from 2 Peter 1:4, has a long history in Christian thought. Developed by Athanasius, Irenaeus, and the Orthodox tradition most prominently, it also appears in Luther, Calvin, Wesley, and others in the Western tradition.[48] In many of its uses, the idea of participation in God operates within a Neo-Platonic framework, whereby

46. Greenman and Kalantzis, eds., *Life in the Spirit,* 39. On Paul's usage, see, e.g., Rom. 8, 1 Cor. 2, Gal. 5.

47. Athanasius, *On the Incarnation,* 54, in Edward R. Hardy, ed., *Christology of the Later Fathers* (Philadelphia: Westminster, 1954), 107.

48. See Michael J. Christensen and Jeffery A. Wittung, eds., *Partakers of the Divine Nature: The History and Development of Deification in the Christian Traditions* (Madison, NJ: Fairleigh Dickinson University Press, 2007); Norman Russell, *The Doctrine of Deification in the Greek Patristic Tradition* (New York: Oxford University Press, 2004).

participation is the ascent of the human mind through a process of purification to union with divine truth and beauty, similar to the weaker participation of the material world in the greater being of the immaterial forms in Platonism.[49]

I am not using the concept of "participation" in this sense. Rather, I am speaking of participation in God's gracious movement of reaching out to all of creation in reconciliation and service *(diakonia)* in Christ and through the Spirit. We find our missional identity not in our ascent out of the world to God, but rather God's descent *into the world* in Christ. In that descent, we are justified and caught up in God's grace, which extends to, through, and beyond us to our neighbors. Participation in God's missional life is not our work or attainment; rather, it is a free gift received in faith. The integrity and distinctiveness of our created humanity is not confused or lost along the way, for reconciliation and communion are predicated on the very existence of otherness.[50]

Martin Luther understood this kind of deep participation of the believer in Christ in terms of the "happy exchange," according to which Christ takes on all human sinfulness and suffering and gives us the benefits of his righteousness (see 2 Cor. 5:21).[51] We are reborn and freed in Christ in this grace. Yet we are reborn and freed not as an end in itself, as if our individual salvation were a self-contained matter, but rather to share in the power of the Spirit, in God's ongoing work of loving service and reconciliation in the world — the creation and restoration of communion among all kinds of people. In *The Freedom of a Christian,* Luther says:

> We conclude, therefore, that a Christian lives not in himself, but in Christ and in his neighbor. Otherwise he is not a Christian. He lives in Christ through faith, in his neighbor through love. By faith he is caught up beyond himself into God. By love he descends beneath himself into his neighbor. Yet he always remains in God and in his love. . . .[52]

---

49. For a helpful discussion of the Platonic background, see Paul S. Fiddes, *Participating in God: A Pastoral Doctrine of the Trinity* (Louisville: Westminster John Knox Press, 2000), 11-56.

50. See Zizioulas, *Communion and Otherness,* 37.

51. Martin Luther, *On the Councils and the Church* (1539), in *Luther's Works,* 41:93-106 (Philadelphia: Fortress, 1966); see also Carl E. Braaten and Robert W. Jenson, *Union with Christ: The New Finnish Interpretation of Luther* (Grand Rapids: Eerdmans, 1998), 32.

52. John Dillenberger, ed., *Martin Luther: Selections from His Writings* (Garden City, NY: Doubleday, Anchor Books, 1961), 80.

We receive a new identity in Christ that draws us closer both to God and our neighbor. Spiritual formation as missional participation involves an ethical dimension that leads us into the world.

Life "in Christ" means the decentering of the self in a reordering of identity in which our relationship with God is primary. This decentering allows for relationships with others to flourish, for it makes space for them. No longer are we at the center of our own universes, focused on individual self-actualization in isolation from God and others, as a kind of lonely journey of self-construction. Instead, we live *with* and *for* others, just as God, in Christ, gave himself to be with and for us. The Spirit's movement decenters those whose social location affords them privilege and power and empowers those whom society has dispossessed. In the power of the Spirit, new relationships of mutuality and equality become possible.

The focal point of Christian mission is God's utter identification with humanity in the incarnation, passion, and resurrection — an identification that takes place with humans, as we are, in the particularity of human cultures and historical moments. In the Nicene Creed we affirm that Jesus "was crucified under Pontius Pilate," thereby recognizing that God comes to us in the very specificity of our circumstances, even to those suffering under imperial oppression and injustice, to the victims of torture, to those condemned to die the most shameful and horrific deaths, as Christ did. In this sense, compassion is at the heart of God's mission to us in Christ: the sharing of our sufferings, the bearing of our burdens, the commitment to walk in our shoes all the way into the lowest, worst, most unjust, sin-scarred places in human life, the places of greatest despair ("My God, my God, why have you forsaken me?").[53] Christian spiritual formation in mission involves compassionate identification, participation, and companionship with those suffering under sin, oppression, injustice, exclusion, and despair.[54] We are to go where Christ went in order to be formed into his likeness, to walk with others the ways of the world's forsakenness because we are found by him and find him there. As Paul says, "I have been crucified with Christ; and it is no longer I who live, but it is Christ who lives in me" (Gal. 2:19b-20). Sharing in Christ's cruciform mission involves vulnerability, not coercion; weakness, not worldly strength; solidarity and service, not "lording over" or mere benevolence

---

53. See Andrew Root, *The Promise of Despair: The Way of the Cross as the Way of the Church* (Nashville: Abingdon, 2010).

54. See Jürgen Moltmann, *The Crucified God* (Minneapolis: Fortress, 1993), 270-78.

(Luke 22:24-27); embracing others, not excluding them.[55] It is a mission that takes place on the cultural and social terms of those to whom we are sent (as did the incarnation), not primarily on the missionaries' terms. Above all, it is a sharing of the loving communion in which we have been restored and which is a gift given to us so that we might give it away.

The Curriculum of the World

From a missional perspective, God and neighbor (the Other and others) play central roles in spiritual formation. Such formation plays out not just within the limited sphere of church gatherings, activities, or programs (though the formative role of the gathered community is critically important), but also in the workplaces, streets, markets, family rooms, and public squares where we encounter our neighbors, especially those who are strangers. Missional theology insists on the importance of the curriculum of the world in spiritual formation, not as a place to be shunned, rejected, or withdrawn from, but rather as a place to encounter God — especially in those who have been shunned or rejected.

Benedictine tradition, echoing Matthew 25:35 and Hebrews 13:2, has recognized the spiritually formative promise of the stranger, encouraging that strangers be "welcomed as Christ."[56] Missional theology leads us one step further. A Trinitarian theology of otherness and communion invites us to recognize that our neighbors, in all their difference, are integral to our growth in Christ. It is through encounters with strangers, especially those unlike us, that we come to know the richness of the image of God and learn new insights into the gospel. God's own Trinitarian life is reciprocal in its mutual sharing. Our life in Christ must also be open to receiving from others, especially strangers. Indeed, biblically speaking, it is precisely in these encounters with strangers that disciples often are converted, deepened, provoked, and encouraged (see Luke 10:1-12; Luke 24:13-35; John 4:1-42; Acts 9–10, among others). Lamin Sanneh has explored this provocatively in the context of missionary encounters in Africa.[57] Paul Chung

---

55. Miroslav Volf, *Exclusion and Embrace: A Theological Exploration of Identity, Otherness, and Reconciliation* (Nashville: Abingdon, 1996).

56. *The Rule of St. Benedict*, trans. Anthony C. Meisel and M. L. del Mastro (New York: Image Books, 1975), 89.

57. Lamin O. Sanneh, *Translating the Message: The Missionary Impact on Culture* (Maryknoll, NY: Orbis, 1989).

draws on Luther's concept of "irregular grace" to highlight the mutually transformative, enriching potential of dialogue with those from other faiths.[58] Missional theology calls us to an expansive understanding of God's work in those most unfamiliar to us and in God's wider world. I must emphasize that our relationships in mission with diverse others are not merely instrumental to our own self-growth but anticipatory of the eschatological communion that is our destiny, where we will join with people of every tribe and nation at the heavenly banquet.

Discerning God's Reign

Jesus used the image of the banquet as one of many to describe the reign of God, which further defines God's mission. God's reign is now and not yet, hidden but provocatively present. It involves the reordering of human community so that the proud are humbled and the lowly raised up. It en- *Magnifical* compasses healing, forgiveness, mercy, and restorative justice. It springs from the seemingly smallest and most insignificant sources (the mustard seed), yet calls into question the very foundations of empires. The excluded, marginalized, poor, and shunned go to the head of the line in the reign of God — before the socially prominent and powerful do. It is embodied in practices of service, hospitality, peacemaking, reconciliation, care, and witness.[59]

The reign of God gives shape to the formation of Christian disciples. It calls us to a new kind of attentiveness to God's presence and movement as we discern and participate in that reign in our lives and world. We must be prepared to encounter God in unexpected places, moving in surprising and paradoxical ways, often at the edges rather than the center. The reign is fundamentally uncontrollable: it is not something we build or extend; rather, it is a reality that we are invited to seek, enter, receive, and inherit.[60] As we discover and name the reign of God in our midst, we are called to testify to it, even in the face of the ambivalence, hostility, misunderstanding, or the persecution of society. The reign is fundamentally connectional, bringing people into right relationships with God, one another, and

58. Paul S. Chung, *Christian Mission and a Diakonia of Reconciliation: A Global Reframing of Justification and Justice* (Minneapolis: Lutheran University Press, 2008), 46-52.
59. See Guder, *Missional Church*, 87-109.
60. Guder, *Missional Church*, 93.

right relationship?

all of creation. Discerning and participating in it leads us into relationship with our neighbors.

When we understand mission as primarily God's movement in our lives and in the world, we are confronted with a significant challenge: discernment. Given human sinfulness, how can we faithfully identify what is, in fact, God's mission in our time and place? The history of the *missio Dei* concept is riddled with contention in this regard, for its expansiveness encompasses a wide range of interpretations of God's missionary activity.[61] This accounts both for the concept's attractiveness and the limits of its usefulness: it can become a vacuum for us to fill. Ditches lie on either side of faithful interpretation. The first ditch, which emerged most prominently with J. C. Hoekendijk's secularized approach in the 1960s, is that God is primarily or exclusively at work in the processes of secular history, eclipsing the role of the church.[62] The other ditch tends to equate the church with God's mission or reign too narrowly.[63] The solution is communal discernment that must be rooted in the biblical narrative, theological tradition, and the leading of the Holy Spirit as the Christian community engages its neighbors in the world. Spiritual discernment is one of the gifts of the Spirit to the body of Christ (1 Cor. 12:10).

In the lives of many congregations today, "discernment" is seen as an episodic or extraordinary activity, often associated with preparing to call a new pastor, launch a capital campaign, or select candidates for ordination. There is a specific outcome in mind, after which discernment can be put aside until the next project or problem arises. However, missional theology calls for a quite different approach.

In the congregation where I serve part-time, we have engaged in a series of practices and processes over the past several years aimed at building the congregation's capacity to discern God's presence and movement in its own life and in the surrounding community. These have included using

61. See Georg F. Vicedom, *The Mission of God: An Introduction to a Theology of Mission* (St. Louis: Concordia, 1965); H. H. Rosin, *'Missio Dei': An Examination of the Origin, Contents and Function of the Term in Protestant Missiological Discussion* (Leiden: Interuniversity Institute for Missiological and Ecumenical Research, Department of Missiology, 1972).

62. Johannes Christiaan Hoekendijk, *The Church Inside Out* (Philadelphia: Westminster, 1966).

63. For a more detailed mapping of interpretations of *missio Dei* and the reign of God, see Van Gelder and Zscheile, *The Missional Church in Perspective*.

Appreciative Inquiry,[64] Dwelling in the Word,[65] Dwelling in the World,[66] and various forms of small-group exercises. At a recent annual meeting, when the fruits of some of these discernment exercises were presented by members of the church board, a particularly astute lay leader commented that he had not liked "discernment" in the past because he thought it was just a way to get a problem solved. However, he now realized that it is really about a process of *wondering* that must be ongoing.

This comment captures a powerful idea: missional Christian formation means cultivating a posture of *wonder:* wonder about the Bible's narrative of God's surprising and powerful acts in history; wonder about the mystery of God's presence and movement in our own lives; wonder about what God might be up to in our neighborhoods and world. A posture of wonder and awe means surrendering many of the plans, programs, and projects by which we in late-modern society seek to manage and control the future. It invites us to open our hearts and hands to God, one another, and our neighbors. It expects surprise. It anticipates God's promised future of reconciliation and communion to break into the present.

When we engage in this kind of discernment and wondering, we use our imaginations. Missional spiritual formation involves the shaping of imagination. I began this chapter with the challenge of Christian formation in a culture whose social imaginary remains deeply secularized. By "social imaginary" I refer to the ways in which ordinary people understand their social existence, how they assume the world works, the expectations that are normally met, the "largely unstructured and inarticulate understanding of our whole situation, within which particular features of our world show up for us in the sense they have."[67]

In using the term "imagination," I'm referring specifically to its socially embodied sense.[68] A socially embodied view of imagination recog-

---

64. See Mark Lau Branson, *Memories, Hopes, and Conversations: Appreciative Inquiry and Congregational Change* (Herndon, VA: Alban Institute, 2004).

65. See Keifert, *We Are Here Now.*

66. Dwelling in the World is a practice developed by South African churches whereby members are invited to think of a time during the past week when they had an opportunity to share the peace with someone in their daily life. They are encouraged to revisit that moment imaginatively and consider what God might have been doing and what God might have wanted to do in that encounter.

67. Taylor, *A Secular Age,* 171-73.

68. For a discussion of alternative views of imagination and its long history in Western thought, see Richard Kearney, *The Wake of Imagination* (New York: Routledge, 1988).

nizes the formative power of social and cultural relationships to shape human thought and perception.[69] When we speak of Christian spiritual formation, we are talking about the shaping and formation of the social imaginary within which Christians live. As Charles Taylor notes, social imaginaries are highly complex, influenced by a variety of conscious and unreflected-on forces and norms. For most of us, they are the air we breathe, something we take for granted, something by which we make sense of our lives and world.

Imagination is shaped by practice.[70] As a number of works in recent years have explored, such practices are deeply formative, particularly when socially embodied in communities.[71] Spiritual formation happens when we engage in mission. Simultaneously, practices of spiritual formation have a missionary dimension. At times in the church's life, spiritual formation has been construed distinct from relationships of service and witness with our neighbors. Yet, biblically speaking, there is no distinction. The disciples learn what it means to follow Jesus as they experience ministry with him; their formation takes place in the context of mission. The posture of wonder and awe that missional theology invites us to adopt suggests an understanding of missional spiritual formation in which action and reflection, service and contemplation, individual and community are deeply integrated in a seamless rhythm.

Being Conformed to Christ

One of the primary ways in which the New Testament talks about spiritual formation is imitation or being conformed to Christ. Paul sees the Christian life as a modeling or patterning after the life and ministry of Christ. Moreover, he is unhesitant to offer his own life as an example to be imitated, recognizing that those to whom he writes must have living examples of Christian discipleship to see and experience (see Phil. 3:17; 2 Tim. 3:10). This imitative approach accords with the predominant Greco-Roman par-

---

69. See Graham S. Ward, *Cultural Transformation and Religious Practice* (New York: Cambridge University Press, 2005).

70. Taylor, *A Secular Age*, 173; see also Alasdair C. MacIntyre, *After Virtue: A Study in Moral Theory* (Notre Dame, IN: University of Notre Dame Press, 1981).

71. See Miroslav Volf and Dorothy C. Bass, *Practicing Theology: Beliefs and Practices in Christian Life* (Grand Rapids: Eerdmans, 2002); Dorothy C. Bass, *Practicing Our Faith: A Way of Life for a Searching People* (San Francisco: Jossey-Bass, 1997).

adigm of education as *paideia,* or character formation through a process of relational apprenticeship.[72] When understood in this mode of relational and experiential patterning, imitation remains a fruitful way to conceive of Christian spiritual formation.

Imitative approaches to spiritual formation and mission, however, have also fallen prey to distortions in which God's active presence is minimized, especially in the modern period. In the church-with-a-mission approach that I have referred to above, mission is primarily construed as something done *on God's behalf,* often through trying to imitate what Christ did.[73] Not only does the reality of human sinfulness severely constrain our ability to imitate Christ effectively, but God's own primary role in mission is underacknowledged. For Paul, imitation of Christ was only possible through the power of the Spirit. It must be so for us, too.

The paradigm of *participation* must be set alongside imitation, for it places the priority on God's agency in mission and spiritual growth.[74] The epistemological revolution in Western thought that began with Descartes made the individual self the center of the universe. Human knowledge came to be seen as constructed by the self. This has led, in part, to approaches to Christian theology and mission focused on human self-growth or actualization, understood in terms of individual autonomy and self-determination. There is little space within these conceptions for God's role. In late-modern Western cultures, many people still inhabit this modern social imaginary in which God has set moral laws for us to follow but isn't directly involved in our daily lives. Missional theology invites us to something of a reverse revolution: a God-centered view of mission that stands in care of the other.

What does it mean to direct our focus on God's presence, movement, and activity in mission and spiritual formation? This calls for a healthy dose of hermeneutical humility and disciplined discernment. The Word and Spirit must be at the center of discernment. We must always take into

72. See Ellen T. Charry, *By the Renewing of Your Minds: The Pastoral Function of Christian Doctrine* (New York: Oxford University Press, 1997); David H. Kelsey, *To Understand God Truly* (Louisville: Westminster John Knox, 1992), 63-75.

73. Much of the contemporary literature that claims the term "missional" perpetuates this approach, often through an incarnational emphasis without a sufficiently Trinitarian framework.

74. For further discussion on a participatory approach to mission, see Scott Hagley et al., "Toward a Missional Theology of Participation," *Missiology* 37, no. 1 (Jan. 2009); Van Gelder and Zscheile, *Missional Church in Perspective.*

account our propensity to misconstrue and distort our views of God. One of the key avenues to correct for this is a relational approach in which otherness and difference play a pivotal role. We are more likely to recognize God's missional movement faithfully when we do so in dialogue with others whose social location, life experience, and perspectives may challenge our own.

At root, a theocentric approach to missional spiritual formation expects that God is up to something big in our lives, in Christian community, and in the surrounding world. We are caught up through the Spirit in the reconciliation of the world by God in Christ (2 Cor. 5). This movement generates communion as it unfolds within relationships with God and our neighbors. It breaks down divisions while retaining created differences. Through the power of the Spirit we are conformed to Christ. The way of the cross, of descent, disempowerment, and loving service becomes the way of resurrection, empowerment, and human flourishing in a new and just human community.

These movements are focused in the church's life in the sacraments of baptism and Eucharist. Through baptism, we find our new identity as people of the new creation, forgiven and initiated into a community of promise. In the Eucharist we participate in God's self-giving grace as diverse people united in Christ. The symbols of daily life (the bread and wine) are broken open in solidarity with all the brokenness of the world. Through the brokenness of the body and blood of Christ comes grace that heals and reconciles, offering a foretaste in the Spirit of our destiny. We participate partially but meaningfully in that end toward which the Christian spiritual life moves: that great heavenly banquet around which people from every imaginable tribe and culture gather with God in love.

Conclusion

In this chapter I have emphasized *participation:* God's mutual, *perichoretic,* participatory life in the Trinity; Christ's participation in human life and suffering in the incarnation and passion; our participation through Christ and the power of the Spirit in mission in the lives of our neighbors; and our promised participation in Christ's resurrection and eternal communion with the Trinity. Missional spiritual formation is a multifaceted, participatory endeavor that unfolds within and outside the gathered community in a web of relationships and influences with God and others in the world. The core Christian practices, such as worship, prayer, service, Sabbath, fellowship, and witness all have missional dimensions. Through them God shapes us into a called people who are sent to testify to the inbreaking of God's reign in a world of many faiths and no faith. That testimony unfolds in part through the public practices of the Christian community as it lives a way of life marked by mercy, forgiveness, generosity, reconciliation, and hope. Through the Spirit this community offers a living, visible alternative to a society rent by enmity, division, greed, injustice, and hopelessness.

If the emergence of Christendom in the late patristic and early medieval period brought a turn inward in Christian spiritual formation, away from the world, today's post-Christian cultural context invites us to reimagine formation in deep engagement with the world. The advent of new monastic communities in the West, which are intentionally choosing to live a covenantal life of Christian formation *amid* their neighbors in society, is a fruitful sign. Rather than abandoning the places of empire, as the desert fathers and mothers did, these communities in many cases are choosing to dwell in the "abandoned places of empire," where they live in relationships of hospitality, service, and witness with those on the underside of society.[75]

These communities represent contemporary expressions of the many streams of monasticism that have historically found their identity in engagement with, rather than withdrawal from, the world. Such monastic communities function as parables of Christian life for the wider church and society. They embody gospel values in their sacrificial service and illustrate a depth of life in Christ and community for others to see. At the same time (and in collaboration with these communities), Christians in ordinary congregations must innovate new ways of living as disciples. Now is a time in which the whole church would benefit from the mutual sharing of lived stories, parables, and illustrations of vital and risky Christian witness and service.[76] Every context is different, yet such stories are integral to enriching our communal imagination for mission.

The church's vocation to serve as the body of Christ in the world — a living community that continues in Christ's ministry of reconciliation in

75. See Jonathan Wilson-Hartgrove, *New Monasticism: What It Has to Say to Today's Church* (Grand Rapids: Brazos, 2008).

76. For an example from the United Kingdom, see Susan Hope, *Mission-Shaped Spirituality* (New York: Seabury, 2010).

the power of the Spirit — requires us to go more deeply in Christian formation at the same time that we go more deeply and broadly in loving our neighbors. Ultimately, the two movements coincide. Without cultivating a renewed identity as a community of disciples, the church loses its ability to witness to salvation in Christ and serve in God's world. Yet that very cultivation occurs in part through witness and service as the church and its members discover their identity in participating in the triune God's communal mission in all of creation.

CHAPTER 2

Formation in the Missional Church: Building Deep Connections between Ministries of Upbuilding and Sending

Richard R. Osmer

In this chapter I will work with a model of practical theology that carries out four interrelated tasks: the descriptive-empirical, interpretive, normative, and pragmatic. Congregational leaders carry these tasks out by exploring four questions:

> Descriptive-empirical: What is going on in particular episodes, situations, and contexts?
> Interpretive: Why is this going on?
> Normative: What ought to be going on?
> Pragmatic: How might we best respond?

I have described these more fully in my book *Practical Theology: An Introduction.*[1] In that book I also argue that academic practical theology shares this same set of tasks but pursues them in ways that are appropriate to scholarly research.

These four tasks provide the structure of this essay, which examines the nature of formation in missional congregations. Since I will be using the concept of *missional vocation* throughout this essay, I begin by very briefly describing the meaning of this concept in the missional church discussion. This discussion is closely identified with the Gospel and Our Culture Network, which emerged in the late 1980s as an extension of the

---

1. Richard Osmer, *Practical Theology: An Introduction* (Grand Rapids: Eerdmans, 2008).

Gospel and Culture discussion initiated in Great Britain by Lesslie Newbigin.[2] As it has developed, a variety of theological perspectives have emerged.[3]

Missional Vocation: A Preliminary Sketch

Missional vocation finds its meaning in relation to two important concepts that are central to the missional church discussion: *missio Dei* and election. *Missio Dei,* the mission of God, marks a shift in thinking about mission from an ecclesiocentric to a theocentric perspective. Instead of thinking of mission as activities the church does (i.e., outreach programs, evangelism, sending missionaries overseas, etc.), it views mission, first and foremost, as something God does in sending the Son and Spirit into the world. David Bosch puts it like this: "We have to distinguish between *mission* (singular) and *missions* (plural). The first refers primarily to the *missio Dei* (God's mission), that is, God's self-revelation as the One who loves the world. . . . *Missions* . . . refer to particular forms, related to specific times, places, or needs, of participation in the *missio Dei*."[4] Missional vocation refers to missions (plural), to the particular ways congregations participate in the *missio Dei* in concrete times and places. Congregations find their missions within God's mission.

A second concept that is important to the meaning of missional vocation is *election.* In the Christian tradition, this concept has commonly been used to describe God's creation of a special covenant people, Israel and the church, who give witness to God's purposes in a fallen world. Across the tradition, however, election has often been associated with the special privileges, blessings, and status of the church.[5] The church is the

2. This discussion was initially sparked by Newbigin's *The Other Side of 1984: Questions for the Churches,* published originally by the British Council of Churches for a yearlong discussion and, subsequently, reissued by the World Council of Churches. For an overview of Newbigin's writings, see *Lesslie Newbigin: Missional Theologian* (Grand Rapids: Eerdmans, 2006). A link to the Gospel and Our Culture network is: http://www.gocn.org/.

3. For an excellent overview of the theological streams of the missional church discussion, see Craig Van Gelder and Dwight Zscheile, *The Missional Church in Perspective: Mapping Trends and Shaping the Conversation* (Grand Rapids: Baker Academic, 2011).

4. David Bosch, *Transforming Mission: Paradigm Shifts in Theology of Mission* (Maryknoll, NY: Orbis, 1991), 10.

5. For an excellent discussion of this issue, see Darrell Guder, *Be My Witnesses: The Church's Mission, Message, and Messengers* (Grand Rapids: Eerdmans, 1985).

"dispenser of salvation," giving it control over those who desire eternal life. Or it is the "community of perfect righteousness," which alone understands and obeys God's will. Or it is a community of individuals who are predestined for salvation before the foundation of the world and may look to their experience for evidences of God's favor. Or it is the evangel of "saving truth," elected to save individuals from eternal damnation.

In contrast to these understandings of election, many theologians in the missional church discussion describe election in relation to the *missio Dei*. God elects a particular people to give witness to the divine saving mission toward the whole of creation. Election is calling to service and witness, not primarily the reception of special blessings, benefits, and privileges. Or, as it is commonly put in the missional church discussion, the elect people whom God has called into being are a "sent" community.

Missional vocation seeks to capture the ways this "sentness" is embodied in a particular congregation. Vocation comes from the Latin *vocare*, to call. In classic Protestantism, it was used to depict the calling of every Christian to service and ministry in their everyday lives. In many ways, it was an outgrowth of Martin Luther's understanding of the priesthood of all believers, which portrays every member of the church as being called to ministry, not the ordained alone. Within the missional church discussion, this concept continues to include the vocation of individual Christians but gives primary attention to the *congregation's* missional vocation. George Hunsberger puts it this way:

> *Personal* vocation is shaped and molded in the context of a community that has clarity about *its* vocation. A Christian's personal sense of vocation is a derivative from that "one hope of our calling" (Eph. 4:4) shared with the whole church, those "called out" *(ekklesia)* into the mission of God![6]

This underscores the importance of leaders, practices, and processes that invite congregations to discern their own particular missional vocations, giving attention to questions like these:

- *where* they are — in a geographic, social, cultural context;
- *when* they are — in the flow of history and change;

---

6. George Hunsberger, "Discerning Missional Vocation," in Lois Barrett, ed., *Treasure in Clay Jars: Patterns in Missional Faithfulness* (Grand Rapids: Eerdmans, 2004), 38.

- *who* they are — in continuity with a tradition, re-forming it in the present;
- *why* they are — welcoming God's call, entering God's coming reign.[7]

Building on the concepts of *missio Dei* and election, therefore, missional vocation refers to a congregation's discernment of its calling to participate in the mission of God in ways that are particular to its place, time, resources, and challenges. While all congregations have a missional vocation, this looks different from congregation to congregation, sometimes even in congregations with similar profiles in the same community. The question I wish to explore in the remainder of this chapter is how we might conceptualize congregational formation with respect to this understanding of missional vocation. I begin by sharing empirical research that may throw light on this topic, the descriptive-empirical task of practical theology.

The Missional Leadership Project

Over the past three years I have been carrying out empirical research on ministers of congregations identified by knowledgeable insiders as involved in the missional church discussion. My co-researcher in this project is Drew Dyson, a doctoral student at Princeton Theological Seminary who was recently appointed professor of evangelism at Wesley Theological Seminary. We call this research the Missional Leadership Project, for our initial research question was: How do pastoral leaders who are deeply involved in the missional church discussion view their role as leaders? We began by conducting in-depth interviews with ten pastors of mainline "missional" congregations located in different parts of the United States. The congregations they were serving were quite different: some were start-up churches, others over fifty years old; some were large and others medium-sized or quite small (under 125 members).

One of the surprising findings to emerge out of this initial round of interviews was the importance of the language of formation and congregational culture among these leaders. To explore this in greater depth, we conducted a second round of twenty interviews, which focused on leaders'

---

7. Hunsberger, "Discerning Missional Vocation," in Barrett, ed., *Treasure in Clay Jars*, 39.

understanding of the meaning of formation, its core practices, and how they view it as related to the discernment of missional vocation. For comparative purposes, we conducted ten of these interviews with leaders who were *not* involved in the missional church discussion but were identified by knowledgeable insiders as having strong programs of spiritual formation. I will refer to them as "spiritual formation leaders," for all of them are immersed in the literature of spiritual formation, and several have even received training as spiritual directors. The remaining ten are pastors who *are* involved in the missional church discussion, and I will refer to them as "missional church leaders." For the purposes of this chapter, I will briefly highlight several points of comparison between these two groups, and then I will focus exclusively on findings from interviews of missional church leaders (altogether, twenty interviews when the two rounds of interviews were completed).[8]

(1) *The language of formation*

Let us begin, then, with several points of comparison of the spiritual formation and missional church leaders. Both groups used the language of formation to describe the ways a congregation shapes the lives of its members and builds up the "culture" of a particular congregation. The language of formation and culture were often used interchangeably, as seen in the following passage from an interview with a spiritual formation leader:

> Well, it's a highly educated congregation. And, to be able to know about something and to speak intelligibly about something is very important. So, what I've said to them is: I can look you up on the Internet and know all about you, but unless I spend time with you, I can't have a relationship with you. And you can know all about God, but unless you spend time with God, you don't have a relationship with God. To me, that's a key to spiritual formation and is the heart of the culture change that we're trying to accomplish here. And it's beginning to happen.

Both groups, moreover, used the language of formation to refer to a process that is broader than Christian education. Some even described Christian education in slightly negative ways. As one missional church leader put it:

8. All interviews were transcribed and coded using NVivo. For a helpful overview of research procedures making use of this program, see Lyn Richards, *Handling Qualitative Data: A Practical Guide* (London: Sage, 2005).

Because what are adult ministries doing, particularly when you think of Christian education? Is Christian education getting the facts straight, believing the doctrine and then still being able to keep God at arm's length from your heart? I think we have a kind of blind spot in the Reformed faith today. To me, spiritual formation is what Paul had in mind in 2 Corinthians 3:18, where he wrote about metamorphosing, the Greek word, from one glory to another when we are beholding Christ. That needs to be our larger purpose over all of Christian education.

Her comments are quite similar to that of a spiritual formation leader:

I've come to believe that what's often missing in Christian education is the formation aspect of it. I think the word "education" is generally associated with learning *about* something and studying a particular topic or studying a particular book of the Bible. Formation is more concerned with the holistic relationship with God and experience of God as well as learning about God and biblical texts.

Members of both groups, therefore, used the language of formation and culture fairly interchangeably, and some in each group viewed Christian education programs as needing to become formational and not merely informational. In spite of these commonalities, there are interesting differences between the two groups in their understanding of the purpose and practices of formation. The spiritual formation leaders described the purpose of formation as cultivating an active prayer life, which enables church members to live prayerfully, that is, to be aware of the Holy Spirit's presence in their everyday lives. The core practices of formation that were mentioned most frequently were teaching and practicing different forms of prayer, modeling "prayer of the heart" in worship, and sharing spiritual experiences with trusted others.

In contrast, the missional church leaders viewed the purpose of formation as cultivating a life of active discipleship in ways that represented both a break with the immediate past of the congregation and was more open to the cultures of people *not* currently in the church. The core practices mentioned most frequently were worship (especially preaching), "discipling" lay leaders, sharing the gospel with others, and small groups (or "mission teams") in which Bible study, prayer, fellowship, and service are significant components.

The differences between the spiritual formation leaders and missional church leaders are interesting, and to my mind they reflect different emphases in the contemporary discussions of spirituality and the missional church.[9] For the purposes of this chapter, however, my focus will be on the missional church leaders. Their understanding of formation as shaping a new congregational culture is well illustrated in passages from interviews of two leaders in the *same* congregation:

> Our last pastor had a DNA that came from Hollywood, and it was true Showtime, with a very limited palette of expression, such as despair, lament, doubts. Anything that would not present well to the world was not preached on, sung about, or allowed into liturgy. And so the church, when we came, had a look of health because it had a lot going on, a lot of activities and lots of full services of worship and a lot of energy in worship. But as we've been here for a while, we've come to realize that it is the same people revolving through the classes and ministry opportunities without taking in and really forming disciples in any depth. It is going to take a culture shift in the congregation for this sort of formation to begin to happen.

> This church and most churches, we find, would really like to attract people "like us," but younger. Well, what does that mean: People like us? Because the next tribes are not like us! They're different than us. So for instance, in this church the ushers were instructed, before I got here, that if anybody walks into the sanctuary wearing a baseball cap, they will be immediately invited to take off the baseball cap or to go worship somewhere else. . . . The rule was, if a baby peeps in church, the ushers were to tap the parents on their shoulders and invite them to take the child out into the crying room so it won't bother anybody else. . . .
> I was in Africa about twenty years ago, in Kenya, and a man who was the principal of St. Paul's Theological College in Lamulu drove me

9. It would be easy to misinterpret these findings, especially without knowing more about the context of the spiritual formation leaders. Nearly all of the congregations of these leaders are actively involved in local and overseas missions, several in exemplary fashion. These leaders viewed their emphasis on spirituality as addressing two needs: rooting the activism of their members in a personal spiritual life and reaching out to young adults and young families who, in the words of one interviewee, "aren't going to come to church any more out of a sense of duty" but need to have a faith "they experience and connects them with others and makes a difference in their lives." At least among the ten spiritual-formation leaders I interviewed, cultivating an active prayer life and encouraging people to live prayerfully does not appear to represent a turn to spiritual inwardness. Rather, it is an attempt to add something that is missing in the lives of congregational members and to reach out to young people in a post-Christian context.

by this warehouse and said, "I just want to show you this warehouse." Inside were probably 300 pump organs in storage, which had been sent by the Church of Scotland. The Ladies Aid Society had saved up pennies for this. Pump organs. And they told the Kenyans early on that the drums were of the devil and that movement in worship was of the devil. They were to sit still, hands folded, and sing hymns with these pump organs. And they did it until the cultural revolution, when they decided to throw them out and recontextualize the gospel into their culture. Now we're very embarrassed in mission history of all the colonial imposition that we did on all these folks and we're chagrined. And I'm saying that the North American church has, by and large, especially the Presbyterian church, done the same thing. We have imposed an alien culture on an emerging generation and said, "Look, if you'll just come here and do it, you'll eventually be just like us." That's not real spiritual formation. In North America we've been as blind to our cultural imposition as we ever were in the mission field context.

These passages capture nicely some of the most important themes associated with formation among the missional leaders. The formation of disciples will not take place unless the congregation itself is willing to change, breaking with the immediate past and "recontextualizing the gospel" in relation to the surrounding culture, as the second passage puts it. Formation is not something the congregation does to others, especially new members. It is something that must first happen to the congregation itself. This leads to two additional findings about the missional church leaders' understanding of formation.

(2) Suspicion of church programs, even as new programs and practices are described as very important in the formation of a missional church and, in some cases, as an expression of the missional vocation of the congregation
One of the most interesting findings of these interviews was the deep ambivalence about church programs articulated by the missional church leaders. On the one hand, leader after leader declared emphatically that programs are *not* the key to becoming a missional church. As one pastor put it, "It is not about going to the session or the congregation and saying, 'Hey, we need to add these programs to be a church that's missional.' Really, it's about working on things that are more basic."

Yet, when asked to describe how congregational formation takes place, the missional church leaders drew attention to new programs and practices. Sometimes they described them as standing alongside traditional programs like the Sunday school or denominational church committees; sometimes they described them as replacing those traditional programs. Here are two examples from different interviews:

> Our idea for spiritual formation is that it will become integral to everything that we do. So, while we're certainly not there, ministry is now done by teams, mission teams. You might be part of a seniors mission team or a finance team or a tutoring team. And we're saying that spiritual formation should take place in those teams. It is not just opening with prayer but a time of spiritual formation, of prayer for each other and fellowship. This supports the team's mission. It's *part* of the team's mission. . . . We're still in culture change, a really big culture change, and that happens slowly.

> The core of formation these days would be something that we call learning communities, which are yearlong communities of about thirty to forty people who stick together for a year studying the same biblical text. . . . This year it's been 1 and 2 Samuel, and next year it's going to be Romans for the whole year. And those communities are committed to biblical, theological engagement, but also to fellowship and mission as a group. The whole experience is formational, we believe, formation for Christian discipleship.

In some cases, new programs and practices were explicitly linked to the pastor's perception of the congregation's missional vocation. To give one example:

> Our special calling is to be a multicultural, missional, postmodern, postdenominational, postideological, postemergent church. And one of the ways that we understand this is to affirm multiple epistemological approaches. . . . We're going to allow Africans to approach God as Africans and through their African-ness. We're going to allow that for the Brazilians in our congregation. We allow people to start from their cultural point of reference instead of the colonial way, which says, "That's not good enough. You've got to go through our epistemological lens if you want to be legitimate." It's not that we delegitimatize the Western approach. We "perspectivalize" it. . . . It's one of a number of valid approaches. So when people ask me, "Are you conservative or liberal?" my response to them is, "Do I look white to you?" That's a

white people's question out of Western dualism. That's not even an important question in this congregation.

This congregation is highly multicultural, with members from around the world. The pastor described the practice of *testimony* as the most important way formation for missional vocation takes place in the congregation. In the context of public worship, members regularly share their testimonies, which are highly personal and self-revealing. These are subsequently posted on the congregation's website. The congregation has established a cell-group program in which this kind of testimony can take place on an ongoing basis across its membership.

In short, the missional church leaders professed skepticism about the power of new programs and practices to form a missional congregation; yet these same leaders pointed to new programs and practices as important avenues of congregational formation and, in some cases, described them as closely related to their congregation's missional vocation.

(3) Leadership is redefined around key tasks of formation for Christian discipleship.

A third set of findings revolves around leadership. When asked to describe their contribution as leaders to congregational formation, the missional church leaders drew attention to three things. First, they emphasized their role in helping the congregation engage Scripture. This was described as taking place in a wide variety of ways: through preaching, retreats for lay leaders, small-group Bible studies, study in the context of mission teams, and other ways. The importance of helping their congregation engage Scripture was described in a variety of ways. If I were to summarize what these leaders said, using different language, it would go something like this: Engaging Scripture is absolutely central because the Bible tells the story of God's mission to the world and God's election of a people who are to participate in this mission. The congregation needs to see its own story as an extension of this story. A key leadership role of the pastor, therefore, is helping this to take place. One missional church leader put it like this:

> If you are going to effect change, there are certain things you have to do. One of the most important is teaching and preaching the Bible as the story of *our* mission. I've done this now in three churches. My strategy early on has been to preach through the book of Acts. I tend to

be an expository lectio-continuum preacher. So, three different times I've preached through the book of Acts. And this last time I called the series "Windows on a Missional Church." To preach through the book of Acts takes about a year. That's a long time to be walking the congregation, every week, through different aspects of what a missional church looks like. . . . And early on I start working with the leadership core in more of a teaching mode, studying the Bible and asking, "What is the missional church?" And in each case, the congregation has said, "You know, I think we want to do this." Then, after a while, they always say, "Now wait a minute, this thing is going to cost us our life." Right. That's the point. It's messing up their nice, safe, comfortable church.

A second theme that emerged when the missional church leaders reflected on their leadership was the importance of sharing leadership, allowing people to take risks, and, even, to expect failure. One interviewee articulated this theme as follows:

My mantra is that every pastor should be a little bit dumb and a little bit lazy because when you're really smart and you're really energetic, the congregation is inclined to just sit back and say, "Isn't he great." [Laughs] They let the pastor do it, and by extension, to kind of live their faith vicariously through their pastor. So I've got a pretty small core area that I assume responsibility for maintaining, namely the theological culture of the congregation, especially the worshiping tone. . . . It's not a staff-led church. It's not really just elder-led. It's lay-led. So lay initiatives that come from the congregation tend to go through a pretty simple screening process to discern whether or not it's appropriate, whether it's a fit for us.

I think that one of the significant things we need to do is to be risky, to take risks . . . because it's not about us. The church is a provisional demonstration of the kingdom of God. It's not the end. . . . There is this foundation that I learned about. When you write a grant proposal, they're looking for success. They want to be able to see your history and how much money's already been raised and how committed the institution is, because they want their money to be well used. Well, there's this *other* foundation that won't award grants unless there is a significant chance of failure. [Laughs] They want an element of risk because they think this more faithfully demonstrates something that the Spirit of God might be up to, rather than a sure thing. It has an element of — this could be a spectacular failure. So that's one of the things I monitor in an evaluative way. Are we playing it safe? Have we gotten comfortable, or are we still risk-takers?

Third, many of the missional church leaders believe that they have an important role in helping their congregation live in the tension between "permission-giving" and congregational accountability and discernment. This theme is already evident in the last sentence of the first passage immediately above. Several pastors I interviewed viewed this as one of the most difficult "balancing acts" of leadership. While they want to encourage a permission-giving culture in the church, they also believe that accountability must be exercised in discerning which initiatives are worth pursuing. As one pastor put it:

> We try to operate with as thin a bureaucracy as possible. But we want there to be some sort of check-and-balance system. We're not just saying, "Let a thousand flowers bloom." We're also wanting to say that it really does matter that we try to work cooperatively so that we can put as great a strength into the things that we commit ourselves to as we can. We don't want to end up having ourselves splattered all over. There has to be some accountability and cooperation.

To summarize, some of the findings about formation to emerge from the Missional Leadership Project include:

(1) Leaders used the language of formation to describe the way the culture of a congregation "builds up" its corporate identity and shapes its members. There were important differences between the ways spiritual formation and missional church leaders describe the purpose and practices of formation.

(2) Leaders were suspicious of programs and practices as the fulcrum of change, even as new programs and practices were described as very important in the formation of a missional church.

(3) Leaders viewed their contribution to formation as including: (a) helping the congregation engage Scripture as the story of God's mission to the world in order to see its story as an extension of this story; (b) the importance of sharing leadership, allowing people to take risks, and expecting failure; and (c) balancing permission-giving and accountability in discerning worthwhile congregational initiatives.

These kinds of research findings are an important part of academic practical theology. The Missional Leadership Project is relatively small and still unfolding. It is important to bring projects like this one into conversation with larger bodies of research that often result in a more fully developed interpretive framework. In the following section we do just that by examining Christian Smith's subcultural identity theory.

Formation and Subcultural Identity Theory

One of the most important developments in sociological theory during the latter part of the twentieth century was a sharp critique of secularization theory and the theories of modernization on which it was based. These theories predicted that, as societies modernized and structural differentiation promoted greater secularization, institutions located in the private sphere would gradually grow weaker when many of their functions were taken over by public institutions of the state and economy.[10] This was especially thought to be the case with regard to religion and the family. Yet the story has proved more complex, and a number of telling criticisms of this perspective have been raised in recent decades.

One criticism is the very obvious empirical fact that religion has not withered away, but continues to play an important role in *both* public and private life in the United States and around the world.[11] It is impossible to imagine the civil rights movement in the United States or the 1989 Solidarity Revolution in Poland without the participation of religious communities. Nor is it really possible to understand political and cultural polarization in the United States and around the world without taking into account the "faith factor."[12] Religion remains an important force in modern life.

The same is true of families. Pankurst and Houseknecht observe:

10. The early work of Peter Berger in the sociology of religion represents an extremely influential example of this perspective. Two of the most important texts in which Berger elaborates on this theory are *The Sacred Canopy: Elements of a Sociological Theory of Religion* (Garden City, NY: Anchor Books, 1969) and *The Heretical Imperative: Contemporary Possibilities of Religious Affirmation* (Garden City, NY: Anchor Books, 1970). For a recent book making a case for secularization theory, see Steve Bruce, *God is Dead: Secularization in the West* (Oxford: Blackwell, 2002).

11. José Casanova, *Public Religions in the Modern World* (Chicago: University of Chicago Press, 1994).

12. For the impact of religion on voting behavior, for example, see John Greene, *The Faith Factor: How Religion Influences American Elections* (Westport, CT: Praeger, 2007).

41

"Little that happens in the public realm is without its private side. Attitudes toward work and spending and leisure and politics are all shaped and nurtured in the family and among friends and acquaintances."[13] Drawing on social capital theory, David Blankenhorn, Sara McLanahan, and Gary Sandefur have presented convincing evidence that families play a crucial role in mediating social relationships, psychological support, educational and economic opportunities, and other assets that enable children to become contributing members of the workforce, civil society, and the political life of a community.[14] The relative health or decline of families has an enormous impact on public life.

Perhaps most important of all, developments in the field of sociology itself have contributed to the critique of the secularization theses, which were based on older theories of modernization. One of the most significant of these developments is increased recognition of the role of culture in shaping a particular region's, country's, or subculture's negotiation of modernization. It is no longer thought to be adequate to focus exclusively on large-scale institutions and macrotrends to depict modernization.[15] In his early work, for example, Peter Berger argued that modernization necessarily has a relativizing effect on religious beliefs and practices, making the "heretical imperative" of individual choice a universal feature of *all* modern societies.[16] Similarly, Anthony Giddens argued that the breakdown of traditional moral systems in the face of institutional differentiation in modern societies gives rise to "pure relationships" in which individuals must negotiate forms of commitment and intimacy in a reflexive fashion.[17] Today,

13. Sharon K. Houseknecht and Jerry G. Pankhurst, eds., *Family, Religion, and Social Change in Diverse Societies* (Oxford: Oxford University Press, 2000), 3.

14. David Blankenhorn, *Fatherless America: Confronting Our Most Urgent Social Problem* (New York: HarperCollins, 1995); see also Sara McLanahan and Gary Sandefur, *Growing Up with a Single Parent: What Hurts, What Helps* (Cambridge, MA: Harvard University Press, 1994).

15. For an overview, see Diana Crane, ed., *The Sociology of Culture: Emerging Perspectives* (Cambridge, UK: Blackwell, 1994). See esp. Robert Wuthnow, *Communities of Discourse: Ideology and Structure in the Reformation, the Enlightenment, and European Socialism* (Cambridge, MA: Harvard University Press, 1989) and *Meaning and Moral Order: Explorations in Cultural Analysis* (Berkeley: University of California Press, 1987). Christian Smith develops subcultural identity theory in his book *American Evangelicalism: Embattled and Thriving* (Chicago: University of Chicago Press, 1998), described more fully below.

16. See Berger, *Heretical Imperative*.

17. Anthony Giddens, *Modernity and Self-Identity: Self and Society in the Late Modern Age* (Stanford: Stanford University Press, 1991), 88-98.

Berger and Giddens are criticized as portraying modernization in a monolithic and unilinear fashion. Their analyses focused too exclusively on macrolevel institutional and cultural trends and failed to give adequate attention to the ways different cultural communities accommodate, resist, or adapt to such trends.

One of the most interesting research projects to explore the way religious culture shapes a community's negotiation of modernization is the Evangelical Identity and Influence Project. The senior researcher of this project was the sociologist Christian Smith, currently teaching at the University of Notre Dame, who has drawn on this project in a number of writings. Here I refer to his book *American Evangelicalism: Embattled and Thriving*. In that book Smith attempts to explain why evangelicalism is thriving in contemporary America. His research found that in comparison to mainline, liberal, and fundamentalist forms of Protestantism, evangelicalism is stronger along six dimensions: adherence to beliefs; salience of faith; robustness of faith; group participation; commitment to mission; and retention and recruitment of members.[18] He explains its strength with a *subcultural identity theory of religious persistence.*

Smith summarizes this theory as follows: "Religion survives and can thrive in pluralistic, modern society by embedding itself in subcultures that offer satisfying, morally orienting collective identities which provide adherents meaning and belonging."[19] He unpacks this thesis in the form of eight propositions.[20]

> Proposition 1: The human drives for meaning and belonging are satisfied primarily by locating human selves within social groups that sustain distinctive, morally orienting collective identities.
> Proposition 2: Social groups construct and maintain collective identities by drawing symbolic boundaries that create distinctions between themselves and relevant out-groups.
> Proposition 3: Religious traditions have always strategically renegotiated their collective identities by continually reformulating the ways their constructed orthodoxies engage the changing sociocultural environments they confront.
> Proposition 4: Because the socially normative bases of identity-

18. Smith, *American Evangelicalism*, 21-22.
19. Smith, *American Evangelicalism*, 118.
20. Smith, *American Evangelicalism*, chap. 4.

legitimation are historically variable, modern religious believers can establish strong religious identities and commitments on the basis of individual choice rather than through ascription.

Proposition 5: Individuals and groups define their values and norms and evaluate their identities and actions in relation to specific, chosen reference groups; dissimilar and antagonistic out-groups may serve as negative reference groups.

Proposition 6: Modern pluralism promotes the formation of strong subcultures and potentially "deviant" identities, including religious subcultures and identities.

Proposition 7: Intergroup conflict in a pluralistic context typically strengthens in-group identity, solidarity, resource-mobilization, and membership retention.

Proposition 8: Modernity can actually increase religion's appeal by creating social conditions that intensify the kinds of felt needs and desires that religion is especially well positioned to satisfy.

The force of Smith's theory is best seen by contrasting it to the above-mentioned widely influential theory of secularization of Peter Berger, who argues that modern rationalization, institutional differentiation, and cultural pluralism have destroyed the sacred canopy of traditional societies and created "cognitive quandaries" at the individual level. This makes it necessary for every individual to piece together his or her own faith in the private realm while relying on secularized moral guidance systems in other parts of their lives — such as work or politics. Berger's explanation of secularization coordinates macrolevel trends with microlevel effects.

Smith's findings lead him in a very different direction. He locates the problems of human meaning and belonging within the larger problem of collective identity, especially at the level of subcultural groups. Such groups may not provide a "sacred canopy" for society as a whole, but they do provide what Smith calls a "sacred umbrella" for the members of their own community.[21] American evangelicalism has thrived precisely because its congregations, parachurch groups, and special-purpose organizations serve as reference groups in which their members can establish strong religious identities. Moreover, what may appear to outsiders as polarized, culture-wars rhetoric by evangelicals is actually less directed toward out-

---

21. Berger, *The Sacred Canopy*, 106.

groups than it is in-group talk designed to strengthen subcultural identity boundaries.

What light does Smith's subcultural identity theory throw on the research findings of the Missional Leadership Project (reported above)? It opens up two lines of interpretation, which I can only explore briefly here.

(1) The use of the language of formation and congregational culture may represent an implicit acknowledgment by missional church leaders of the need to build stronger subcultural identities in their mainline congregations.

If Smith's subcultural identity theory is correct, then many features of late modernity that are commonly interpreted as having a secularizing impact actually create social conditions that may *increase* religion's appeal, intensifying "the felt needs and desires that religion is especially well-positioned to satisfy" (proposition 8 above). The key is whether religious communities — be they evangelical or not — can foster subcultural identities that satisfy the human needs for meaning and belonging. They can do so by serving as reference groups with which people identify and by forming religious identities among their members strong enough to shape their engagement of modern institutions.

A fair amount of social scientific research on mainline congregations appears to indicate that many of its congregations are "loosely bounded" and practice what Nancy Ammerman calls "Golden Rule" Christianity, inculcating noncontroversial values like honesty, kindness, and caring, which do not place them in tension with the surrounding culture or form clear boundaries as a community.[22] In other words, there are good reasons to believe that mainline congregations, for the most part, do not foster strong subcultural identities among their members. This makes sense because, historically, the mainline has been at the center of American culture and could take its privileged status for granted. Unlike many religious groups in the United States, it has not been forced to think like a minority. Little attention has been given to the need to foster, sustain, and hand on a distinctive way of life, or subcultural identity, among its members.

The end of American Protestant Christendom over the course of the twentieth century has left the mainline in a very different social context. It

---

22. See, e.g., Wilcox, *Soft Patriarchs*, cited above, and Nancy T. Ammerman, "Golden Rule Christianity: Lived Religion in the American Mainstream," in David Hall, ed., *Lived Religion in America* (Princeton, NJ: Princeton University Press, 1997), 196-216.

45

can no longer count on the social support of the surrounding culture. What we see, therefore, in the language of formation, congregational culture, culture shift, and so forth among missional church leaders is an implicit acknowledgment of the need to foster a stronger subcultural identity among their own congregations — and perhaps the mainline generally. A clear and resounding theme in the interviews of these leaders is that mainline congregational culture is not missional. It is simply a part of the "background" or taken-for-granted tapestry of the broader culture. Formation, as such, requires a culture shift in mainline congregations, which typically includes renegotiating its relationship with its own past and with the surrounding culture in the present.

(2) Congregational leadership, practices, and programs are viewed as formational by leaders to the extent that they contribute to a new subcultural identity in the congregation.

Smith's subcultural identity theory is also helpful in interpreting what missional church leaders mean when they describe congregational leadership, practices, and programs as formational. Perhaps this becomes most clear in the ambivalence of these leaders toward programs and practices. This ambivalence appears to reflect a sense that established routines in congregations must give way to something new. Yet what this is cannot be prepackaged and imported from elsewhere. New structures will have to emerge out of a difficult process of letting go of many standard scripts and models of what it means to be a church and passing through a period of experimentation, risk-taking, and failure. New programs and practices were highly valued by these leaders as avenues of formation. But such programs and practices emerged and took form at the far end of a process of cultural transformation within the congregation. This kind of transformation takes place at the *congregational* level, the level of collective identity in Smith's terms.

Smith describes leadership in similar ways. Important leadership tasks such as preaching, teaching Scripture, and administration he describes in terms of their contribution to a congregation's transition from one culture to another (i.e., from the "established" routines of the mainline to a congregational culture that was more "missional"). They contributed to formation only to the extent that they led to the emergence of a new congregational structure and culture, which, in turn, formed congregational members.

An important caveat must be added to both of these lines of interpretation in terms of Smith's subcultural identity theory. Further research is needed to explore a clear theme in the interviews of the missional church leaders: the importance of becoming *more* open to the surrounding culture. This included becoming more open to emerging adults, the new media, the post–civil-rights generation, new racial and ethnic groups in the surrounding community, and so forth. Mainline congregational culture was viewed as tied to practices, programs, and models that were rooted in an older and outdated cultural perspective when the mainline was still at the center of American society. The theme of openness to the surrounding culture is thus worth exploring further. How do congregations negotiate this openness and, simultaneously, build stronger subcultural identities?

Formation and Missional Vocation

There are a host of theological issues to emerge from the Missional Leadership Project and Smith's interpretive framework.[23] For the purposes of this chapter, I will confine my attention to the relationship between formation and missional vocation, combining the normative and pragmatic tasks of practical theology. It is important to explore the relationship between formation and missional vocation for several reasons. Even in the small research project I reported above, it is apparent that formation is used in several different ways today, and we may need greater clarity. Moreover, sociological theories like Christian Smith's subcultural identity theory can only take us so far. In fact, it may be true that American congregations will do well in the pluralistic societies of late modernity if they form strong subcultural identities. Yet this alone tells us very little about the moral and religious substance of a particular religious subculture. Nor does it provide

---

23. Of the various issues raised by this research, I will mention only two here. (1) Is it adequate to describe a congregation as having a single, comprehensive missional vocation? A number of the congregations of the leaders interviewed in this project appeared to be committed to more than one form of mission. Do we need to find ways of talking about missional vocations (plural) *within* the same congregation, especially in larger congregations? (2) Similar questions emerged with respect to the importance several missional leaders ascribed to ministry or mission teams in their congregations. These are relatively small groups that combine study, service, fellowship, and worship. Organizational-theory literature leads me to believe that these groups are one of the primary ways their participants experience the "organizational reality" of the congregation. Are such groups appropriately described as having distinctive missional vocations, not at the corporate level of the congregation as a whole but at the level of smaller communities within the larger community?

us with a theological framework with which to assess the adequacy of a religious subculture. On *theological* grounds, what counts as formation in a congregation? How might we distinguish between formation and *misformation*?

Since this represents a step into the normative task of practical theological reflection, it is worth pausing to explore what is at stake in this sort of reflection and why it is a necessary step beyond the social sciences. To illustrate the importance of normative theological reflection in practical theology, let us reflect briefly on the findings of another research project conducted by Christian Smith, in which he and Michael Emerson examined the way white American evangelicalism interprets and responds to racism.[24] This follows nicely on our examination of Smith's subcultural identity theory, based on his research on evangelicalism in the Evangelical Identity and Influence Project.

In *Divided by Faith,* Smith and Emerson share research in which they identify the "cultural tool kit" of white evangelical culture.[25] It comprises three key tools: (1) accountable, free-will individualism, (2) relationalism (attaching central importance to interpersonal relationships), and (3) anti-structuralism (the dismissal of the importance of social structural influences). Smith and Emerson point out that this religious subculture makes it extremely difficult for white evangelicals to interpret racism as a social structure. It predisposes them to view racism exclusively as a matter of personal prejudice that can only be overcome by a changed heart and transformed interpersonal relationships.

In short, there is an implicit theology at work in evangelicalism's understanding of racism. While sociologists can be extremely helpful in describing and interpreting the cultural toolkit of this religious subculture, practical theologians must assess the adequacy of this toolkit on *theological grounds.* They must also offer constructive theological proposals that might guide congregations in different directions if they evaluate this toolkit as inadequate. I will focus on the constructive, action-guiding task of practical theology in the remainder of this chapter, outlining a theological understanding of formation in the form of six propositions that build on the discussion of missional vocation in the first part of the chapter.

24. Michael Emerson and Christian Smith, *Divided by Faith: Evangelical Religion and the Problem of Race in America* (Oxford: Oxford University Press, 2000).

25. I borrow the idea of a "cultural tool kit" from a seminal article by Ann Swidler, which she has developed more fully in *Talk of Love: How Culture Matters* (Chicago: University of Chicago Press, 2001).

Toward a Theological Conceptualization of Formation

(1) God's mission — the *missio Dei* — is universal in scope, comprehending creation, redemption, and the consummation of all creation.

(2) God elects a particular community of people to give witness to the divine saving mission toward the whole of creation. Election is calling to service and witness, not primarily the reception of special blessings, benefits, and privileges.

(3) Congregations find their particular missions within God's mission. Each congregation has the task of discerning its own missional vocation, which is appropriate to its own time, place, circumstances, personnel, and resources.

(4) In discerning their missional vocation, congregations should pay attention to two foci: one focus is the gathering and upbuilding of the congregation; the other is the sending and self-giving of the congregation. Formation is most powerful when deep connections are created between these two foci.

(5) The primary actor in spiritual formation is not the congregation. It is the Holy Spirit as she builds up and equips the congregation for mission, and as she empowers the congregation to carry out its particular vocation.

(6) Spiritual formation is thus the congregation's "taking form" in the Spirit, what might be called *primary missional formation*. This includes the relationships, structures, programs, and practices that emerge as a particular congregation lives into and out of its missional vocation. These, in turn, shape the spiritual lives of those who participate in this missional vocation, what might be called *secondary missional formation*.

Near the beginning of this chapter, I explicated the first three propositions; therefore, I will focus here on propositions 4 through 6. In Proposition 4, I am referring to David Bosch's description of the church as an ellipse with two foci. This is a key dimension of the theological framework with which I understand formation. Bosch puts it like this:

> In and around the first [focus] it acknowledges and enjoys the source of its life; this is where worship and prayer are emphasized. From and through the second focus, the church engages and challenges the world. This is a forth-going and self-spending focus, where service,

mission and evangelism are stressed. Neither focus should ever be at the expense of the other; rather, they stand in each other's service. The church's *identity* sustains its *relevance* and *involvement.*[26]

Bosch is drawing here on the missional ecclesiology of the great German theologian Jürgen Moltmann, who describes the congregation with the bipolar concepts of identity and relevance.[27]

With the *identity* pole, Moltmann portrays the congregation as a contrast society, a community of mature and committed disciples that serves as a sign of the kingdom in its fellowship of equality, mutual acceptance, and care, its worship in joy, and its struggle to live out the Sermon on the Mount as a kingdom ethic.[28] He portrays the congregation as acquiring a distinctive "way of life" as it follows Christ's way.[29] The distinctiveness of its subcultural identity as a contrast society holds before the world an alternative set of possibilities, which is to have a catalytic role in bringing about change in the broader social context.[30]

With the *relevance* pole, Moltmann portrays the congregation as a *kenotic* community, a community of openness, self-giving, and solidarity in its various relationships with the world.[31] This encompasses many things, from the congregation's confrontation of systemic forces of evil to its dialogue with its "partners in history," Israel, and other religions. In his description of the kenotic pole, Moltmann places special emphasis on the way the Holy Spirit leads people to Christ, who is present among individuals and groups that are most vulnerable. It is especially in its solidarity with the poor, the marginal, and the "surplus people" of economic systems that the congregation finds and joins the *missio Dei.*

The church lives in the tension between identity and relevance, be-

26. Bosch, *Transforming Mission,* 385.

27. Jürgen Moltmann, *The Church in the Power of the Spirit: A Contribution to Messianic Ecclesiology* (San Francisco: Harper and Row, 1977). Helpful overviews of Moltmann's writings in English are Richard Bauckham, *The Theology of Jürgen Moltmann* (Edinburgh: T&T Clark, 1995), and Joy Ann McDougall, *Pilgrimage of Love: Moltmann on the Trinity and Christian Life* (Oxford: Oxford University Press, 2005).

28. Among the places Moltmann discusses the Sermon on the Mount, see *The Way of Jesus Christ: Christology in Messianic Dimensions* (Minneapolis: Fortress, 1993), 116-32.

29. Moltmann, *Way of Jesus Christ,* 43.

30. Moltmann, *Church in the Power of the Spirit,* 158.

31. The term "kenotic community" is mine, not Moltmann's; but it is consistent with his description of relevance of the congregation in its relationships and encounters with the world.

tween the pole of gathering and upbuilding, on the one hand, and the pole of sending and self-giving, on the other. It is both a contrast society and a kenotic society. Moltmann grounds this ecclesiology in his social doctrine of the Trinity, which portrays the divine persons perichoretically as existing in *centered openness.* The Father, Son, and Spirit are centers of identity and personhood. Yet their particular identities are constituted by the mutual indwelling of their relationships to one another. They do not merely have their relationships; they *are* their relationships. They subsist in and for one another in centered openness. When the church lives as a community of centered openness, living in the tension between identity and relevance, it serves as an *analogia Trinitatis* (an analogy of the Trinity).

This Trinitarian, missional ecclesiology of centered openness is the key to the relationship between formation and missional vocation. Missional vocation, we can recall, points to the way a congregation discerns what God is calling it to be and do in its own time and place in light of its particular resources, personnel, social context, and relationships beyond the church. It finds its particular mission within God's mission. In an ecclesiology of centered openness, this is best conceptualized as a process of missional formation: the discovery of congregational identity through relevance and, simultaneously, the sustaining of congregational relevance through identity. Missional formation takes place as a congregation lives into and out of its missional vocation. The upbuilding of the congregation takes place as it engages the surrounding world; the self-giving of the congregation is deepened and sustained as its identity is built up. Therefore, missional formation is the process of the congregation "taking form" as it lives into and out of its missional vocation, as it lives in the tension between *identity* and *relevance.*

It is worth noting in passing that this represents an important shift in thinking about how and where formation takes place. In the literature of contemporary spirituality, the language of formation is conceptualized almost exclusively in terms of the pole of identity — that is, as the upbuilding of the members of the gathered congregation through spiritual practices and programs. Within the ecclesiology developed above, this is broadened to include the pole of relevance. The congregation and its members are *formed* as they act with and for others beyond the church in partnership, mutual learning, and solidarity with the vulnerable. Missional formation in a congregation of centered openness includes, but goes beyond, the typical practices we associate with spiritual formation.

An important practical implication of this point is the need to build

deep connections between ministries of upbuilding and sending in formation. Perhaps the best examples of this in my interviews were mission
groups and learning communities. These are relatively small groups — up
to thirty people — that combine worship, fellowship, study, and service.
These groups forge deep connections between the upbuilding and sending. Service builds fellowship and deepens study; worship and mutual care
sustain service; and in this way missional formation takes place.

This leads us to Proposition 5, which portrays the Holy Spirit as the
primary actor in formation as a congregation discerns and embodies its
missional vocation. A more adequate way of putting this would be to say
that the Holy Spirit forms the congregation and its individual members toward the likeness of Christ in ways that are particular to its missional vocation. Christ takes form in the congregation through the Spirit as it embodies its calling in a particular time and place. This has two important
practical implications.

The first implication is that we should not view missional formation
as a form of socialization in which the congregation simply imposes certain
habits and routines on its members. Formation as socialization into a
preexistent community is not adequate theologically. This raises questions
that cannot be explored here about the adequacy of subcultural identity
theory alone to describe what needs to take place in the renewal of mainline
congregations. This is because missional formation is a matter of inviting a
congregation to become open to the Spirit, to enter a dynamic and creative
process in which the Spirit forms the congregation Christomorphically and
transforms its relationships in openness to the surrounding world.

A second practical implication is that missional formation is costly.
It necessarily involves risk-taking, uncertainty, and even failure. It is a matter of openness to the "new thing" the Spirit is calling a congregation to do
and be as it joins Christ's mission in its own time and place. For many
mainline congregations today, this will entail letting go of habits of mind
and practice and creating an open space in which the Spirit evokes new
ways of thinking and acting as a community.[32] Missional formation by the
Spirit toward the likeness of Christ requires leadership that can challenge
and sustain a congregation through a process of creativity and risk-taking.

Proposition 6 builds directly on this understanding of creativity and

---

32. Parker Palmer offers an especially helpful description of spiritual formation as
cultivating an open space for the Spirit in *To Know as We Are Known: A Spirituality of Education* (San Francisco: Harper and Row, 1983).

risk-taking. Missional formation primarily is the process by which a congregation "takes form" as it lives into and out of its missional vocation. By "taking form," I mean developing relationships, structures, practices, and programs that emerge out of missional engagement. This is not a matter of jettisoning ecclesiastical and denominational traditions, but it is a matter of putting them at risk and allowing them to be renewed in order to allow new forms to emerge that are appropriate to a congregation's mission. We saw this in the interviews of missional leaders who were quite clear that congregations cannot become missional simply by instituting new programs, yet pointed to a variety of new structures, relationships, practices, and programs that were now supporting the missional vocation of their congregations. Structures follow creativity; institutions follow movements; and so, too, do new patterns of congregational life "take form" out of the Spirit's shaping of the congregation in mission.

It is thus appropriate, theologically, to distinguish primary and secondary missional formation. Primary formation points to the "taking form" of new patterns of congregational life around the discernment and embodiment of missional vocation. Secondary formation refers to the kinds of habits, practices, and dispositions that are cultivated when a congregation has begun to embody its missional vocation. How long a congregation will find its identity and relevance within a particular missional vocation is an open question. Even the best congregations are likely to rediscern their vocation periodically in light of changes in their local community, the composition of the congregation, and world events.[33]

Let me end by giving you one example of a congregation that embodies many features of the understanding of missional formation developed above, especially living in the tension between identity and relevance, and building deep connections between ministries of upbuilding and sending. The example focuses on a Presbyterian congregation located in a U.S. county with one of the largest populations of Indian immigrants in the United States. It offers a highly abbreviated account of the way this congregation began to "take form" as a result of its annual mission trip to a partner church in India. The congregation was struggling with a question that many churches face when they work with populations that are vulner-

33. Alan Roxburgh and Fred Romanuk, in *The Missional Leader: Equipping Your Church to Reach a Changing World* (San Francisco: Jossey-Bass, 2006), argue that even strong congregations pass through a thirty-year cycle in which established patterns of leadership, practice, and relationship must be renewed. I tend to believe that major shifts may occur more frequently than this, given the speed of change in our world today.

able. How might their members move beyond viewing their relationship with the vulnerable as merely charity work "at a distance" and allow it to become genuinely formational?

The congregation had been on mission trips to its partner church for five years before its leaders began to sense that they were not doing a very good job of helping the participants to "spiritually" (their term) appropriate what they were experiencing. So they asked the members of the next trip to carry out three tasks while they were in India: they were to make a journal entry every night about significant experiences of the day; they were to lead one "listening group" of children, youth, women, or untouchables and record the conversation on a tape recorder; and they were to interview one adult and record that conversation as well. All the while, they engaged in manual labor on a project their partner church set up before they arrived. When the travelers returned home, they met in small groups for three months to process what they had experienced. They shared from their journals and listened to their tape recordings. They prayed for specific people they had encountered. They studied a passage of Scripture chosen by the senior pastor each time they gathered, and sometimes he preached on this passage.

Over time, a new openness to Indian immigrants in their own community began to emerge in the congregation, which at that point was almost entirely white. This, in turn, led a Sunday school class to study the W-2 visa problem of many Indian women in the United States, something that prevents them from seeking employment outside the home and often creates unhealthy dynamics in the family. The Sunday school class then invited a group of local Indian women to meet with them, and they eventually established a community organization supported by the church to meet these women's particular needs. For the first time, this congregation had begun to engage in evangelism, which its members had previously viewed as a coercive way of convincing people to join the church and become like them. It now began to reimagine evangelism as offering welcome and hospitality to the immigrants in the community, which required certain changes on the congregation's part.

Obviously, we would need a fuller story to gain a more complete picture of missional formation as this congregation began to take form through the discernment of its missional vocation. But I have said enough here to illustrate what occurs when a congregation begins to live in the tension between identity and relevance. What began as mission viewed as charitable work refracted back on the congregation's internal life. This, in turn, gave rise to new forms of local mission. The process of missional formation is still unfolding and is likely to impact the congregation's relationship with its partner church in India.

It is no accident that I end with a concrete example of practice in a chapter written from the perspective of practical theology. I began with empirical investigation of the language of formation and congregational culture among pastoral leaders. I then interpreted some of our findings from the perspective of subcultural identity theory. This led to a normative theological perspective on formation and missional vocation, which issued in practical guidelines. But it is fitting that we end with an open-ended example of missional formation. Such practice is both the grounding point and ending point of practical theology.

CHAPTER 3

Exiles on Main Street:
Reframing Short-Term Mission

Scott J. Hagley

> *For I know the plans I have for you, declares the* LORD. *Plans to prosper you and not to harm you. . . .*
>
> Jeremiah 29:11

> *Do not worry about your life. . . . And why do you worry about clothes? See how the lilies of the field grow. They do not labor or spin. . . .*
>
> Matthew 6:25-28

Introduction

It was not, at all, in the plan. I heard each of these verses from two different high school students, as if for the first time, while standing in the desert sandwiched between the soft-orange glow of two smoldering fires. The fire on my left was, of course, the last gasp of sunlight as day turned into night. The fire on my right, less predictably, was the steady smoldering of a burning bus. Flames had devoured it during the previous hour along a Mexican road, while thirty high school students walked barefoot in the scrub brush and sang worship songs (with the help of the lone guitar rescued from the fire). The bus popped and hissed in the background, and our driver — unable to call dispatch — waited by the road to flag down the next bus or truck that might pass along our way.

The initial adolescent euphoria wore off as the sun dropped below the horizon. The reality of what had just happened began to sink in. We had managed to get only one fire-damaged bag (and a perfect guitar!) off the bus. We were without shoes, water, food, and blankets. We just might have to spend the night exposed in a foreign desert. The students formed a circle and prayed: the above verses, which were shared in prayer and conversation, jarred me. This, of course, was not the plan. It was a disruption — disorienting and worrisome. When the fire had started, we were two hours from Monterrey, the bus packed with t-shirts, soccer balls, clown costumes, computers, work supplies, and our own clothing for a short-term (week-long) missions trip. Now, if we could get to Monterrey at all, we would arrive empty-handed. A student from a middle-class family said in tears, "I have always wondered what it would be like to have nothing but my faith," while another had nightmares for a couple weeks. The church that received us — weary and dirty — about 3:00 a.m. the next day hosted us with generosity, joy, and great sensitivity. This disruption and disorientation unveiled for us a new future and a different kind of mission than we had anticipated: "For I know the plans . . . ," the Lord says.

Of course, when the prophet Jeremiah penned those words to Hebrew exiles, it bore little resemblance to the sentimentalized notions of God's plan we tend to refer to in graduation cards or even in the midst of a relatively safe missions trip gone wrong. "For I know the plans I have for you . . ." bore witness to God's future in the midst of violence, chaos, and upheaval. It was written to those who had survived the violent seizure of Judah's cities, only to relive its events in memory.[1] Judah had been conquered, the temple destroyed, her sons and daughters taken into the service of Babylon and families forcibly resettled. Like many displaced people, this was both a material and religiocultural crisis.[2] The psalmist cries, "How can we sing the songs of the LORD while in a foreign land?" (Ps. 137:4); Jeremiah sets about writing a letter (Jer. 29). In essence, the letter

---

1. Recent biblical scholarship has begun to emphasize the likely violence and terror of the experience of exile. This challenges a long-standing assumption among scholars that since Jeremiah and Deutero-Isaiah are relatively positive toward exile, the Babylonian and later Persian rule must have been benign. For an overview of these developments, see Daniel L. Smith-Christopher, *A Biblical Theology of Exile* (Minneapolis: Fortress, 2002).

2. I am also convinced here that this crisis is not something easily abated by the "restoration" in Ezra-Nehemiah or the nationalism of 1 and 2 Maccabees. Rather, I follow N. T. Wright, who argues that the crisis of exile is carried into the diversity and identity of first-century Judaism and thus the New Testament documents.

tells Judah to settle in where they are, to seek the welfare of the city in which they live, for God has neither abandoned them nor forgotten them. Like Ezekiel's vision in which the presence of God lifts up from the temple and moves east, Jeremiah testifies to the exilic life of God. God exiles Godself amid the horrors and disorientation of Judah's passion. "For I know," then, bodies forth gospel to an anxious Judah, expressing the possibility of a future in the midst of an ambiguous present.

Many contemporary thinkers and theologians describe the church in the United States within an exilic narrative of dispossession and diaspora.[3] The various disestablishments of mainline Protestantism from circles of cultural and political influence are well-documented.[4] The disorientation and powerlessness that many congregations experience amid the fluid and fast-paced cultural changes of the last few decades is real. It is this ambiguity and disorientation that calls for a transformed vision of mission: disestablishment and exilic conditions create the possibility for a re-formation of Christian identity characterized as a "new missional era."[5] That is, exile creates the conditions for a new kind of engagement with society and world. However, despite rhetoric that might suggest otherwise, North American Christians live lives of relative comfort and privilege. Their experience of exile is not one of forcible removal or violent persecution, but rather hybrid identities and discontinuous change.[6] This is why many on

3. One of the most recent (and perhaps most popularized) is Michael Frost, *Exiles: Living Missionally in a Post-Christian Culture* (Peabody, MA: Hendrickson, 2006). But exilic tones also carry throughout Stanley Hauerwas's insistence that a post-Christendom church is to understand itself as a resident alien. See Stanley Hauerwas, *The Peaceable Kingdom: A Primer in Christian Ethics* (Notre Dame, IN: University of Notre Dame Press, 1983); Stanley Hauerwas and William H. Willimon, *Resident Aliens: Life in the Christian Colony* (Nashville: Abingdon, 1989).

4. This is often traced in "missional church" literature. See Darrell L. Guder, ed., *Missional Church: A Vision for the Sending of the Church in North America* (Grand Rapids: Eerdmans, 1998), 46-76.

5. Patrick R. Keifert, *We Are Here Now: A New Missional Era* (Eagle, ID: Allelon, 2006).

6. Again, this is a theme that runs throughout the missional church and emergent church literature. See, for example, Alan J. Roxburgh, *The Missionary Congregation, Leadership and Liminality* (Harrisburg, PA: Trinity Press International, 1997). But the issue of hybrid identities and transnationalism is of much broader interest than just missional church literature. It is a part of many postmodern and globalization theories. See, for example, Zygmunt Bauman, *Liquid Modernity* (Malden, MA: Polity Press, 2000). See also Arjun Appadurai, *Modernity at Large: Cultural Dimensions of Globalization* (Minneapolis: University of Minnesota Press, 1996); Jehu Hanciles, *Beyond Christendom: Globalization, African Migration, and the Transformation of the West* (Maryknoll, NY: Orbis, 2008).

the religious "right" and "left" still entertain visions of governing majorities and enjoy a general trust in their own cultural and political agency despite diminishing returns.

But exile is not agency. It is, rather, suffering thrust upon a people. Exile is disruptive, and yet a site for a kind of reformation of identity, a space in which old words can be heard in new ways. This essay asks whether the seemingly benign practice of short-term mission (STM) trips can facilitate a kind of exilic awareness for North American congregations. Can STM generate missional formation attuned to the fluidity, loss, and disorientation of exile? Can STM help congregations hear God's "for I know . . ." anew while finding themselves in uncharted territory? In what follows I will suggest that, under the right circumstances, short-term mission creates an experimental space within the life of congregations in which the exilic disruption of the U.S. church can be noticed and discovered, for STM can open eyes and ears to the voice of the exilic God who claims a future for the church amid the ambiguity and pluralism of late modernity.

The argument proceeds in three different movements. First, I consider the phenomenon of STM trips and the relevant research regarding both their effectiveness and integrity. Based on the research, I will argue that STM trips are somewhat ambiguous practices both in their perceived effectiveness in the field and the life change for those on the trip. If STM does not provide measurable results in the field or in the group sent, what might it accomplish? I will suggest that the very ambiguity of STM as a practice points toward its disruptive possibilities: that it is an exilic event rather than a planned pilgrimage. But how might disruption understood as exile help form congregations in and for participation in mission? This leads to the second section. I argue that Israel's identity and theological crisis in exile make possible an expanded horizon for interpreting God's mission marked by an abiding hope in God's future. That is, the ambiguity, loss of power, and crisis conditions that mark exile are also spaces in which God cultivates hope in God's future. This is good news for U.S. congregations. In the final section I explore some concrete ways in which this theme of exile can reframe STM trips in the life of the congregation as experimental spaces for experiencing, interpreting, and narrating the church's exilic disruption for the sake of encountering again the God who promises and gives a future.

Short-Term Missions in North America

Robert Priest and colleagues estimate (conservatively) that over 1.6 million Americans engage in STM trips overseas each year, with perhaps many more engaged in STM trips within the United States. As a type of grass-roots movement, STM trips have risen dramatically in the past twenty years, but they are difficult to track because they do not always go through mission agencies or existing denominational structures.[7] The growth of Youth-Works, a short-term mission agency in Minneapolis, embodies the explosion of STM trips by United States congregations. YouthWorks was incorporated in 1994 to resource youth ministries for STM experiences.[8] That summer, thirty-five congregations took roughly 400 participants to two different work sites. By 2002, 1,600 congregations took 27,000 participants to fifty-eight different sites. By 2009, the number of participants increased to 35,000. As a nondenominational organization, YouthWorks understands its mission at three different levels: as a resource for congregations sending teams for STM trips ("the church that pays"); as a partner for "the church that stays";[9] and as a kind of service-learning organization for multidenominational partnerships.[10] YouthWorks provides only one window into STM in the United States, but its incredible growth and multidenominational work mirrors what is generally true about STM in the United States.

For many congregations, STM trips are not isolated and optional events. Rather, organizing such trips is now considered a regular part of a youth or mission pastor's job, and many organizations exist (YouthWorks included) to help these pastors partner with one another and organizations or congregations open to receiving STM teams. The majority of these trips last seven to fourteen days, and they have become, according to Priest and colleagues — a kind of pilgrimage:

> Like pilgrimages, these trips are rituals of intensification, where one temporarily leaves the ordinary, compulsory, workaday life "at home"

7. Robert J. Priest et al., "Researching the Short-Term Mission Movement," *Missiology: An International Review* 34, no. 4 (2006): 432.

8. "History," YouthWorks: http://www.youthworks.com/about/history.asp (accessed Sept. 24, 2010). All numbers come from the YouthWorks Web site.

9. Noted by Eric Iverson, servant leader for MultiCultural Integrity for YouthWorks, in a personal conversation with the author, and confirmed via email, Oct. 2010.

10. "About Us," YouthWorks: http://www.youthworks.com/about/cpv.asp (accessed Sept. 24, 2010).

and experiences an extraordinary, voluntary, sacred experience "away from home" in a liminal space where sacred goals are pursued, physical and spiritual tests are faced, normal structures are dissolved, *communitas* is experienced, and personal transformation occurs. This transformation ideally produces new selves to be reintegrated back into everyday life "at home," new selves which in turn help to spiritually rejuvenate the churches they come from, and inspire new mission vision at home.[11]

But is this the case? No doubt many pastors and church members can tell well-rehearsed stories like the narrative of the burning bus, where *something* happens that brings persons back home changed, renewed, and transformed. The missiological, theological, and social-science research, however, is sparse. Christian scholars, theologians, and teachers have largely overlooked short-term missions; therefore, many seminarians graduate without doing theological reflection on STM, and yet they are expected to lead them when they enter a congregation.[12] In the absence of research, the conventional narrative of STM trips tends to hold that these trips provide an important service to the church abroad and renew the church at home.

Recent research, however, has called the conventional narratives into question.[13] Several studies have looked for strong correlations between STM trips and changed attitudes and/or practices at the local level. These correlations have been less clear than initially assumed. As such, two different conventional narratives have been called into question: that STM leads to personal transformation of the participants, and that STM provides spiritual and material goods and services to communities in need.

The Transformational Effectiveness of Short-Term Mission

As Priest and team observe above, a crucial hope for STM leaders is that the liminality of the experience will make possible a renewed spirituality

---

11. Priest et al., "Researching the Short-Term Mission Movement," 433-34.

12. Priest and team say that, in an informal survey given to incoming students at Trinity Evangelical Divinity School, over 62 percent of students had traveled outside the United States on a short-term mission trip. When compared to the fact that only 1 percent of college students engage in study-abroad programs, this number is quite remarkable as a sign of the popularity of these trips. See Priest et al., "Researching the Short-Term Mission Movement," 434.

13. Both Priest and Ver Beek provide short summaries of the available research. Kurt Alan Ver Beek, "The Impact of Short-Term Missions: A Case Study of House Construction after Hurricane Mitch," *Missiology: An International Review* 34, no. 4 (2006).

for participants. In my experience as a youth pastor, STM trips were designed with the express hope that students would come back changed and transformed. And in many cases (even on trips without buses catching fire) students obliged. They would arrive home safely, step off the bus and exclaim, "We went on the trip expecting to do things for others, but afterwards I feel like we received way more than we gave. I will never be the same again." Not surprisingly, this sentiment has been explored in several studies.

However, such a narrative remains fairly ambiguous in the research. As any youth pastor might testify, long-term change in students after such a trip is both difficult to assess and subject to various incongruities. For example, Kurt Ver Beek's research demonstrates how measurable changes in attitudes after STM trips do not necessarily translate into changed practices.[14] And even when persons report changed practice in areas that can be measured, this *perception* can be (in Ver Beek's research) inconsistent with actual data.[15] Part of the problem is that spiritual transformation remains a vague concept to study. Several studies concretize this sense of spiritual transformation by pointing toward particular results that STM experiences will bring about, such as better interethnic relationships, a rejection of consumeristic materialism, and increased missions support.

This concretization of spiritual renewal makes inherent sense. If STM trips are truly cross-cultural experiences, then it does not take a leap of faith to imagine that the vague sense of renewal reported by STM participants might be demonstrated through increased cultural sensitivity. Again, however, this is a difficult metric to study. Some studies have noted how STM trips tend to exhibit behavior patterns similar to the "tourism effect," where persons are likely to cross social and cultural boundaries when traveling, but unlikely to do so at home. Certainly, some of the data suggest that this is what happens, in that cross-cultural STM trips serve as a kind of "service tourism" with marginal impact on one's return home.[16] Although changes in actual practice have not been correlated with STM experiences (there are not necessarily well-publicized multicultural con-

14. Ver Beek argues that the largest reported change is in intangibles that cannot be measured, such as attitudes. However, Ver Beek found that this change in attitude was less likely to be seen in changed behavior.

15. Such as giving money to the CIDO mission agency. See Ver Beek, "The Impact of Short-Term Missions," 484-89.

16. Miriam Adeney, "Shalom Tourist: Loving Your Neighbor While Using Her," *Missiology: An International Review* 34, no. 4 (2006).

gregations who became this way because of STM experiences), there is some new research among Korean-American churches that demonstrates a correlation between STM experiences and a higher score on a metric called the Other Group Orientation (OGO).[17] Although this research is still in process, the initial findings demonstrate the strongest correlation between those who engage in children's ministries (such as VBS programs on the mission field) and OGO score. However, other research has shown that levels of ethnocentrism (a scale different from OGO) tend to drop immediately after an STM trip, but over time those with STM experience tend to be no different from those without in terms of ethnocentrism. In the end, STM trips are only ambiguously related to changed attitudes and relationships across cultures.

Still another hope for STM experiences is that they will expose and challenge the attitudes and practices of Western materialism.[18] This is often what participants report, but what exactly this transformation entails is much more difficult to assess. Priest and team offer a telling narrative from a personal conversation with a neighbor who served on an STM to an impoverished country. "I will never be the same," the neighbor swore. When pressed, the neighbor said that this change is one of gratitude: he is now much more thankful for what he has. The data that Priest and his team have points in this direction.[19] Contact across cultures and socioeconomic levels often does register (for participants) a deep sense of change, which is often expressed as gratefulness or a new awareness of Western materialism.

This is true in my own experience. After the infamous bus-burning STM trip, I noticed how quickly students went back to practices of the material acquisition they had sworn off only a week before. The incredibly liminal space we lived in for a week with one change of clothing was something left behind and across the border amid the poverty at the outskirts of Monterrey. With the reimbursement money from the bus company in hand, students rushed to the mall to replace whatever brand-name clothing or gadgets they had lost. They certainly consumed with a renewed gratitude, swearing that they will never be the same again. But they consumed

---

17. Sokpyo Hong, conversation with author at American Society of Missiology annual meeting (Chicago, 2010). Confirmed in personal correspondence with the author, July 23, 2010.

18. David A. Livermore, *Serving with Eyes Wide Open: Doing Short-Term Missions with Cultural Intelligence* (Grand Rapids: Baker Books, 2006).

19. Priest et al., "Researching the Short-Term Mission Movement," 440.

nonetheless. The siren song of the mall, with its concomitant practices of consumer culture, does not fade away with a renewed sense of gratitude or an awareness that people can be happy with fewer things.

A final hope for transformation placed on STM trips is that such experiences will increase involvement in missions through an uptick in career missionaries and giving. Proponents of STM often assume that these trips facilitate some kind of vocational change or spiritual formation that can be expressed as an increased interest in missions. But this has clearly not been the case. Although STM trips have increased exponentially over the past twenty years, the number of career, long-term missionaries has actually decreased.[20] Studies show that STM participants have a more positive view of a missionary vocation after a trip, but this change in attitude has not translated into missionaries in the field. Admittedly, this is most likely due to a host of issues unrelated to STM trips or personal attitudes (such as a general crisis in the identity of global missions and cash-strapped denominations and congregations). Similarly, though Ver Beek found that STM participants were most likely to *claim* increased financial support to mission work, giving records show only a marginal increase in giving.[21] Again, we see that changed attitudes and claims that "I will never be the same again" are difficult to substantiate in any concrete expression.

As compelling as the transformation narrative is, we must conclude that it is significantly oversold as a purpose for STM trips. We see, again and again, reported changes in attitudes unsubstantiated in the actual practice of STM participants. To be clear, I am not suggesting that the transformation narrative has no merit, just that it is quite often overstated.

In general, this brief overview of research shows that too much can be claimed for STM trips. Ver Beek and Priest and his team do not necessarily call into question the narrative that links STM to spiritual renewal. But they do provide research that can support what any honest Christian leader already acknowledges: that spiritual renewal and transformation are messy, fluid, and ambiguous aims not easily measured or defined. This leads, of course, to the second narrative for STM trips: STM brings vital and important change to communities, missions, and persons in need.

---

20. A. Scott Moreau, Gary Corwin, and Gary B. McGee, *Introducing World Missions: A Biblical, Historical, and Practical Survey*, in the Encountering Mission series (Grand Rapids: Baker Academic, 2004), 279.

21. Ver Beek, "The Impact of Short-Term Missions," 485-86.

The Missionary Effectiveness of Short-Term Mission

In recent years, STM trips have come under a good deal of criticism as a direct rebuttal to the narrative that short-term mission provides important spiritual and material resources for communities in need. Some have compared STM to tourism, which underscores the ethical ambiguity of such engagements. This ambiguity is clearly expressed in two different essays by Miriam Adeney: "When the Elephant Dances, the Mouse May Die" and "Shalom Tourist: Loving Your Neighbor While Using Her."[22] Others argue that from the perspective of a cost-benefit analysis, a great deal of money is spent on travel to perform a relatively cheap service. They suggest that this travel money should be sent to those already on the ground; that is, more service work can be done if the money is not "wasted" on expensive travel for undertrained personnel to engage in "mission-tourism."[23] Still others argue that a kind of ethnocentrism is actually sustained in STM trips rather than critiqued, because sending churches remain in a position of power and are often ill trained in terms of cultural sensitivity and social-systemic issues of injustice.

Ver Beek's research tests these criticisms by comparing groups in Honduras who received a new home after Hurricane Mitch from STM teams from the United States and those who received a home from the social-service agency on the ground. Are there spiritual and/or cultural benefits bestowed on those who received a home from the STM teams as compared to those who received a home from the aid agency? Or are there significant negative effects left by the STM teams? Against both the critics and proponents of STM, Ver Beek found in seventy-eight interviews conducted in six different regions of Honduras that "little or no difference" existed between STM or agency families who received homes in terms of the expressed level of spiritual impact, level of satisfaction, and other long-term differences. That is, the interviews, when compared, expressed neither a positive nor negative impact of the STM teams as compared to Christian agencies operating on the ground without STM help. Furthermore, when Ver Beek asked both North American and Honduran groups whether next time it would be better to send money rather than travel in

22. Adeney, "Shalom Tourist"; see also Miriam Adeney, ed., *When the Elephant Dances, the Mouse May Die* (Pasadena, CA: Into All the World Magazine, 2003).
23. For a brief overview of this argument, see Ver Beek, "The Impact of Short-Term Missions," 477-78.

order to provide more resources, the answers were quite nuanced. North American teams tended to both assert the value of their experience while also acknowledging a desire to do greater good by only sending money, whereas Honduran respondents tended to acknowledge the benefit of more money while also emphasizing how they do value the relationships built with STM teams. Again, it is clear that STM results are less clear and more contingent than both those who are critical of and those who are op- timistic about short-term mission maintain. They may not do as much damage as those critical of the trips claim, but they also might not bring the kind of benefit to local communities as advertised.

Reframing Short-Term Mission

So far we have explored the contemporary discussion regarding short- term mission trips. Based on the research, I have suggested that the relative merits and liabilities of such trips are difficult to gauge and measure. That is, STM trips do not necessarily create spiritual renewal or cultural sensi- tivity, nor do they necessarily run roughshod over local communities and "use them." As Ver Beek has shown, both the locals and STM participants tend to have fairly nuanced views of the merits and challenges of such trips.

The uninspiring results of the research might seem, at first glance, to tip the scales toward those that argue against STM trips. All things being equal, why not do the expedient thing and just send money to agencies al- ready at work "on the ground"? But should we be so quick to dismiss the testimonies of so many who come back saying, "I will never be the same again"? I think not, because the studies cited are limited by their emphasis on before-and-after measurement of select attitudes and behaviors. This is a distinctly linear and teleological frame for STM. Although this may not be out of line, this linear framing tends to treat something as profound and mysterious as spiritual formation and the transmission of faith as a rela- tively "thin" human phenomenon with discernible relationships of corre- lation. It is perhaps not surprising (nor do the researchers themselves seem surprised) that such studies find minimal measurable impact: a thin test- ing of mission will yield a thin result. Statistical models and generaliza- tions drawn from interviews are always generated from within an interpre- tive frame. In this case, current research tends to test the potency or efficacy of STM as an instrument or technology for certain kinds of personal or community transformation. It is a *teleological* and *instrumental* frame for STM in that it either tries to generalize or consider the end inherent in STM practice, or it looks for correlations between certain desired outcomes and STM experience.

This account surely flattens the STM experience. The research shows us that it is clearly not a technology for delivering certain results, or at least not an effective one. Moreover, STM participants will often report stories of disruption, confusion, and failure as much as perceived success. One does not need to lose a bus to fire in order to see that things do not always go as planned. What if, rather than looking for a transformation between home and away, between pre- and post-trip, we reframed STM by considering it as a disruptive event, where certain settled assumptions are challenged (at least for a week)? If this were the case, STM stories of disruption and even failure could rest alongside stories of success and triumph; and the ambiguity that accompanies the phrase "I will never be the same again" can be affirmed without being reduced. Furthermore, if STM were understood as exile, the present disruptive experience of the church could be seen in connection with the experience of dependence on God and strangers that marks a cross-cultural STM trip. Drawing attention to the ways in which God brings hope and a future in the midst of ambiguity and relative impotence (because of language barriers, conflict, burned-out buses, etc.) can generate new eyes and ears for discerning God's future amidst congregational exile back at home. That is, an exilic reframing of STM not only draws attention to overlooked aspects of the STM experience, but it also provides an experimental space within the life of the congregation for noticing and discovering God's presence in the exilic disruption of congregational life.

In order to reframe STM as an experience of exilic disruption, one must reconsider the conventional metaphors and narratives for STM experiences and explore new theological and congregational resources for describing and interpreting STM. I do not have space to do this work in great detail, but I will suggest the outline of such a reframing in the space that remains. As a metaphor, "exile" challenges a number of the assumptions that accompany the use of traveling metaphors such as "journey," "trip," or "pilgrimage."[24] In other ages, the prospect of a pilgrimage or journey evoked fear and demanded faithful courage, for a host of forces — real,

---

24. The Priest team uses "pilgrimage" to describe the common interpretation of STM. See Priest et al., "Researching the Short-Term Mission Movement," 433-34.

imagined, and largely unknown — conspired against the pilgrim. Vehicles could not carry individuals quickly through dangerous stretches of land, nor could hospitality arrangements be made with the help of Travelocity or a Smartphone. As such, a pilgrimage denoted a kind of journey into an unknown set of risks in hope of meeting a desired spiritual (and/or physical) end.[25] Travel (and perhaps the term "journey") carries a different meaning in the modern world. Rather than a risky and dangerous endeavor, it is a mark of one's power and potency. The educated and the socioeconomically elite are now the mobile class who can move from city to city across the globe (both geographically by air travel and virtually onscreen). STM participates in this reality. As a pilgrimage or journey, it is a well-organized and executed trip to accomplish certain missionary and formational tasks. As such, "pilgrimage" names STM (albeit unwittingly) as a privilege of the mobile classes and as a mark of potency and power. Thus, in the emphasis on life change, the STM pilgrimage is framed as a technology for certain predetermined ends (mission support, Bible study, lessened ethnocentrism).

This use of travel metaphors — with their teleological frame and assumption of potency — certainly draws on the inherited vision of Christendom. For the church in the United States still carries the institutional memories and social practices from an era of relative power and influence. Overseas mission often functioned within a paradigm of benevolent activism, and STM carries this set of assumptions. But if the United States has entered a postfunctional Christendom social reality, and if *exile* names its current experience of dispossession and displacement, then perhaps STM also needs a different theological frame, because "trip," "journey," and "pilgrimage" all suggest that the STM experience is one directed at a clear end, and the realities of modern mobility frame it as an act of privilege and power. We can state the implicit message of STM as pilgrimage baldly as such: If the church experiences exile at home, it need not when it exercises its privileged mobility and acts benevolently across a cultural or national boundary. But it is also difficult to imagine *mission* in relationship to exile, or as an experience of disruption and displacement.

25. This is, of course, a major theme in Augustine's work. It carries a teleological but also an eschatological sense in that the pilgrim is journeying to a future (city of God) that God will provide. My point here is to emphasize how our modern sense of travel emphasizes our initiative and power and eclipses the eschatological gift inherent in a metaphor like pilgrimage. For a discussion of Augustine's use of *peregrina* ("pilgrim"), see Peter Brown, *Augustine of Hippo: A Biography* (Berkeley: University of California Press, 2000), 312ff.

In the final section of this chapter, then, I will look to a theology of exile as a resource for understanding how it is that sustained disorientation might relate to God's ongoing work and the Spirit's creation of new and fluid identities in mission for Christian communities. My hope is that, by drawing on Israel's theological work in light of exile, we might find theological and biblical resources for recognizing and reframing the exilic and disruptive experiences of STM *as mission*. This is both a theological and a contextual argument, for if the church in the West is, in fact, experiencing the collapse of a functional Christendom arrangement, then we might read the explosion of STM as a significant way in which God is shaping the church. Finally, I will close with some theses regarding STM as disruption or exile, and what this might mean for planning and taking trips.

Disruption, Return, and Exile

It is commonplace for the binary "exile-return" to be applied to the Deuteronomic and exilic texts in the Hebrew Bible. As it is sometimes interpreted, the building of the second temple marks a "return" for Israel that was anticipated by the prophets, as Yahweh brings Israel "back to this place" after seventy years (Jer. 29:10). But there is a lingering sense in the Old Testament text that this return is not a return.[26] The text of Deuteronomy expects God to gather the exiles from the ends of the earth so that the Hebrews will again possess the land and be more prosperous than their ancestors (Deut. 30:3-5). But these expectations are not met. Indeed, the narratives that chronicle Israel's return are remarkably ambiguous. Ezra prays in front of the "faithless returned exiles" that "we are slaves; yet our God has not forsaken us in slavery, but has extended to us his steadfast love before the kings of Persia, to give us new life to set up the house of our God, to repair its ruins, and to give us a wall in Judea and Jerusalem" (Ezra 9:4, 9). It is a return and yet not a return. They are in the land but still slaves. A "remnant" is in Jerusalem, but the great majority remain scattered in the Diaspora. They build a wall and a temple, but it is not cause for celebration; it only underscores what had been lost, while the exilic crisis of identity remains. The disruption of exile persists.

26. The symmetry of the phrase "a return and yet not a return" comes from Patrick Keifert, "The Return of the Congregation: Missional Warrants," *Word and World* 20, no. 4 (2000).

What is at stake theologically in this persisting disruption? How is it that exile shapes Israel and Yahweh? This is a question that could occupy much more space than I have left in this chapter. However, given our concern for short-term missions and missional spiritual formation, I will focus our discussion on two different crises provoked by exile. First, Israel's exile creates a full-fledged identity crisis for the people. The experience of mobility in exile is not one of power and privilege, but rather of weakness and dislocation. This feature of exile calls into question Israel's symbolic and narrative self-understanding, as the psalmist asks how one can sing the songs of the Lord while in a foreign place (Ps. 138:4). Israel's response is a messy and multifaceted retelling and reappropriation of the tradition for the sake of accounting for the new, the return that is not a return. Second, the exile marks a theological crisis. What does exile have to do with Yahweh? Israel affirms both Yahweh's sovereign freedom as a judge of Israel and Yahweh's *pathos* as God identifies Godself with exilic Israel's suffering. Finally, I will suggest that the tensions that emerge in response to these two crises — of identity and theology — come together (though remain unresolved) in an expanded horizon for mission.

Identity in Exile: Who Will We Become?

Walter Brueggemann argues that a powerful and pluralistic Jewish counterimagination is unleashed in exile. Amid daily reminders of imperial hegemony ("we are slaves"), the exilic testimony "refuses given imperial reality and summons its hearers to an alternative reality": that Yahweh is God even in captivity, when land, temple, and priesthood have all been taken away. The question "How can we worship God while in a foreign land?" is answered in a score of ways, as prophets reinterpret and renarrate the written and oral traditions in light of their dislocation. Brueggemann writes: "In the generation of this text, there were no obvious lines of certitude, no ready formulations of assurance, no self-evident reliabilities. Therefore, it is not surprising that the exile is a moment of enormous literary generativity, when a variety of daring articulations of the faith were undertaken."[27] Since the old (somewhat stable) certainties for Israelite theology and worship — city, land, temple, monarchy — had been taken away, questions of identity needed to be re-addressed.

27. Walter Brueggemann, *Theology of the Old Testament: Testimony, Dispute, Advocacy* (Minneapolis: Fortress, 2005), 75-76.

This is not unusual among displaced peoples. Studies of modern-day refugee populations demonstrate the need for displaced peoples to reconstruct their history, for in this reconstruction they are able to recover meaning and also accept a new future. This reconstruction, then, is necessarily a personal and historical task:

> Several anthropologists working with refugees have found that one of the important components in the recovery of meaning, the making of culture, and the reestablishment of trust is the need and the freedom to construct a normative picture of one's past within which "who one was" can be securely established to the satisfaction of the refugee. The refugee's self-identity is anchored more to who she or he was than what he or she has become . . . for the refugee this is the foundation on which a meaningful world can be rebuilt.[28]

The reconstructive, imaginative, and meaning-making task of dislocated and traumatized populations is to *reconstruct* the past in order to *receive* a new future. The question "who are we?" becomes, in moments of traumatic displacement, both "who were we?" and "who will we become?" An exilic identity crisis seeks to understand the past so that a future can be recognized and received.[29] The exilic prophets demonstrate this task.

An example of the re-formation of identity can be seen in Deutero-

28. E. Valentine Daniel and John C. Knudsen, "Introduction," in E. Valentine Daniel and John C. Knudsen, eds., *Mistrusting Refugees* (Berkeley: University of California Press, 1995), 5; quoted in Smith-Christopher, *A Biblical Theology of Exile*, 80.

29. Patrick Matlou, "Upsetting the Cart: Forced Migration and Gender Issues, the African Experience," in Doreen Marie Indra, ed., *Engendering Forced Migration: Theory and Practice* (New York: Berghahn Books, 1999). Matlou shows the danger in this identity-work in modern refugee populations. He emphasizes the way in which divisions and inequalities before exile are frequently reinforced and magnified during exile. A "negative" retelling of history can just as easily create negative and destructive behaviors as it can generate more positive and reconstructive behaviors. It is perhaps counterintuitive, but scholars note that a negative retelling of a community's history (we are suffering because of our own sins, or because of the failure to follow our best traditions) serves to reinterpret and reinforce its identity and god in a time of dislocation, for if it is God's punishment, then God is still present and powerful; if it is bad karma, then Buddhism helps to interpret the suffering and promises that the worst is past. See Smith-Christopher, *A Biblical Theology of Exile*, 78-83. Brueggemann argues that Israel's theology of creation was drawn on and given a more substantive role in the exile for this reason. The fact of Yahweh's punishment of Israel at the hands of Babylon means that Yahweh is not a territorial god but God of all creatures, of all creation. Brueggemann, *Theology of the Old Testament*, 149-54.

Isaiah, who draws on the Exodus and reconstructs history so that "wilderness wanderings" can be seen in light of exile. Just as Israel learned God's faithful leading in the wilderness, so also God leads Judah in the exile. But exilic circumstances also reshape this theological memory as Yahweh declares through the prophet: "See, the former things have come to pass, and the *new things* I now declare" (Isa. 42:9; italics added). The shocking announcement of the Persian emperor Cyrus as God's "shepherd" who will carry out God's purpose is, of course, among the "new things" proclaimed by the prophet (Isa. 44:28). How can the memories of the Exodus be revived when the shepherd is a pagan? A foreign king? A similar juxtaposition of images also shapes the Ezra-Nehemiah narrative, as historical-prophetic images such as "remnant" and "return" collide with empirical realities of divisiveness and Persian dominance. How can the "return" of Judah's remnant be marked by "faithlessness" and continued "slavery" while still claiming God's "steadfast love before the kings of Persia" (Ezra 9:4, 9)? The biblical texts hold this tension and do not resolve it. It is the exodus, and yet it is new, shockingly new. It is a return — and yet not a return.

Yahweh in Exile: Where Is God?

Theologically, of course, this account of the exile raises all kinds of questions.[30] If the return is marked by such ambiguity with regard to land, temple, and monarchy, what can be made of the promise? If Yahweh is indeed the Creator-God, can this God be trusted in light of recent events? Is God good for the promise, or is God fickle and untrustworthy? The exilic identity crisis is also a theological crisis in which Yahweh is identified with "Israel-at-risk," thus disclosing *God's* vulnerability.[31] But this vulnerability also makes possible new horizons for mission and God's promised future.

In exile, Israel again discovers what Brueggemann calls Israel's "oddest theological testimony," that Yahweh is both committed in solidarity with Israel and yet relates to Israel in freedom. For Brueggemann, the testimony in Exodus 34:6-7 is paradigmatic in that a statement describing

---

30. Brueggemann calls this Israel's "counter-testimony." See Brueggemann, *Theology of the Old Testament*, 317-18.

31. Of course, this vulnerability is not a new addition to the Israelite narrative in exile. It is present throughout biblical literature in the fact that God continually identifies Godself with fickle and contingent human beings. Being the God identified with Abraham, Isaac, and Jacob is risky business.

God's steadfast love "for the thousandth generation" and forgiveness for "iniquity and sin" is interrupted with "yet by no means clearing the guilty, but visiting the iniquity of the parents upon the children. . . ." In Israel's testimony, the two statements are not reconciled; rather, they are held in unresolved tension. In solidarity and commitment to Israel, God seeks partnership with Israel. Israel is identified with Yahweh, and Yahweh with Israel; and yet Yahweh enters this relationship freely, for Yahweh is not subsumed by the covenant. That is, "Yahweh is committed to Yahweh's partners in *freedom* and in *passion*."[32]

The usual binary of exile-return tends to emphasize God's freedom in relationship to Israel, that God — as a righteous and holy God — punishes Israel for her sins and iniquities before bringing her back to the land. Working from this framework, it is easy to see how the exilic experience, ironically enough, expands Israel's theological horizons in relationship to Yahweh.[33] For at the same time that God brings judgment on Israel through the nations, these same nations are brought within Israel's story of blessing and judgment. Jürgen Moltmann expresses this dynamic well: "[O]n its political deathbed Israel brings the nations, as it were, into the hands of its God and into his future."[34] It is perhaps not a surprise, then, that exile is also associated with a kind of universalism, in which Israel proclaims Yahweh's profound act of creation vis-à-vis the other national gods and in which the prophets (especially the book of Isaiah) imagine the nations sharing in Israel's blessing. That is, what is initially interpreted as God's act of judgment also becomes the context for revealing a broader horizon for God's promise; for "it is too light a thing that you should be my servant . . . and to restore the survivors of Israel; I will give you as a light to the nations, that my salvation may reach to the end of the earth" (Isa. 49:6). To be clear, this is not a universalism that overlooks sin, for the image of the nations pouring into Jerusalem suggests a "turning," or a humbling, of the nations as well.[35] Regardless, the dream of universal peace and justice, where age-old enemies come together in worship of Yahweh as the fulfillment of God's promise to Israel demonstrates an expanding theological horizon.

Here Jeremiah's encouragement to the exiles to seek the welfare of

32. Brueggemann, *Theology of the Old Testament*, 270, 410 (italics added).

33. For a nuanced account of exile and mission, see Smith-Christopher, *A Biblical Theology of Exile*, 125-36.

34. Jürgen Moltmann, *Theology of Hope: On the Ground and the Implications of a Christian Eschatology* (Minneapolis: Fortress, 1993), 129.

35. Smith-Christopher, *A Biblical Theology of Exile*, 125-36.

their new cities takes on a more profound theological tone. The Diaspora attempt to reconstruct their history unveils God's contemporaneous relevance to their displacement among the nations. That is, by telling the story of exile as God's freedom to fight against Israel, to punish Israel for her sins, God also reveals Godself as the God of world history, the God of creation. Israel can seek the peace of the city because Yahweh is God there, too. And Yahweh's judgment is not the last word: "for I know the plans I have for you. . . ."

But we must not forget the human and divine cost of this expanded horizon. The same prophets who interpret exile as Yahweh's freedom vis-à-vis Israel also show the tortured relationship of Yahweh's steadfast love and *passionate* appeal to Israel. Like a jilted lover, Yahweh gives voice to an open wound recalling the collapse of the Northern Kingdom and expresses incredulity at Israel's refusal of Yahweh's love: "I thought you would call me Father, and would not turn from following me. Instead, as a faithless wife leaves her husband, you have been faithless to me" (Jer. 3:19-20). God continues to identify Godself with Israel and Judah in her faithlessness, and also in her exile. Ezekiel sees God's glory rise up from the temple and move east (Ezek. 10:18-19), and then later Yahweh remarks that God's name has been "profaned" among the nations because of the weak disposition of Israel (Ezek. 36:20). That is, the exiles discover God's freedom *and* suffering in exile. They seek the peace of the city because God is both the God of the nations and because Yahweh is the exilic God who has gone before them, and whose name is identified with Israel. God's act of global freedom and strength in gathering the nations against Israel is also God's disclosure of vulnerable love. Yahweh's mighty acts are witnessed to by a displaced and marginalized people. In this way mission is organically related to passion, to vulnerability and suffering.

Mission as Exile: Disruptive Hope

Several scholars note that mission emerges more explicitly in the exilic texts, both as a strain of universalism (imagining the salvation of the nations) and an explicit reference to Yahweh's servant bearing witness to the Gentiles.[36] This argument can certainly be overblown; the Hebrew Scrip-

---

36. Smith-Christopher, *A Biblical Theology of Exile*, 125-36; see also Christopher J. H. Wright, *The Mission of God: Unlocking the Bible's Grand Narrative* (Downers Grove, IL: InterVarsity, 2006); Brueggemann, *Theology of the Old Testament*.

tures understand Israel's vocation with respect to the nations in a variety of texts. But attending to the theme of mission can clarify the *hope* sustained in the midst of a persisting exilic disruption. We are accustomed to think of mission — and particularly short-term mission — in terms of a sending agency in which a group intentionally collects resources and goes out to share with another group of people. Under such assumptions, Israel's exilic experience would seem like a disruption of mission from the expansive and heady days of David and Solomon. Exilic mission subverts this sense of agency in that mission is what happens while Israel tries to make sense of its exilic life in its full vulnerability and suffering. The servant in Deutero-Isaiah is a light to the nations even while being publicly humiliated and crushed — a narrative that is easily recognized in the life and ministry of Jesus. Even in the book of Jonah, the prophet is sent against his will to a people that he does not trust or like. And yet there is a sustaining hope throughout much of the exilic literature. The servant bears witness to God in suffering; God is merciful to a pouting Jonah. And Jeremiah's encouragement to seek the peace of the city is a profound testimony to a kind of missional promise while in the midst of exile. That the biblical tradition sustains hope in the midst of this trauma can be understood as an affirmation of Israel's sense of vocation rooted in a dynamic faith in a dynamic God.

Exile as mission, or mission in exile, is an ambiguous affair. It is no longer a teleological quest like a pilgrimage, in which a group sets out for a certain place or end, but rather a way of discovering and naming God's presence — activity and passivity — in and among the nations with an exiled people. As such, Israel's exilic mission required several creative and daring interpretations of the Israelite story. Thus we see images that suggest a kind of universal saving action of God alongside celebrations of God's judgment on the nations, and movements that reinforce Israelite boundary markers (such as Ezra-Nehemiah's injunction against intermarriage) rest in the canon alongside stories that emphasize the faithfulness of the pagans (such as Jonah). God's work is placed within a broadened horizon, such that exile makes possible the affirmation of Israel's Diaspora as a kind of participation in God's mission to the nations.

But it is decidedly not the kind of triumphant narrative — even with the return to Zion and the rebuilding of the temple — in which Israelite identity is clarified and the ambiguity of exile is resolved. It is a return, and yet not a return. Nor does this kind of naming and discovering produce an abidingly clear picture of God's presence and work. Indeed, the exilic tensions persisted even in first-century Palestine, as several Gospels tell the story of Jesus as a performance of Israel's return from exile.[37] The naming and discovering work of exilic mission, then, is done within the kind of humility, suffering, and finally hope that marks the space between exile and return, cross and resurrection, promise and fulfillment.

"How can we sing the songs of the Lord in a new land?" This question is both answered and hauntingly open in the biblical tradition. I have outlined two kinds of irresolvable tensions that characterize exile. On the one hand, the suffering and physical displacement of a people requires that the national stories are retold and reinterpreted so that meaning can be recovered. And yet, this recovery of meaning opens up the possibility for interpreting the new, discontinuous, and unexpected. On the other hand, the fluidity of identity and the experience of both God's judgment and promised presence create an expanding theological horizon in which God is revealed as *over* the nations and yet *vulnerable* in suffering love for Israel. The tensions come together (though are certainly not resolved) in an expanded horizon for mission. These tensions that lead to an expansive mission underscore why there cannot be a return, why the construction of the temple and the completion of Jerusalem's wall only lead to public mourning for what was. Exile is not only physical displacement but also narrative displacement. There is no return because the story has lurched into a different direction. "For I know the plans . . ." is not the soft romanticism of a God who orders our life, but rather an invitation for renewed trust in an open sky even though it might be falling. It is an invitation to risk with the God who also risks identification with God's created partners.

Exiles on Main Street

The North American church has not experienced the kind of violent displacement that ancient Israel or modern-day refugee populations have. And yet exile has become an increasingly common metaphor for understanding the experience of the church. Although not physically intimidated and displaced, the Christendom narrative emphasizing Christian expansion and power has run out of steam. Historical downtown church

---

37. I am following N. T. Wright's interpretation of the Gospels here: that the Jesus story is told in response to a continued sense of exile in Jewish identity. See N. T. Wright, *The New Testament and the People of God*, vol. 1 (Minneapolis: Fortress, 1992).

buildings are now libraries or nightclubs; many church budgets are contracting, including budgets for mission societies; and the cultural influence of the Protestant mainline has waned. As these examples demonstrate, exile is an appropriate metaphor for the loss of Christendom precisely because it is experienced as the sudden absence of power, influence, and agency.[38] Attentive observers of the Western church have insisted on the emergence of post-Christendom cultural reality, and have called for a new performance of the gospel in Western cultures.[39]

However, old habits die hard. Such calls are often met with a renewed productivity in "missional" congregational work. Mountains of books have been generated to teach missional leadership, missional small groups, missional evangelism, and missional worship for the sake of reengaging Western society.[40] This work is important and often profound for the life of congregations. However, it still fails to address the fundamental loss of agency, influence, identity, and resources that characterizes exile. "Missional" becomes another church-growth technology that alleviates some anxiety without doing the creative and daring retelling of God's story that characterizes the Israelite exilic community. That is, "missional" can create the illusion of cultural agency through the production of new initiatives, which (ironically) keeps the church from recognizing its exilic instability and vulnerability.

Within this context, it is not surprising that short-term mission trips tend to institutionalize a kind of benevolent activism. But perhaps they can be reframed in light of mission in exile, for on a lonely Mexican highway fire consumed an embarrassingly long list of goods, props, and gifts brought for the sake of mission. The student teams had prepared Vacation Bible School and park presentations months in advance. We brought our mission in a bus; we had a message to share and resources to give — until cigarette ashes fell into a T-shirt box during the border inspection. At that

---

38. This has been most recently picked up by Michael Frost, *Exiles: Living Missionally in a Post-Christian Culture.*

39. I am referring here to the work spawned by the Gospel and Our Culture Network (GOCN). See, for example, Guder, *Missional Church;* George R. Hunsberger and Craig Van Gelder, *The Church between Gospel and Culture: The Emerging Mission in North America* (Grand Rapids: Eerdmans, 1996).

40. A survey hardly seems necessary here. Those familiar with the conversation can fill in the blanks; those unfamiliar with it should consult Craig Van Gelder and Dwight J. Zscheile, *The Missional Church in Perspective: Mapping Trends and Shaping the Conversation* (Grand Rapids: Baker Academic, 2011), for a concise overview and critique of this literature.

point our pilgrimage became a kind of exile. We no longer had a clear "end" toward which to focus our aim. We were not sure we could stay the rest of the week, so we turned to our hosts for material, spiritual, and emotional hospitality. When one student prayed the words of Jeremiah 29 and named God's presence — God's activity *and* passivity — our exilic mission emerged. We tried to bring a "mission"; we were surprised to discover something altogether different, as God met us in the hospitality of our Mexican brothers and sisters.

A local news station greeted us when we returned to our church parking lot ten days later. Many students proclaimed to the cameras, "I will never be the same again." But time has a way of softening novelty, and things certainly *seemed* to be the same in just a few weeks. Ver Beek's research held even in this extreme circumstance. And yet, a disruptive event became a part of our church story. What we had planned, intended, and worked toward went up in smoke. We started our trip as pilgrims and ended up exiles. We began with the intention of benevolence and instead found we had little to offer. After ten days we returned safely, but such a disruption did not conform easily to the stories we tell about our agency, our benevolence, and our mission. The trip might not have translated into the kind of tangibles sought after in STM research. Maybe some in the church began to give more to missions, or students read their Bibles and prayed more often, but this is most likely not the case. However, the trip did introduce a new and disruptive narrative into the life of the congregation; as such, the trip offered a subtle challenge to congregational identity. The exilic nature of the experience offered the narrative resources for recognizing exile at home. As such, it is precisely the ambiguity of the trip and its consequent intangible "results" that offers a theo-practical disruption to the congregation.

Not every STM includes a bus fire. But trips do facilitate experiences of dislocation and disruptive surprises. Every STM participant seems to have an "up-in-smoke" story that articulates broken plans and unfulfilled intentions. The theological work I have attempted in this chapter is to reframe and recontextualize the "up-in-smoke" narratives as needing more careful attention. Mission in exile means that, rather than approaching these disruptions as challenges for the team to overcome, they are opportunities for discovering the surprising presence and work of God in our passivity and vulnerability rather than our potency and agency. That is, exile suggests a theological reframing of STM, not as an instrument or pilgrimage to bring certain services to a community while fostering spiritual maturity in the participants, but rather as a practice that creates the possibility for a subversive counternarrative to the dominant North American assumption of agency and initiative in mission. And it is in this reframing that we can perhaps be more likely to take our congregants at their word when they confess, "I will never be the same again," even if they cannot verbalize what has changed or if we cannot see any evidence of such change. It is possible that their narrative has just been disrupted, and they sense that their return is not a return. In such a case, we would be wise to watch for what catches fire next.

Conclusion: To Start a Fire . . .

Thus far we have noticed the ambiguous results of STM for United States congregations and explored the way in which exile might provide a theological reframing of such trips. Drawing on the tensions present in the exilic biblical literature, I suggest that the disruptive experience of exile opens up settled and stable identity markers that make possible the recognition and reception of a new future. Moreover, Israel's account of exilic helplessness and passivity discloses an expanded horizon for mission while also testifying to God's vulnerability in suffering with Israel. That is, the crises of identity and theology yield surprising hope in the midst of ambiguity and sustain anticipation of "the new" while many certainties crumble. Israel's testimony of hopeful anticipation in the midst of exile, of daring storytelling in order to receive the new, of recognizing God's vulnerability in the midst of their own, is a compelling basis for discovering mission in exile — or mission as exile. Throughout this chapter I have argued that this reframing is not only compelling but also potentially illuminating for the sense of dislocation that congregations are experiencing in the United States. If STM is to be an experimental and disruptive space for congregations in which *mission* is discovered in the midst of exile, then we need to try a different kind of theological framing and storytelling. STM can be an experimental narrative and experiential space for congregations to recognize and discover God's presence — action and passion — in the midst of displacement, disruption, and exile. Such experiences, when nurtured in congregational theological storytelling, where God's mission is recognized and sustained in moments of displacement, ambiguity, and disruption, will certainly generate an identity receptive to and discerning of "the new" that God is cultivating in America's exilic landscape.

In conclusion, I will offer three suggestions for reframing STM as a disruptive and exilic event for the sake of recognizing God's future in the midst of exile. (1) *Pay attention to and nurture stories of disruption and ambiguity.* STM stories — even STM research — tend to emphasize the triumph of the mission. We face certain obstacles, we learn to grit our teeth, trust God, and voila! — it all ends well. But this is not the story of exile and return, of living in the tension of the already-but-not-yet. STM provides an opportunity to begin the habit of discovering God in the moment of loss, insecurity, and ambiguity rather than in the story of triumph. What would it mean for these kinds of stories to become part of our identity? This is the beginning of mission in exile, or even exile as mission.

(2) *Allow your host community to teach and train you.* By this, I do not mean imposing an unbearable burden on a host community, but finding ways of depending on the hospitality and expertise of a host community in a way that gives life to both groups. This was my experience when the bus burned. Sadly, I have not encountered this kind of mutuality in any trip since. Some East African communities who have received groups of mission teams over many years have suggested reframing STM as "mission training" rather than simply short-term mission.[41] This subtly changes the focus of the trip from "bringing" mission to actually learning ministry from those already at work in a context.

(3) *Take advantage of failure.* One of the marks of an exilic disruption is the loss of identity. What this means is that long-standing assumptions are now questioned and long-standing practices are now impotent. STM is essentially an action-reflection engagement, and so it can be a kind of experiment in Christian community and mission. It is a space for new experiences. But these experiences — and, perhaps, experiments — must be reflected on theologically. STM should be accompanied by constant questions: What are we learning here? About ourselves? About God? Where have we seen God? A mission failure that reflects deeply on these questions can be a worthwhile one, even without a burning bus.

41. Edwin Zehner, "Short-Term Missions: Toward a More Field-Oriented Model," *Missiology: An International Review* 34, no. 4 (Oct. 2006).

CHAPTER 4

Living into the Big Story:
The Missional Trajectory of Scripture
in Congregational Life

Allen Hilton

The action of Plato's *Symposium* begins when Phaedrus identifies a gaping hole in Greek literature: "While all [manner of] screeds have been written on such trivial subjects [as the uses of common salt], the god of love has found no one bold enough to sing his praises as they should be sung" (177.b-c).[1] Once Phaedrus has issued this challenge, Eryximachus easily persuades his drinking mates to join him in answering it. This will not be a night of drunkenness or the entertainments of flute girls; instead, this company will speak properly the praises of Eros.

The dialogue will reach its climax in Socrates' splendid mystic vision of love. But earlier, when Aristophanes gets his turn (freshly recovered from a bout with the hiccups), he traces out love's origins. In Aristophanes' myth, human beings were once of a much different form than ours — "globular with rounded back and sides, four arms and four legs, and two faces, both the same, on a cylindrical neck, and one head, with one face one side and one the other. . . ." These very capable creatures wax ever more arrogant, until their hubris drives them to crash heaven's gates. In response, Zeus and the gods decide not to obliterate humanity (from whence then would their offerings come?), but rather to weaken them by means of bisection. Each creature is to be sliced down the middle "like an egg with a hair," then sewn together with the skin pulled tight and gathered at the belly. Each half is to be fully separated from its other half. Predictably, this surgery "left each half with a desperate yearning for the other." The human

---

1. *Plato's Symposium*, trans. Michael Joyce (New York: Everyman's Library, 1935).

is no longer fully sufficient in him/herself, so each seeks another passionately, day and night. Eros is born. The company raises a glass in reverence.

We, too, have gathered to sing praises to a God whose nature is love. But this divine love is of a kind different from the one Plato's Aristophanes imagined. Eros, once it has entered a human soul, pursues its beloved urgently, night and day, out of a hunger that will only be sated by union. But this God's love, which is even more urgent and tireless, pursues all the peoples of the world — not to complete itself but to complete them. Its story is told in pictures: of chaos becoming order by God's word, so that the beloved may have a home; of the divine Lover weathering the beloved's rejection in Eden; hearing and heeding her suffering cries from beneath the scourge of Egyptian slave-owners; reaching to her derelict destitution in Nineveh; hearing the choked anger of her cry from the side of a Babylonian river; seeking her as a shepherd chases one lost sheep or a woman scours the house for one lost coin; sprinting from the old home's porch breathlessly to welcome her home from blind wanderings; dying on a tool of torture so that she might live; undoing death to be reunited with her; and building a new heaven and a new earth where the beloved may dwell with the Lover forever.

This brilliant love, so bent on blessing all peoples, is the very mission of God. It is what God does always, from the dawn of creation through eternity. Its story is told, not in the annals of an imagined drinking party, but in the world God's Holy Spirit has built for us by the hands of the ancient authors, whose words became Scripture. So let us put aside the strong drink and send the flutists away. It is time to sing praise to the God who eternally is this ever-seeking, never-dying, people-blessing Love.

Our Project

My charge here is to trace the missional trajectory through Scripture.[2] One simple way to meet this challenge would be to gather all of the passages in

---

2. Defining the term "missional" is notoriously difficult. I will feature four characteristics of missional Christianity.

    (1) *God's act is primary:* A missional congregation understands that God's activity in the world precedes, succeeds, and is independent of its own initiative. God is ever and always building God's kingdom in our world, and it is a Christian's and a congregation's call to participate in that ongoing activity of God.

    (2) *God's act is for everyone:* A missional congregation knows the international (even cosmic) reach of God's blessing.

    (3) *Church is not all about us:* A missional congregation has a primary and consum-

the Bible that picture God actively loving the whole world; I could then add all the parts in which God calls persons and communities into that redemptive activity and feature especially the ones in which those persons and communities actually consent and participate in God's loving reach to the world. I could close with an inspiring call to form congregations with those words.

In the burgeoning field of missional hermeneutics, this has been the tendency: to trace out the central theme of God's mission through Scripture. Christopher Wright is representative when he writes: "In short, a missional hermeneutic proceeds from the assumption that the whole Bible renders to us the story of God's mission through God's people in their engagement with God's world for the sake of the whole of God's creation."[3] Wright's subtitle, *Unlocking the Bible's Grand Narrative,* reiterates the claim. There is much in Scripture that tilts in this direction, so Wright and others have plenty of passages to mine. I could follow their lead and discharge my duty in that way, and perhaps this would help you. I have a feeling, though, that if this topic interests you enough to prompt the exquisitely self-sacrificial act of reading a long academic paper, you already know some of the several articles and books that do something like what I have described. And my suspicion is that you know the Bible passages well but remain frustrated that your congregation or group or class is either not heeding or not reading them. The missional God has caught you, and you want that God to catch your people. You just want to know how.

There is another matter. Perhaps you have tripped on your own missional walk over ambiguities that litter the biblical way, as I have. A missional thread clearly winds its way through Scripture, but the people of God and the authors of Scripture who record their movements register another impulse, alongside the missional one; this thread is internally fo-

---

ing devotion to continue God's work in the world as the body of Christ. Discipleship is not merely a compliance with commands of Jesus, but rather the playing out of a spiritual cooperation with the God who "so love(s) the world" in Jesus.

(4) *All Christians are called to mission:* A missional congregation cultivates this devotion to living Christ toward the world in each member of the congregation. Every member of a missional church knows that he or she is called into life-giving ministry as the body of Christ.

There are many other ways to slice the pie, and this definition is not comprehensive. But it will help us to be specific and to limit the definition in this way.

3. Christopher Wright, *The Mission of God: Unlocking the Bible's Grand Narrative* (Downers Grove, IL: InterVarsity, 2006), 122.

cused, xenophobic, and world-conquering. These authors and characters imagine God on their side against the other, rather than reaching with them *to* the other. And this attitude is not rare or isolated. It appears in Genesis and Revelation, and frequently across the landscape in between.

To help with this practical matter of forming congregations, I want to do two things in this chapter that I have not seen done in the growing literature on the Bible in missional Christianity. First, I'll try to balance the thoroughly missional reading of Scripture that has characterized recent missional hermeneutics, noticing the places in the text where God and God's people are not pictured as missional. This project may seem heretical in a book of this purpose, but I'll try to make the case that an honest reading of the good, the bad, and the ugly of biblical peoples will actually help our cause of forming missional Christians.[4]

The second project here is to identify a pedagogy, a set of practices, that will help your congregation members to actually read the Bible and begin to see themselves in its pages. The Moses of Deuteronomy commanded his charges to announce to their priests, "[A] wandering Aramean was my father . . ." (Deut. 26:5). How can you and I instill such immediacy and relatedness in our folks? As a professor of Bible who now ministers in churches, I've had the profound privilege of helping two congregations become "people of the book." In these pages I will share with you some of the means God has used to bring about those transformations.

Two parts, then: first, an honest rereading of Scripture's story; second, a very practical run at moving that story into the lived lives of our people through communal Bible study.

The Missional Trajectory?

I draw the comparison with Plato's *Symposium*, not ornamentally but heuristically. Noticing the important differences between Aristophanes' Eros and the love of God in Scripture will help us to understand the sometimes

---

4. George Hunsberger, in "Proposals for a Missional Hermeneutic," has helpfully raised a similar question without attempting an answer. He writes, "This framework [i.e., that the Bible is primarily or even univocally missional] is fundamental to all the other proposals, and they all have in one way or another affirmed this understanding of the Bible as a whole. This may be a point for further serious engagement . . . with biblical scholarship (does it propose more unity than is present in the writings?) . . ." (http://www.gocn.org/resources/articles/proposals-missional-hermeneutic-mapping-conversation).

bleak history of nonparticipation by Israel and the early Christians in God's missional purposes.

The plot line of Aristophanes' myth and the Genesis 11 story of the Tower of Babel feature obvious and well-chronicled similarities. In each, the gods/God notice a human conspiracy that threatens to tear down the wall between divine and human. And in each the divine acts to thwart the conspiracy by separating humans in a way that undermines their shared power. Both are etiologies, explaining through story a well-known part of "the way things are."

For our purposes, the differences between Aristophanes' legend and the biblical story are more significant than the similarities. One concerns timetable. In the *Symposium*, Eros is born of separation. But in Genesis, God's love simply *is* — from the beginning. Love preexists and explains creation itself, as God makes space for an other who will receive divine love. When the beloved themselves separate from God in the Garden of Eden, the same love that created the beloved and gave them a home simply finds new form. And when the beloved force their own separation at the Tower of Babel, that new form is clarified: God will bless all humanity. It is God's unchangeable nature to bless them. But after the distancing damage of Eden and Babel has been done, God's love seeks a people through whom to bless the world, and suddenly love takes on a horizontal and interfamilial dimension. After clans and nations and languages have split humanity, God's love sets out toward reconciliation, and so God calls Abram and Sarai and their family (and, eventually, anyone else) who will join God's mission to become agents of blessing.

Missional Family?

It is at the pivot point of Genesis 12 that we recognize a second crucial difference between Aristophanes' story and ours, and it concerns motivation and participation. When Eros is born in the *Symposium*, its hungry urgency appears within every human as standard equipment. As Aristophanes has it, humans are "always looking for our other half." We incessantly desire our "meeting and melting" with one another. The driver that moves lover toward beloved is planted internally, so that the lover will not rest until she/he has found and joined the beloved. Indeed, the myth has it that all humanity shares this other-seeking nature.

When God calls Abram and Sarai, however, God installs no such internal driver in them. The promise is beautiful: "Now the Lord said to Abram, 'Go from your country and your kindred and your father's house to the land that I will show you. I will make of you a great nation, and I will bless you, and make your name great, so that you will be a blessing. I will bless those who bless you, and the one who curses you I will curse; and *in you all the families of the earth shall be blessed*" (Gen. 12:1-3; italics added).

There is much for Abram and Sarai in this promise: a great nation, a blessing, a great name. But the promise does not picture Abram and Sarai's clan as the sole and final destination of divine blessing. Rather, the last clause tells the larger story of God's love: God intends to extend the divine blessing beyond Abram and Sarai — better, through them to all peoples. In this moment of divine communication, Abram's kin are enlisted in God's plan to resolve the fragmentation wrought by the Tower of Babel. God's love now has a focused entry point for its activity. Abram's soon-to-be family will be a means of God's blessing to all peoples. As splendidly missional as this promise is, however, it offers no assurance that divine love will ever burn in Abram and Sarai, or in any others who would open themselves to be a blessing to all nations. In fact, if we peruse the story of this family in Genesis, Abram/Abraham and Sarai/Sarah never once acknowledge the last clause of the blessing. Abraham complains to God about the delay of off-spring; he negotiates his fortune. His fame rises accordingly. He relishes the way God curses those who curse him. But not a word about being a blessing or being the conduit through which blessing flows to all the earth's families.

This is an astonishing aspect of the story, is it not? A couple hears the very voice of God and veritably ignores its climactic call. But even commentators from a missional perspective have not, to my knowledge, noted the incongruity. The chosen family appears throughout to be oblivious to its role in God's reach to the world. Missionally sensitive ears prick up when Abram and Sarai plan a trip to Egypt. Perhaps they will begin quickly to live out blessing to the world. But, alas, they venture out not to bless Egyptians but to survive a famine. And the impact of their visit on the people of Egypt is far from redemptive: when Abram passes Sarai off as his sister and Pharaoh takes her into his bed, "the Lord afflict[s] Pharaoh and his house with great plagues" (Gen. 12:17).[5] Apparently, God is "cursing those who curse [Abram]" (12:3); but our first family of blessing has not yet joined God's international intention.

The rest of Abram/Abraham's career continues along those same

5. This will happen twice again, differently, with Abimelech (20:1-18).

lines: in any contact with "all the nations," he clearly intends, not to bless them, but to preserve and acquire wealth for himself and his family. He amasses an army to free Lot and plunder his captors (14:1-16), a victory that Melchizedek attributes to God (14:19-20). Abram does have the good sense not to plunder Sodom, but only to clarify how God is blessing Abram (14:22-23). He seems to have earned the neighbors' respect when he buys a burial plot for Sarah from the Hittite people (23:1-20). But, on the whole, Abram seems unconcerned with blessing the nations. In fact, even the portrait of God in these chapters seems devoid of the stated divine attention of Genesis 12:3 to bless the nations. Indeed, in a reiteration of the promise, God defines the promised land by listing the nations that God will drive out from it, with no redemptive end in sight (15:18-21). The only hint that Abram is conscious of the nations as other than threat or source of wealth is his pleading for the people of Sodom in Genesis 18:22-23.

Clearly, God has not chosen Abram and Sarai for their developed humanitarian habits or internationalist instincts. Because this family comes to this project unformed, pedagogy will be required. And while the two learn much about how to trust God in the story of Genesis 11–24 (e.g., in Abraham's willingness to sacrifice the child of the promise in Gen. 22), a missional pedagogy really plays no part in that learning. If God is to teach Israel how to bless the nations, the learning must begin after Abraham and Sarah. In fact, God reiterates the promise to Isaac after his parents have died, clarifying that "in your offspring all the nations of the earth shall be blessed" (Gen. 26:4); and then again to Jacob in even more expansive terms (Gen. 28:14). But again, in those next two generations, the story offers no hint that this family is taking its international role to heart. In fact, the involuntary journey of Abram to Egypt — to acquire food during famine rather than to carry God's blessing (Gen. 12:5-17) — initiates a biblical theme that is particularly visible through our missional lens: time and again God's people, whether Israel or the earliest Christian church, must be dragged kicking and screaming toward the nations.

The theme continues in the story of Joseph. Interpreters routinely explore the Joseph cycle to address the theological category of providence, because in it God demonstrates an ability to use even the jealous and spiteful actions of Joseph's brothers to prepare the way for Israel's survival. In Joseph's profound words to his brothers, "Even though you intended to do harm to me, God intended it for good, in order to preserve a numerous people, as he is doing today" (Gen. 50:20).

However, from a missional perspective, which seeks signs that the people of God have taken to heart God's call to bless nations, the story is very disappointing. Joseph does not intend to bless Egypt. He is literally dragged to that land, bound and gagged by slave traders. And Jacob and his other sons only reunite with Joseph because famine forces them there. Even Joseph's salutary service to Egyptian officials is presented as a matter of course rather than a generous benefaction. Our narrator never draws a thought bubble above Joseph's head featuring the words "How shall I bless Pharaoh and so live out the promise God gave to my great grandparents, my grandparents, and my parents?" God does bless the Egyptians through Joseph, but the outcome seems incidental to Joseph's abilities and character. It does not seem like Joseph's intention to bless nations.

Liberation theologians are among many Jews and Christians who celebrate the Exodus as a window to the character of a God who hears the cries of suffering people, and it surely is that. At the burning bush Moses hears God's compassion and ultimately volunteers himself as a vehicle of that compassion. Slaves are set free. But the God pictured in the Exodus story is ethnocentrically inclined toward Israel at the expense of Egyptians. In that event, we again see most of Genesis 12 honored and acknowledged: God reopens the possibility of keeping the promise to bless Israel with a land and numerous offspring; and God curses those who curse Abraham's family. But that beautiful last line of the promise goes wanting once again.

For those keeping score at home: when God speaks to Moses on Sinai in the twentieth chapter of the book of Exodus, not a single Israelite has displayed even a hint of recognition that God has called the family to bless nations. Nor has this family shown a trace of desire to join God's nation-blessing activity. Egypt has prospered because they have Abraham's great grandson in their midst, and so God has blessed a family of the earth through Joseph. But as you and I imagine how to form our congregations missionally, we look closely for conscious participation in God's mission, and we find no such thing.

Missional Nation?

When we follow the Deuteronomistic voice of Deuteronomy itself, Joshua and Judges, 1 and 2 Samuel, and 1 and 2 Kings, the period of Israel's occupation and residence in Canaan may be its most inward-turned of all.[6]

6. Space does not allow a survey of the Psalms, but they would bear out this observa-

There the editorial voice sees nations in two ways: either as potential conquests or as perpetual threats. Putting it mildly, blessing all the families of the earth is not a chief priority. In fact, kings who mingle with the nations usually receive the back of our commentator's hand for opening Israel to foreign idols. This bunker mentality pervades the narrative with rare exceptions. Our narrator is so bent on maintaining monotheism that he looks fearfully, rather than opportunistically, at the nations.

So it is that Israel's and Judah's next major international ventures, aside from military attempts by David and Solomon to expand the national territory, would be forced on them by the conquering Assyrian and Babylonian empires — in the form of forced exile. In 622 B.C.E., Assyria conquered Samaria and shipped the people of the Northern Kingdom away. In 597-87 B.C.E., Nebuchadnezzar followed suit and burned Jerusalem and Judah to the ground, taking its leaders captive to Babylon.

Missional Church?

To our formed Christian sensibilities, the first seven chapters of the book of Acts should be the counterpoint to Israel's general complacency about God's call toward the world. They feature perhaps the fastest expansion of the church in its history. The narrator carries us with breathtaking speed from an upper-room-sized gathering in a Jerusalem home to 5,000 believers meeting in each other's homes all across town (Acts 1:13-14 through 4:4). Not only because of that remarkable growth in numbers, but also because of the inspiring pattern of loving community those multitudes lived out toward one another, we would imagine that the first Jerusalem church should be missional church headquarters. When we factor in the multitude of nations represented in those first Jerusalem crowds, it appears that every base has been touched — a true missional home run! And in a way it is. The red thread of missional identity is prominent here.

And yet. . . . And yet, even in this missional wonderland of enfleshed love and evangelism, we discover an early Christian resistance to looking outward toward the geographical and cultural other. New Testament scholars often point out Luke's tendency to airbrush blemishes out of his subject in the account of the earliest Jerusalem church in Acts. To their

---

tion: the psalmists spend much space calling God's vengeance down on the other, and little to none asking God's blessing on the other.

eyes, the blissful summaries of Christian love lived out through a community of goods (Acts 2:42-47; Acts 4 and 5) are a bit too good to be true. However that may be, the gilding of this gang is not thoroughgoing. In Acts 1–7 the church has its less than savory moments: Peter retells the treachery of Judas the betrayer (Acts 1:16-18); the blatant dishonesty of Ananias and Sapphira stands in chapter 5 for all the world to see. Most important among these flaws for our purposes is a more subtle characterization: in these first chapters of Acts, the Jerusalem church benignly, but negligently, declines Jesus' directive toward the nations.

At the outset of Acts, the resurrected Jesus gives his followers a significant fourfold task: "You will receive power when the Holy Spirit comes upon you, and you will be my witnesses in Jerusalem, in all Judea, Samaria, and to the ends of the earth" (Acts 1:8). Jerusalem. Judea. Samaria. The ends of the earth. It is true that in the long haul of this twenty-eight-chapter book, the church will obey each specific part of this command. Their witness to one another shines forth from the very first chapters. Philip will move the gospel into the Judean countryside and start churches in Samaria (Acts 8:4-8, 26-40). And over the course of Acts 9–28, Peter, Paul, and others will extend the witness to all the nations. The church of Acts will indeed get around to engaging all four parts of Jesus' plan within the long haul of the book. However, a full seven chapters into the story, these Jerusalem Christians appear very content simply to fulfill the first of the four geographical mandates and call it good. Just as Jesus has imaged it for them in Acts 1:8, the Holy Spirit does come powerfully upon the community not long after he ascends. They immediately stream into the streets of Jerusalem and witness to the gathered nations. Peter preaches, the community flourishes, thousands embrace the message and the life of discipleship. The church is a rousing success in Jerusalem — despite persecution. By the time chapter 6 rolls around, the church has even outgrown its simple infrastructure, necessitating a corps of deacons who will see to the distribution of shared goods (6:1-7). The action is compressed, so we do not know how much time the narrator imagines passing; but numerical and bureaucratic growth imply a good deal of elapsed time.

The blemish on the church that our narrator never explicitly identifies — but loudly implies — is the utter failure of any Christian in Jerusalem to initiate a mission beyond the walls of that city throughout the first seven chapters of this story. We might have imagined that conversation beginning immediately after Jesus' promise, even during the time of waiting before Pentecost. Peter turns to the gathered company and says, "Brothers and sisters, I don't know what this Spirit and power will look like, but whenever it comes, I'll take Jerusalem, Andrew, you take Judea, John, how does Samaria sound for you? And — we'd better put a few of you on that part about the ends of the earth. May I ask for volunteers?" But we see no such thing. Apart from replacing Judas, the church takes no strategic or tactical initiative. They are content to pray and wait.

Or perhaps the initiative outward would have been better placed in chapter 4, where we read about new thousands joining the church. "Our growth is a blessing!" one of them might say. "Now we are equipped and ready to take that blessing out into Judea and Samaria and to the ends of the earth." Again, it doesn't happen. The organizational instincts do prompt them to consider a new infrastructure for the distribution of their material goods, but "Judea, Samaria, and the ends of the earth" still do not appear in their conversation.

By the end of Acts 6, then, the church has enthusiastically embraced only one fourth of Jesus' directive, and these Jerusalem Christians seem content to leave the other three parts alone. In fact, it is not until angry opponents stone Stephen that the Christians of Jerusalem become curiously interested in mission! "That day a severe persecution began against the church in Jerusalem, and all except the apostles were scattered throughout the countryside of Judea and Samaria" (8:1b). The specificity of this verse's last three words, and their echo of "Judea and Samaria . . ." from Acts 1:8, can hardly be accidental. God will wait one chapter to rather violently call Paul to the ends of the earth. Like a little bird that needs her mother to shove her out of the nest, the cozy Jerusalem Christians had to be scared out of their homes and into the world Jesus had clearly and directly commissioned them to reach.

When we observe the behavior and attitudes of our three called communities, we see that they lack an internal motor that would drive them toward the other in blessing. Each group had to be pushed by circumstances into the world, despite having received an explicit mandate to bless and witness to the nations. It turns out that we must seek the solution to this problem, not in human nature, but in the formative power of the calling God.

Missional God!

At this point I could be accused of chronicling a countermissional trajectory in Scripture. Abraham's family, the nation Israel, and even the earliest

Christian church in Jerusalem blatantly ignored the divine call to be a blessing to all families. Where is the hope in this story? How in the world can you and I even begin to expect any success in forming our own congregations, given this bleak biblical track record?

Friends, I bring you good news: Despite their strong and protective inclination toward themselves and their familiar homelands, each company that God dragged into the nations did ultimately learn there the deep truth of God's international love. And even against strong resistances, that bright light shone through. The nations-loving character of God will inevitably come out. Consider Abraham's family after their experience of a four-century sojourn in Egypt. We noticed above that, prior to Sinai, not a single member of that clan had evidenced even a trace of consciousness that she or he was built to bless nations. However, the Law of Moses breaks that long losing streak.

While God has been making space for an "other" since the dawn of creation in Genesis 1:1, it is at Sinai that we first see the Israelites joining the divine act, and their deference takes shape in a spate of commands pertaining to "sojourners" and "aliens." Beginning with the Sabbath command in Exodus 20:8-10, Israel's story features a heaping handful of legal material protecting the alien/sojourner/foreigner who lives among the people. The human tendency to disregard or degrade the other that has so characterized the story of the patriarchs and Moses up to now — that ego- and ethnocentric tendency is here countered with consistent reminders that cluster sojourners with widows, orphans, and Levites, other groups who might normally be disregarded and degraded.

God calls foreigners in Israel's midst to pause on the Sabbath with the rest of the family (Exod. 20:10-11). God lovingly feeds and clothes sojourners (Deut. 10:18), partly by reserving the third year's gleanings for them, the widows, and orphans (Deut. 14:29; 24:19ff.). And Israel is commanded to follow God's lead by supplying sojourners with justice (Deut. 24:17) and full participation in the congregation of Israel (Deut. 29:10-13).

This new element in Israel's consciousness requires explanation: What changed them from a fully clan-focused people into one that can hear commands to open themselves? The agent of transformation is clearly experience. God's voice at Sinai grounds this new call to benefaction in Israel's collective experience: "You shall not wrong sojourners or oppress them, for you were sojourners in the land of Egypt" (Exod. 22:21), and "You shall not oppress a sojourner. You know the heart of a sojourner, for you were sojourners in the land of Egypt" (Exod. 23:9; see also Exod.

23:7). In a Golden Rule-like call to empathy, God turns Israel's gaze toward regard of the other.

This widening of the people's world also happens to the people of Judah during the Babylonian exile. Judah's first experience of this new land and people must have been utter disorientation. Psalm 137 registers the desperate plea: "How can we sing the Lord's song in a foreign land?" However, this harsh disorientation proved crucial in producing the largest and most world-embracing image of God in Hebrew history. For it is during and after exile that the prophets help Israel imagine the multinational company that will stream to the mountain of God. Isaiah's voice rises and the people hear their calling afresh: "The Lord says, 'It is too light a thing that you should be my servant to raise up the tribes of Jacob and to restore the survivors of Israel; I will give you as a light to the nations, that my salvation may reach to the end of the earth'" (Isa. 49:6; see also Isa. 60:1-3). The lamp of the people of Israel shall shine again, and this time it will not be a private viewing. Israel will be a blessing to all the families of the earth. God's prophets did not speak that way before the people had been trained by exile.

Nor, of course, does the stay-put church of Jerusalem hold onto its preference for hearth and home forever. True, it takes Stephen's stoning to scare them into the world; but once they are forced out into Judea and Samaria and all points on the way to the ends of the earth, they discover that God is acting there as well, and they enjoy joining that act. We don't imagine Philip returning from his encounter with Samaritans or the Ethiopian eunuch and saying, "Whew, I got that out of the way!" The experience of God's Spirit reaching through him to the other drew him in to God's caring (Acts 8:4-8, 26-40). Soon their experience shows up in their dreams and discussions. Peter sees a sheet lowered with unclean animals, and the scandal of Gentile inclusion is raised (Acts 10:9-15). The Holy Spirit inhabits their audiences even before they can get them circumcised (Acts 10:44-45). And not much later the unthinkable is happening: a company of Jewish Christians gathers in Jerusalem and decides that, since God so obviously loves and includes Gentiles without their being circumcised or kosher, they should, too (Acts 15:13-29). By the time Paul has reached the intellectual and imperial capitals of Athens (Acts 17:16-34) and Rome (Acts 28:11-31), God's mission has become their mission. God has taught these earliest Christians the mission through their experience.

Missional Formation

Step One: Trust God

The good news about our biblical observations is that our ancient brothers and sisters in faith did finally learn and join God's mission in the world. The divine Teacher formed their communities in ways that extended their vision beyond themselves to God's redemptive activity around them, both nearby and among the nations. This formation produced insights (and sometimes even habits) that show up in the Scripture passages one usually hears in a session like this, texts telling Abraham's family to embrace the stranger and the alien; telling the nation of Judah that God will make their light shine to all nations; telling the early Christians that God's reach is much wider than they ever would have thought. This collection of insights comprises the canon of missional Scripture.

The bad news of our Scripture survey is that God's methods may not be available to us. God's vehicle of formation in the stories we've surveyed can be captured in two words: forced experience. Harsh famine forces Abraham and Sarah's family to Egypt and slavery, where they glimpse the significance and value of people outside their family; a foreign ruler drags the nation(s) of Israel/Judah into rough exile, where they realize that God's operation has been international all along; and the earliest Christians dash desperately away from flying stones aimed at them and into a world where they find God actively at work. Each of these ancient "congregations" learned to look outside their circle by being forced to experience life outside their circle.

Fortunately or unfortunately, you and I cannot control the larger movements of history. So how are we to imitate God's ways? How are we to attain God's level of success forming our groups? I put the questions in this ludicrous way because the first answer must be obvious: we don't and we can't. God is God, and we are not. God is the former and transformer. If our people are to learn to love strangers and aliens, learn to be a light to all nations, learn that God's activity in the world is exciting to join, it will be God who changes them. God did it then, and God can do it now.

But if that first question has an obvious answer, the answer to a second serious question is not nearly so obvious. How will God form us? If God is the primary actor in formation, God has chosen you and me to be vehicles of that work in our congregations and communities. It is our task here today to discern how we can become means to divine ends. So how?

Step Two: Open Wide the Classroom Door

One part of the answer that you and I knew before we opened this book is biblical formation. In Deuteronomy 6, Moses foresees the problem of Israel's complacency and complicity with surrounding cultures, and prescribes as a remedy sheer repetition: "Keep these words that I am commanding you today in your heart. Recite them to your children and talk about them when you are at home and when you are away, when you lie down and when you rise. Bind them as a sign on your hand, fix them as an emblem on your forehead, and write them on the doorposts of your house and on your gates" (Deut. 6:6-9). The psalmist writes, "Thy word I have hidden in my heart that I might not sin against thee" (Ps. 119:11). Paul urges the Romans "not [to] be conformed to this world, but [to] be transformed by the renewing of your minds" (Rom. 12:2).

Step one on that journey is to help our people begin to learn from the Bible in the first place. All kinds of evidence tells us that biblical literacy is low and declining — both in the wider culture and in churches. Missional folks know that Christendom is dying, so we are not surprised by these statistics and observations. In fact, most of us experience the reality of biblical illiteracy in our congregations. But why? Why do our people not read the Bible? Here are three observations that may help us move practically toward greater engagement with Scripture in our congregations. First, our people are busy; second, our Bible illiterates are intimidated by those who have read the Bible (and they think everyone else has read more than they have); and third, our people think that the Bible is a big ancient book, rather than many shorter, community-based communications. What follows is a case study from a suburban Minnesota church that illustrates these observations.

When I arrived eighteen months ago to begin as teaching minister in a Twin Cities UCC congregation, I asked about Bible study attendance and found that in a 3,000-member church there were about forty adults studying the Bible together each week. In the United Church of Christ that is not a particularly unusual number; nonetheless, it seemed a shame to me. Through some amateur anthropological work, I discovered two things: first, people in the congregation did not like being biblically illiterate; second, their reasons for not attending Bible studies were social and practical, not spiritual or theological. Even during my interviews, as I asked my way around the search committee circle, only three of the twelve members regularly studied the Bible in a group, and one of those three was getting his

Bible study outside the church. The adult Christian education recruiting team was batting .167 at church Bible study. Not promising.

When I listened longer, though, I discovered that these people were hungry to learn more about the Bible. In fact, it was why they had accepted invitations to serve on the team. Their nonattendance had origins, not in an aversion to the ancient book, but in the social realities of Bible study at the church. First, studies were being offered at times that were inaccessible to the majority of the congregation: mid-morning on weekdays and early Saturday mornings. Second, those who could attend at those times made gallant efforts, but many found themselves on the outside looking in, either because of what they perceived as a cliquish impenetrability in the group or because the shared group literacy and language made the visitor feel inferior. Several confided their ironic predicament: they wanted to learn Bible, but they didn't feel like they knew enough to attend a Bible study group. When I arrived, I found that the search team was a representative sample. So I planned.

Steps one and two became clear: offer a Bible study at times when everyone could attend, and then make everyone feel unconditionally welcomed once they arrived. Accordingly, we named our class "Bible for Dummies," and we offered it on Wednesdays at 7:00 and 10:00 a.m., 4:30 and 7:00 p.m. The congregation sensed that amnesty had been declared. There would be no guilt about what they did not know. They also perceived that we were coming to them with the Bible, rather than making them go out of their way. With a Wednesday full of options that a colleague has dubbed the "no excuses schedule," they could imagine fitting study into their week. So they showed up.

On the first day of Bible for Dummies, we had 110 in the four classes. We were adding chairs all day. And when they sat down, they heard me say, "To get to Psalms, open to the very middle of the Bible. . . . The New Testament begins about three fourths of the way through the book. . . . Isaiah is one of the big books to the right of the Psalms. . . ." A buzz spread, and the attendance started to expand. All of this happened before anyone really knew what class would be like. They heard "Bible" and they came running — just because we got rid of a couple obstacles for them.

The good news is that the initial buzz has not subsided. Fourteen months later, the "Bible for Dummies" class is averaging 150 students, and last week I taught 210 people in six classes over the course of the church week, including one on the book of Isaiah and one with parents and children on the history books of the Old Testament. Around the church, sixty others met in other small-group Bible studies, for a grand total of about 270. Our goal is to steadily draw 400 weekly (half our worshiping population) by the middle of the 2011-2012 program year. In addition, we have a growing number of our parishioners and their friends (a number we haven't yet figured out how to monitor) watching our "Bible for Dummies" video podcast on the website.

I am not citing these numbers for the purpose of self-promotion. I give them out here for the same reason that Luke tells the story of expansion in the early chapters of Acts: to show that God is doing something in our church. Luke wrote: "And day by day the Lord added to their number those who were being saved" (Acts 2:47), and "many of those who heard the word believed; and they numbered about five thousand" (Acts 4:4). God is doing this work, and God is very, very good at it! The point is that we have seen God do a whole lot more obvious work as we have opened the doors wider to let more people in. My overwhelming experience from the start of this project has been that God draws people to Scripture, as long as we make "a highway in the desert" for our people. After trusting God, the next step for you and me is to ask what obstacles keep people away from our program of Scripture education — and then to get rid of those obstacles.

Step Three: Make the Story Their Story

Scripture study is not a simple answer to our question. We know that some Christians and communities who know Scripture very well are anything but missional. The Puritans who brazenly exterminated large chunks of the Native American population knew Scripture well and counted themselves a new Israel in a new promised land. Analogies to different ways of reading the Quran are vivid in our time, as some readers become instruments of peace and others carry terror into the world. Simply becoming biblical doesn't seem to ensure missional success.

How will we help our people learn Scripture in a way that forms them missionally? The broad arc of our learning in this hour has been that God teaches the Hebrew people, the nation of Israel, and the early church through experience. That observation alone should cure us of the notion that our formational strategy must not begin and end with a Bible on our laps. If we cannot control the broad course of history, and if we cannot even control the migratory patterns of our congregants or community members, we can at least provide incentives for active outreach. Getting people outside comfortable circles and into the realm of the other worked then, and it works now. Please do not leave this chapter with any notion that I think Scripture study alone is the solution. Bodies need to move into the world.

Granting that praxis and experience of the other are crucial to transformation, I nonetheless believe that the time-honored dichotomy between "learning" and "doing" is a false one — at least with Bible study. In the space that remains, I hope we will discover together a kind of Bible reading that is experiential in its very nature. When Moses instructs Israel to take its sacrifice to the holy place, he gives each faithful one a script: "My father was a wandering Aramean . . ." said those ancient Israelites as they appeared before their priests. Each worshiper was saying, "God's history with Abraham is my history."

The immediacy of that scene from Deuteronomy makes a good start toward imagining experiential Bible study. It is one thing to know when the exile occurred, which nations ruled when, and how many Judeans traveled east to Babylon. It is another thing to feel one's way to an ancient gathering by the river and feel with the psalmist the ridicule of belittling captors, the futility of forcing mirth into one's singing voice "in a foreign land" (Ps. 137). There is a kind of Bible study that brings readers into that ancient experience, a study that sets the scene and reconstructs the meeting room and knows the joys and sorrows, hopes and fears of brothers and sisters long dead. That is the kind I recommend.

There are other options. The first is the literary reading. This approach seeks God's revelation on the narrative level of the text. It has the merit of embracing the biblical writings as they are, but the disadvantage that the whole text as it stands is not a continuous narrative but a collection of types of literature. Story is interrupted by vast patches of legal material. Even the most faithful person who sets out to read Scripture, given a New Year's resolution or some other impetus, will hardly make it past Leviticus, because the story stops being dramatic by then, and the legal minutiae become overwhelming. The experience of the Bible as literature, therefore, does not fit her experience, because the stories she usually reads are not so disjointed. Even if she can make it through Torah undaunted, the Bible isn't arranged with Isaiah 40–55 between 2 Kings and Nehemiah, though that is where it fits in the drama. Nor is Jeremiah interspersed in the last chapters of 2 Kings. The Psalms do not appear in the communities that first uttered them, but as a collection. This organization of Hebrew

Scripture into the groupings of history, poetry/wisdom, and prophecy does not lend itself, as is, to the categories our people bring along with them.

A second option for reading is a strictly historical one. Some mainline church leaders take pride in thinking critically and cultivating that critical approach among their people; and so they lead Bible studies that endeavor to get behind the text to the minimal history. They host speakers who can help them arrive at the historical Jesus or Paul or Mary Magdalene. Unfortunately, this enterprise often winds up informing more than forming or transforming. By the time a group has finished the task of distilling out the history behind the story, they have become detached evaluators of the record, rather than invested participants in it.

The experiential approach is a hybrid that joins these two ways of reading into one, and then tilts them toward empathetic listening. Each week in "Bible for Dummies" we find our way to an ancient community that received a part of Scripture, look around at what they are experiencing, and then listen to the words of Scripture through their ears. Finally, after all that, we feel our way back to the present, asking how many of the questions the ancients asked were our questions, too.

Here is an example. For three weeks last fall we gathered by the rivers of Babylon with the exiles, experiencing their anguish and disequilibrium amidst an alien people and their gods. Using 2 Kings 24–25 and Lamentations, we pictured the ruin of Jerusalem, our six-hundred-year home and imagined the march to the east; we listened to Gilgamesh myths that gave us a sense of the religion in the streets; and we sang the plaintive cry of Psalm 137: "How can we sing the Lord's song in a foreign land?"

Having set and entered the scene, we listened as priests spoke the two creation stories out into the room: one, which we had heard around the hearth for generations, about a near God who formed us out of clay (Genesis 2); and one that pictured a more orderly and majestic God, the God who spoke all creation into existence (Genesis 1). Suddenly we had left the creation-evolution debate and had begun feeling instead the ancient healing of a people who needed a God both transcendent and immanent, needed the company of their kindred of the past, needed hope for a better future. When we read in Genesis 2 that Eden lay between the Tigris and Euphrates rivers, we felt the comfort of knowing the land was not alien to God. When we heard Isaiah's "Comfort, comfort . . ." it was real comfort to us. And as we realized that God had plans to redeem nations beyond our own, our worlds widened. Sitting alongside the exiles helped us experience Scrip-

ture from seven different biblical books in one session as a message to us —
living and ready to be brought with us back to the twenty-first century.

In the weeks after exile, we did the same thing with Paul's church in
Corinth and the community that received Mark's Gospel. During the winter we spent six weeks hearing Philippians through the ears of the Christians who received it, a series that culminated in "A Night in Paul's
Philippi," complete with ancient Macedonian food, togas, a woman named
Euodia and a woman named Syntyche, and a full reading of the text into
the room.

The folks who walk this path together don't retain everything they
learn, by any means. But they are realizing more every day that what they
thought was a religious anthology can actually be a vital communication
that meets their lives. They experience Scripture now in a way that makes
them want to listen longer. It's not all success story, but God is doing mar-
velous things.

Step Four: Move beyond the Classroom

After tracing missional themes through Abraham's family, the nation of
Judah in exile, and the Christian community in Acts, you and I concluded
that God taught those ingrown communities the value of the other
through experience of the other. After surveying one church's experiential
reading of Scripture, perhaps my formational convictions are becoming
evident. I believe that a good hope for missional formation lies in an intensive, guided reading of Scripture, which relives the experiential learning of
ancient Israel and the early church. I see our people opening themselves,
not only to the book, but to their role in God's love toward the world.

The practical next step for us is a praxis-based discipleship group
that commits itself to live into the story of Acts 1–8. This will be the first
formational experience I've attempted that has missional goals at the very
center of the curriculum. We will feel our way into the Jerusalem church,
breaking bread together in each other's homes, praying, listening to the
apostles' teachings, and contributing as any among us have needs. We will
also covenant intentionally to share the gospel and its healing acts with the
people we encounter on our way in life, telling the stories of success and
failure, acceptance and rejection — then finding refuge in one another as
we do. By the time we reach chapter 6, we will feel in our bones the comfort and sense of belonging that kept the earliest church nested securely in

Jerusalem. However, when Stephen is stoned, we will feel the disorientation of being chased from that comfort. At the end of our weeks together, these twenty will be pushed out of the nest and into the streets of Minneapolis and St. Paul and beyond, on short- and long-term mission to the world. If the biblical communities were forced out by their circumstances, we will count ourselves forced out by the text.

The ultimate measure of success for these formation programs will not ultimately be the number of bodies we gather in rooms. Participation numbers help us gauge progress. But it is culture change we seek. We will have succeeded when the God who loves all peoples everywhere infinitely and eternally has broken through our status quo and turned us inside out toward one another and toward the world.

A Last Word

How might Christian leaders cultivate the missing internal passion of Aristophanes' myth in the minds and hearts of our congregations? This conference and this book univocally name Christian and missional formation as our best hope. Through an honest reading of Scripture that can recognize in ourselves the inertia and resistance of called people, we gain access to the God who changed them and can change us. To that God be praise and glory, now and forevermore.

CHAPTER 5

Practices of Dispossession:
The Shape of Discipleship in a
Church Taken, Blessed, Broken, and Given

Christian Scharen

> To live as a Christian in the world today is necessarily to live an
> exposed life; it is to be stripped of the kind of security that tradi-
> tion, whether ecclesiological or institutional, easily bestows.
>
> Donald M. MacKinnon, *The Stripping of the Altars*

"To Live an Exposed Life"

I begin with a parable I first heard from Peter Rollins. It is called "Salvation
for a Demon."[1]

> In the center of a once-great city there stood a magnificent cathedral
> that was cared for by a kindly old priest who spent his days praying in
> the vestry and caring for the poor. As a result of the priest's tireless
> work, the cathedral was known throughout the land as a true sanctu-
> ary. The priest welcomed all who came to his door and gave com-
> pletely without prejudice or restraint. Each stranger was, to the priest,
> a neighbor in need and thus the incoming of Christ. His hospitality
> was famous and his heart was known to be pure. No one could steal
> from this old man, for he considered no possession his own, and while
> thieves sometimes left that place with items pillaged from the sanctu-

1. Peter Rollins, *The Orthodox Heretic: And Other Impossible Tales* (New Brewster,
MA: Paraclete Press, 2008), 24-26.

ary, the priest never grew concerned: he had given everything to God and knew that these people needed such items more than the church did.

Early one evening in the middle of winter, while the priest was praying before the cross, there was a loud and ominous knock on the cathedral door. The priest quickly got to his feet and went to the entrance, as he knew it was a terrible night and reasoned that his visitor might be in need of shelter.

Upon opening the door he was surprised to find a terrifying demon towering over him with large dead eyes and rotting flesh.

"Old man," the demon hissed, "I have traveled many miles to seek your shelter. Will you welcome me in?"

Without hesitation, the priest bid this hideous demon welcome and beckoned him into the church. The evil demon stooped down and stepped across the threshold, spitting venom onto the tiled floor as he went. In full view of the priest, the demon proceeded to tear down the various icons that adorned the walls and rip the fine linens that hung around the sanctuary, while screaming blasphemy and curses.

During this time the priest knelt silently on the floor and continued in his devotions until it was time for him to retire for the night.

"Old man," cried the demon, "where are you going now?"

"I am returning home to rest, for it has been a long day," replied the kindly priest.

"May I come with you?" spat the demon. "I too am tired and in need of a place to lay my head."

"Why, of course," replied the priest. "Come, and I will prepare a meal."

On returning to his house, the priest prepared some food while the evil demon mocked the priest and broke the various religious artifacts that adorned his humble dwelling. The demon then ate the meal that was provided and afterward turned his attention to the priest.

"Old man, you welcomed me first into your church and then into your house. I have one more request for you: will you now welcome me into your heart?"

"Why, of course," said the priest, "what I have is yours and what I am is yours."

This heartfelt response brought the demon to a standstill, for by giving everything the priest had retained the very thing that the demon sought to take. For the demon was unable to rob him of his kindness and his hospitality, his love and his compassion. And so the great demon left in defeat, never to return.

What happened to that demon after this meeting with the elderly priest is anyone's guess. Some say that although he left that place empty-handed he received more than he could ever have imagined.

And the priest? He simply ascended his stairs, got into bed and drifted off to sleep, all the time wondering what guise his Christ would take next.[2]

This chapter is in part merely a long commentary on this powerful parable that sets as its horizon a discussion of mission through an engagement with the practice of dispossession. I work with this practice, drawn from the writings of Rowan Williams and his key theological teacher, Donald MacKinnon, as a means to speak of how, in a situation of advanced secularism, congregations are beginning to find it necessary, as MacKinnon says above, "to live an exposed life" as integral to their "sent-ness." From the start, however, I must be honest and acknowledge that feminist scholars have made clear how such a posture is intimately tied to positions of power. Women, children, racial-ethnic minorities, and other vulnerable peoples need the space and empowerment to take possession of their lives and spaces of habitation and worship first, before the parable above can feel like much more than violence.[3] That said, my case studies in this chapter are the established churches of Christendom. They clearly are churches that have possessed (and in many cases still possess) enormous wealth and power — economic, political, and spiritual. In this chapter I engage the practice of dispossession with respect to three secular contexts and particular congregations within them; I reflect on that theologically; and I conclude with a pastoral provocation for congregations similarly situated.

2. While Rollins does not say so explicitly, this parable recalls Victor Hugo's kindly and faithful bishop, Monseigneur Bienvenu, who welcomes Jean Valjean to his home when no one else will have him, and who, when faced with Valjean's theft of his silverware, gives him also his silver candlesticks. The bishop's actions and his words, "Jean Valjean, my brother, you no longer belong to evil but to good," stand not only at the heart of Valjean's transformation but of the transformative heart of the novel's juxtaposition of the law and grace, of glory and the cross. See Victor Hugo, *Les Misérables*, trans. Lee Fahnestock and Norman MacAfee (New York: Signet Classics, 1987 [1862]), 106.

3. Take, for example, the stunning fact that in the United States one of every four women has experienced sexual assault. Among other powerful resources, I have learned much from Christie Cozad Newger, *Counseling Women: A Narrative Pastoral Approach* (Minneapolis: Augsburg Fortress, 2001).

Statistics on Church-Going

Of the many gifts of Charles Taylor's work over the last decade or so, I want to lift out his demolishing of the myth that modernity is a "single process destined to occur everywhere in the same forms, ultimately bringing convergence and uniformity to our world."[4] His careful phenomenological approach brings him to speak of "multiple modernities," each sharing common characteristics: the modern bureaucratic state, market economies, science and technology. Along with these he has spoken of the ways that these modernities and their various social imaginaries — the "ways people imagine their social existence . . . and the deeper normative notions and images" — are secular.[5] They are not uniformly secular in the sense that with modernization societies become less religious; clearly, something much more complex has happened, and religious decline and resurgence coexist next to one another throughout much of the contemporary West.[6] Rather, Taylor writes, "religion occupies a different place, compatible with the sense that all social action takes place in profane time."

One important aspect of this view, expanded and deepened in Taylor's magisterial book *A Secular Age*, is that insofar as there has been a religious decline (largely underscored by depressing statistics about churchgoing across most of Europe and North America), it was the result of developments internal to Christianity and its reforms as much as anything.[7] Aspects of Christian history — for example, the claim that priests could confect the sacraments *ex opere operato* — set off centuries of reform rooted in the protest against making the sovereignty of God subject to magical manipulation by any drunk who could manage the proper formula. In this example, the energy of religious reform internal to Western Christianity, motivated by the desire to protect God's freedom, opened the way to the disenchantment of society that Taylor finds constitutive of our secular age.[8]

4. Charles Taylor, *Modern Social Imaginaries* (Durham: Duke University Press, 2004), 195.

5. Taylor, *Modern Social Imaginaries*, 23.

6. Peter Berger, ed., *The Desecularization of the World: Resurgent Religion and World Politics* (Grand Rapids: Eerdmans, 1999); José Casanova, *Public Religion in the Modern World* (Chicago: University of Chicago Press, 1994).

7. Charles Taylor, *A Secular Age* (Cambridge, MA: Harvard University Press, 2007).

8. Taylor, *A Secular Age*, 72-73; Marcel Gauchet, *The Disenchantment of the World: A Political History of Religion* (Princeton, NJ: Princeton University Press, 1997).

Further debates are continuing in the wake of Taylor's arguments, especially in terms of understanding the varieties of secularisms.[9] In an effort to make a modest contribution to this conversation, I will describe three secularisms within this secular age, and the way specific Christian congregations practice a kind of formation by dispossession, a formative stripping that has, among other things, "pruned" and perhaps made more fruitful these congregations' patterns of communal discipleship ("by their fruits you will recognize them" [Matt. 7:16]). I will move in order from the "more" secular cases (Norway and England) to the "less" secular case (United States), pointing out distinctive aspects in each case, but also remarkable similarities both in context and congregational response. In briefly introducing each case, I obviously can do no more than gesture toward a much longer and more careful history that would be necessary in order to do justice to a study of this kind.[10] However, even gesturing in the direction studies need to take can offer helpful direction for dialogue.

The Norway case involves the Church of Norway, the official religious home of 83 percent of the population. The Church of Norway is Lutheran by confession and has been established as the state church since King Christian III declared it so in 1537. While official membership is high, participation rates have been in a steep decline. Currently, weekly church attendance is between 3 percent and 5 percent, one of the lowest church attendance rates in the West.[11] One measure of decline can be seen in comparing numbers of births to baptisms, a traditional rite of passage for all children. As recently as 1960, church statistics reported that 97 percent of children born in Norway were baptized; the most recent statistics, available from 2006, report a 24 percent drop in baptisms, now at 76 percent of births. This relatively high level of participation in baptism, however, does

9. See, for example, Michael Warner, Jonathan Vanantwerpen, and Craig Calhoun, *Varieties of Secularism in a Secular Age* (Cambridge, MA: Harvard University Press, 2010), as well as the excellent blog entitled "The Immanent Frame: Secularism, Religion and the Public Sphere" sponsored by the Social Science Research Council at New York University: http://blogs.ssrc.org/tif/.

10. I hope to take on such a study over the next few years, using the shape of this paper as a starting place for a much-expanded research project.

11. Attendance: UofMich World Values Survey on religiosity and church attendance; adherence: Pew Research Global Attitudes Project; the problem of self-reporting inflation: C. Kirk Hadaway and P. L. Marler, "Did You Really Go to Church This Week? Behind the Poll Data," *The Christian Century*, May 6, 1998, 472-75.

not mean that significant religious observance exists among the broader population. In his fascinating study of secularism in Denmark and Sweden, Phil Zuckerman records this exchange:

> Lise is currently engaged, and I wondered, if she were to have kids, would she raise them to be religious?
> *No.*
> Will you have them confirmed?
> *Yeah, and baptized.*
> Because . . . ?
> *It's the norm. It's what we do.*
> And that was that. When I pushed her on why she would baptize her baby even though she doesn't believe in the central tenets of Christianity, she just shrugged her shoulders and again explained that it is simply what Danes do.[12]

Norwegians speak of the west of their country as the "Bible belt," and of the area in the east surrounding Oslo, the capital city, as the most secular. It is there that I want to explore congregational response to this remarkably secular society.

The Oslo Domkyrka has gone through a renovation in body and soul, opening itself to a broader public. This process, shared among a number of city churches in the Nordic countries, seeks to reintroduce the faith to the wandering seeker, whoever she is, whenever she wants to come inside. The approach includes, on the one hand, how the church presents itself and, on the other, when it makes itself available. First, the church presents itself as "a church for everyone," where one should "feel free to come as you are." It is a "church for the whole person — and for all people." They seek to live their Lord's "receptiveness towards life and all expressions of life." They acknowledge the pain and brokenness of life, and in doing so, they seek to witness to "the light that shines through our cracks."[13] Second, they have expanded the times they are open, including many of the weekday hours, but also what is called *Natt Åpen*, Friday evenings from 3:30 p.m. until 8:00 a.m. Saturday morning. It offers an open space, a place for an alternative approach to God compared to the High

---

12. Phil Zuckerman, *Society without God: What the Least Religious Nations Can Tell Us About Contentment* (New York: New York University Press, 2008), 9.

13. http://www.oslodomkirke.no/artikler/1183/oslo-cathedral/ (accessed Aug. 23, 2010).

Mass Sunday mornings. A meditative prayer service is offered, and staff are available for private conversation should someone desire it.[14]

When one enters the Domkyrka, the space is set up to allow what amounts to self-interpreted wandering with stations for prayer, reflection, and action scattered throughout the full extent of the building. For example, in one transept (the area set crosswise to the nave in a cruciform — usually Gothic — church building), next to an obviously ancient font, one finds a beautiful wrought-iron globe held up at body height by a pole; its center holds a large, beautifully lit candle, and many places to set smaller candles both outside and inside the globe. A nearby sign by a box of candles invites passers-by to "light a candle — words do not always suffice — even silence may be your prayer" along with a quote from Psalm 139. Nearby, a large brass sculpture of the Last Supper has become a prayer station: Jesus' open hands are packed full of folded slips of paper. Again, a sign explains the practice, and slips of paper and pencils are provided: people are invited to read and make prayers left by others their own, or, for privacy, a box just to the left of the statue is for prayers to be left. A young man, about thirty, reflected on his experience:

> As I enter the room, I get a feeling of tranquility and peace. In the beginning, I regarded the Night Church as a house of prayer. I didn't know the people there. Today, I know a lot of the people and I'm a part of the twilight congregation. To me, the Night Church is prayers by night, singing, friends, the coffee table, and the silence lying underneath it all. This peace fills me.[15]

All in all, the feeling is of a place prepared for those who might not have planned to come, and are not at all sure they are welcome, but find despite themselves a place to be, to breathe, to find peace, and perhaps to pray.

The English case involves the Church of England, the official religious home of 40 percent of the population. The Church of England is Anglican by confession and has been established as the state church since King Henry VIII declared it so in 1534. Both membership and participation have been in significant decline for generations, with some reports sug-

---

14. This practice began at the Church of our Lady in downtown Copenhagen. See Christina Mertz Fundrup, "The Night Church of Copenhagen," *International Review of Mission* 96 (July-Oct. 2007): 248-55.

15. This example is from Copenhagen Cathedral's night church. Fundrup, "The Night Church," 249.

gesting as low as 3 percent attendance at least once monthly.[16] The official church statistics measure any attendance at any service during a given month; thus they report a 30 percent attendance, clearly an inflated figure. Recent research has suggested that the decline is accelerating, including — as in the case of Norway — traditional "rite of passage" events and practices usually held onto after weekly churchgoing has been discarded: marriages, baptisms, and even funerals have been falling as much as 3 percent per year.[17] Yet, as the Church of England's own research shows, their more than 16,000 churches (including 14,500 with special historic designations) are surprisingly valued. Nearly seven in ten Britons say these buildings are important, including nearly five in ten who claim no religion at all.[18]

All Saints, Threxton, in Norfolk in southeast England, is part of a region of the country with an unusually rich architectural heritage. With proximity to early Roman settlements and to France, this small section of England has nearly a tenth of all churches in England, and most were built during the Middle Ages. Within a popular trekking region of the country, with a beautiful rural countryside that holds significant historical interest, these churches have together embarked on an active campaign called "Open Churches," which includes an "Open Churches" week during the height of the summer holiday each August. During that week all churches are open, prepared for stoppers-by of all kinds, and special events are held throughout the region.[19]

The project extends throughout the year. It acts as an invitation to the public to explore these amazing historic sites as places of contemporary spiritual pilgrimage. It also acts as a goad to the wardens of each to make the necessary preparation and local commitment to being open.

16. http://www.timesonline.co.uk/tol/comment/faith/article3890080.ece (accessed Aug. 26, 2010). Among many important works, see Grace Davie, *Religion in Britain since 1945: Believing without Belonging* (New York: Wiley-Blackwell, 1994); Steve Bruce, *God is Dead: Secularization in the West* (New York: Blackwell, 2002); Robin Gill, *The Empty Church Revisited* (Burlington, VT: Ashgate Publishing, 2003); Peter Berger, Grace Davie, and Effie Fokas, *Religious America, Secular Europe? A Theme and Variations* (Burlington, VT: Ashgate, 2008).

17. Ruth Gledhill, "Church of England Congregations Fall Again," *The Times*, Jan. 23, 2010: http://www.timesonline.co.uk/tol/comment/faith/article6999268.ece (accessed Aug. 28, 2010).

18. The Church of England Today: http://www.cofe.anglican.org/about/thechurchof englandtoday/ (accessed Aug. 28, 2010).

19. http://www.norwich.anglican.org/visiting/openchurches/ (accessed Aug. 28, 2010).

Those who have wandered in and deeply appreciate the shift in stance of the church are sometimes amazingly eloquent regarding its import. Simon Knott, a regular visitor to these churches, writes:

> We will never benefit spiritually from churches which are locked when a service isn't on, churches where we have to hunt for the key before entering a building which is little more than a preaching space. Ironically, evangelical congregations who usually inhabit such churches are mortified when their buildings are described as museums. But churches that are no more than mere accommodation for the Sunday club, however holy its members may be, can never be anything other than dead to strangers. To be a living church, the building should be one that speaks to the stranger and pilgrim alike, touching them with something like beauty and mystery, one where they can sense the presence of God, and know Him, perhaps for the first time.[20]

Knott has personally visited every church in Norfolk, producing one of the most loving and impressive photographic tributes to local churches that I have ever seen.

Knott's commentary about All Saints, Threxton, is a beautiful example. While no town remains, a nearby farm and surrounding pasture set the church in fields of green. Its eleventh-century Norman tower, distinctly round in style, connects to a simple church. Upon approaching the church, one finds this notice tacked onto the heavy wooden door, written in beautiful calligraphy: "Welcome to Threxton Church. The Door is never locked. Please stay as long as you wish and enjoy the Peace." Entering through the door, one finds a snug, simply adorned church with a very old font against an old pillar in the rear. Just behind the font one finds photography showing the twentieth-century renovations, during which beautiful medieval paintings were discovered on the plaster walls of the arches and restored. Looking down the aisle toward the altar, one can pause before remarkably detailed stained glass windows from the late thirteenth century.

The case in the United States involves the Episcopal Church, a relatively small mainline denomination in the United States that is tied to the global Anglican Communion. The Episcopal Church began shortly after the American Revolution to distinguish its own ecclesiastical life separate from the monarchial allegiance required of Church of England clergy. At

---

20. Simon Knott, "St. Mary, South Creake," found at: http://www.norfolkchurches.co .uk/southcreake/southcreake.htm (accessed Aug. 28, 2010).

roughly two million members, the Episcopal Church has under 1 percent of the US population. While the United States is still considered the most religious of the Western nations, in part because of vibrant new immigrant Christian communities, membership in many of the so-called mainline denominations, including the Episcopal Church, has experienced dramatic declines in the last half century.[21] Over that period the Episcopal Church has lost an average of 1 percent a year. Denominational decline, argues Kirk Hadaway, sociologist and chief researcher for the Episcopal Church, is not the same as congregational decline. While many congregations are healthy, many more are declining. In Hadaway's view, the "renewed culture-wide interest in spirituality" offers the church a remarkable opportunity to reach beyond its historic constituency. However, he concludes, the Episcopal Church remains "largely unprepared to deal with the interest that unchurched seekers are directing towards our churches."[22]

St. Gregory of Nyssa Church, an Episcopal congregation in San Francisco, was founded in 1975. The founding priests, Richard Fabian and Donald Schell, met in seminary and discovered that they shared a common vision for liturgical mission. Their choice of a location for a church plant, the increasingly secular west-coast city of San Francisco, placed them squarely in what has since been termed the "none" zone. This region of the United States is distinguished for its fast-rising population of people who, when asked about their religious affiliation, respond, "None."[23] Current statistics from a major religious affiliation study found that, for the country as a whole, an average of 16 percent respond "none"; in California, however, the number is almost 25 percent.[24] In response, among many in-

21. On new immigrant Christianity, for example, see Moses Biney, *From Africa to America: Religion and Adaptation among Ghanaian Immigrants in New York* (New York: New York University, 2011); see also Mark Gornik, *The Word Made Global: African Christianity in Motion* (Grand Rapids: Eerdmans, 2011). On the fate of the U.S mainline churches, see David Roozen and James Nieman, eds., *Church, Identity and Change: Theology and Denominational Structures in Unsettled Times* (Grand Rapids: Eerdmans, 2005); see also Robert Bacher and Kenneth Inskeep, *Chasing Down a Rumor: The Death of Mainline Denominations* (Minneapolis: Fortress, 2005).

22. C. Kirk Hadaway, "Is the Episcopal Church Growing (or Declining)?" (New York: Domestic and Foreign Missionary Society, 2004), 18: http://www.episcopalchurch.org/109378_105233_ENG_HTM.htm (accessed Sept. 30, 2010).

23. See Patricia O'Connell Killen and Mark Silk, *Religion and Public Life in the Pacific Northwest: The None Zone* (Lanham, MD: Altamira, 2004).

24. See the Pew Forum on Religion and Public Life U.S. Religious Landscape Survey: http://religions.pewforum.org/ (accessed Sept. 30, 2010).

novations meant to respond to these social factors, Fabian and Schell sought above all to create a community centered on open communion. Their idea was to recover the radical nature of Jesus, the savior who was accused of "welcoming sinners and eating with them" (Luke 15:2). In a paper entitled "First the Table, Then the Font," Fr. Fabian describes the practice:

> We are all guests at Jesus' table, so we welcome all without exception to share the bread and wine that are Christ's Body and Blood. These are not some vaguely holy symbols which they might find elsewhere, or which mean whatever seekers might think comfortable. When Christ's Spirit blows newcomers in our church doors to share his table with us, we know these gifts will transform their lives mysteriously.[25]

Remarkable for its humility, this perspective nonetheless firmly grasps hold of the promise of Christ's Spirit to "blow wherever it pleases" (John 3:8). Perhaps St. Gregory of Nyssa's most famous open-communion convert, author Sara Miles, writes the following in her memoir of coming to faith, *Take This Bread:*

> One early, cloudy morning when I was forty-six, I walked into a church, ate a piece of bread, took a sip of wine. A routine Sunday activity for tens of millions of Americans — except that up to that moment I'd led a thoroughly secular life, at best indifferent to religion, more often appalled by its fundamentalist crusades. This was my first communion. It changed everything.

Miles returned, week by week, only gradually understanding the deeper meaning of this meal and its connection to the deep hunger she felt welling up within her. Her baptism came even later. She describes the way the very architecture prepared the church for her arrival.

> St. Gregory's very floor-plan, designed by Donald Schell with the architect John Goldman, spoke of a mission centered on inclusive communion. In most churches, I learned, the baptismal font is planted at the entrance, and the altar far away at the end of the church, behind a rail, making it clear to visitors that initiation is required before receiving bread and wine. The font serves as a gate to keep the wrong people

25. This article, originally written for the Association of Anglican Musicians in 2002, is posted on the church's website: http://www.saintgregorys.org/worship/resources_section/233/ (accessed Oct. 2, 2010).

from the feast, and the table remains mysterious and distant, something only priests can approach. But at St. Gregory's, the front doors
opened on an empty space under a soaring cupola, with a round table
right in the middle, the first thing visitors saw upon entering. . . .
[O]utside the doors, set into the hillside, stood the baptismal font: a
huge chunk of rock with a basin hewn out, spilling forth water for anyone who wanted it, after dinner.

Part of what is so remarkable was Miles's openness to take communion,
and as she eloquently puts it, let "communion take me, too — wherever I
was going."[26] As anyone who has followed her story knows, she has drawn
her congregation into an amazing food-pantry ministry shared from that
same communion table in the same open worship space, and she has written beautifully about the experience so that many can share in her experiences along the way.[27]

The Practice of Dispossession

I now turn to make the argument that these three case studies are all examples of a missional congregational practice — the practice of dispossession
— that signals the kind of discipleship formation needed in a secular age.
We should find help in thinking through the theological implications
these congregations and their practice of dispossession raise in conversation with missional theology.[28] Here I want to show both how this is and is
not the case because of particular developments in missional theology.
What I want to suggest is that there are clear benefits, but also limitations,
to the move to begin with Trinitarian theology and from there move to
congregational practice. The theological "big picture" can move too
quickly past the actual shape of congregational practice, thus potentially
misleading the effort to understand the theology implicit in practice.

26. Sara Miles, *Take This Bread: A Radical Conversion* (New York: Ballantine Books,
2007), xi, 79-80, 83.
27. Her follow-up book is *Jesus Freak: Feeding, Healing, Raising the Dead* (San Francisco: Jossey-Bass, 2010).
28. By "missional congregational practices," I have in mind the kind of perspective
outlined in Guder, ed., *Missional Church*, chap. 6, "Missional Community: Cultivating
Communities of the Holy Spirit," 153ff. I say more about how I think about practice(s) as a
theoretical concept below.

Let's take, for instance, the classic text *Missional Church*. In the main theological chapter, George Hunsberger draws on Lesslie Newbigin and David Bosch to describe the shift from the church as a place to the church as a people. Bosch traced the way theological developments in the West led to understanding the church as a place where certain things happen. He cites the Augsburg Confession's Article VII on "Concerning the Church" as a well-known place where this pattern is evident: "The Church is the congregation of saints, in which the Gospel is rightly taught and the Sacraments are rightly administered."[29] Bosch admits that this can be understood as a kind of missional faithfulness under the conditions of Christendom, a place where a Christian population gathers for worship and where the Christianity of the population is cultivated.

However, Bosch goes on to say that, as a result of the missionary movement throughout the nineteenth and twentieth centuries, this understanding of church began to shift. One might say that the cumulative impact of sending so many missionaries over decades of church life began to suggest the image of the church as a "sent people." Theologians through the twentieth century began to speak of a theocentric view of mission rather than the prior ecclesiocentric view. The concept of the *missio Dei* has been one way of speaking of this shift, leading to the aphorism "it is not God's church that has a mission but rather that God's mission has a church." Bosch puts it more carefully: "The classical doctrine on the *missio Dei* as God the Father sending the Son, and God the Father and Son sending the Spirit was expanded to include yet another 'movement': Father, Son, and Holy Spirit sending the church into the world."[30] As is evident in this quotation, a revival in Trinitarian theology has gone hand in hand with the development of missional theology.[31]

I would like to pause here and return to the limitations of this Trinitarian-informed missional theology hinted at above. While on the one hand Trinitarian life and our theological reflection on it is essential to mission (a claim that I embody in this chapter and that is richly portrayed in Dwight Zscheile's chapter in this book), I worry about what might be missed when conversation moves immediately — or too quickly — to sys-

29. Timothy Wengert and Robert Kolb, eds., *The Book of Concord* (Minneapolis: Fortress, 2000), 42-43.

30. David J. Bosch, *Transforming Mission: Paradigm Shifts in Theology of Mission* (Maryknoll, NY: Orbis Books, 1991), 373.

31. "Theocentric mission theology recovered the Trinitarian character of mission." Guder, ed., *Missional Church*, 82.

tematic reflection on the Trinity as the starting point for a theology of mission. Beginning with the Trinity, a common approach in the missional church conversation offers the clear advantage of tools for thinking carefully about the muddle of actual beliefs present in particular congregations. In fact, the reason for the renewed emphasis on the doctrine of the Trinity as integral to mission, according to Lesslie Newbigin, derives from this conviction: "The church continues to repeat the Trinitarian formula but — unless I am greatly mistaken — the ordinary Christian in the Western world who hears or reads the word 'God' does not immediately and inevitably think of the Triune Being — Father, Son, and Spirit. He thinks of a supreme monad." That concern is an important one, and there are excellent discussions of the historical and cultural reasons for it.[32] The obvious limitation of working from a systematic theological understanding of Trinity and mission is that, from the perspective of the person wandering into the Oslo Domkyrka on a Friday night or Sara Miles wandering into communion at St. Gregory of Nyssa on a Sunday morning, personal experience is unlikely to be understood explicitly in Trinitarian form, even if the Trinitarian fullness is implicitly there.

The benefit of beginning "on the ground" theologically is, as this chapter aims to show, that one can take account of the particularity of local performances of the Christian life. From these local performances, such as I have described in each case-study congregation (Oslo, Threxton, and San Francisco), one can turn to the fruitful Trinitarian frameworks that missional theology offers, but entering into them contextually rather than dogmatically. That is, rather than unfolding certain loci such as creation, spirit, Christology, and so on, one can reach for these categories building out of the particular explicit and implicit theology present in the practices of a particular congregation. Among the most articulate and sophisticated theologians working this way, James Nieman has argued that the richness of embodied local theology is rarely adequately understood.[33] Mary McClintock Fulkerson seeks to take up this challenge in her study of the practices in one diverse North Carolina congregation.[34] While neither Nieman or Fulkerson is part of the "missional church" conversation ex-

---

32. For instance, Gary Simpson's wise article "No Trinity, No Mission: The Apostolic Difference of Revisioning the Trinity," *Word and World* 18, no. 3 (Summer 1998): 264-71.

33. James Nieman, "Attending Locally: Theologies in Congregations," *International Journal of Practical Theology* 6:2 (Fall 2002), 198-225.

34. Mary McClintock Fulkerson, *Places of Redemption: Theology for a Worldly Church* (New York: Oxford University Press, 2007).

plicitly, both are friends of such a conversation and inform the approach I seek to offer here. And while I am appreciative of approaches that begin with systematic theological claims, my worries about them drive me to begin from theological approaches that seem implicitly present in the cases I have presented, and to move from these approaches to a theology of the Trinity — rather than the reverse.

What theological approaches seem implicit in my case studies above? As I have hinted at in my opening, these cases all embody a kind of "stripping away" of the assurances of the Christian establishment. Such establishment is nicely described in the book *Missional Church* as "the system of church-state partnership and cultural hegemony in which the Christian religion was the protected and privileged religion of society and the church its legally established form." Guder and colleagues continue that, even when the official legal structures of Christendom are removed, the power of this pattern endures in what they call "functional Christendom."[35] The conditions of secularity — of post-Christendom — in each of my cases suggest the force of "stripping away" rather than letting go. Each case has, in its own context, responded with some version of letting go of their possessions, from the worship and devotional practices to the very holy space in which the congregation gathers week by week. At St. Gregory's this is explicitly shaped according to eucharistic practice of Christ's own self-giving in the bread broken and wine poured out for the sake of the world. Yet the cases all have this deep structure of the Eucharist implied in their actions, breaking open their fear and closed-fistedness to give themselves away for the lost, lonely, hungry, and hurting stranger. This is the territory theologians describe as Christology, and I'd like to explore one trajectory of theological reflection that takes special account of Jesus' self-giving — sometimes summarized by the term *kenosis*. I'll do that briefly, and then I will conclude by returning with this theological understanding to speak pastorally about what we might take from the consideration of these cases.

The language I have been introducing from the beginning — of "being stripped of the security tradition easily bestows" — comes from a lecture entitled "*Kenosis* and Establishment," which Donald MacKinnon delivered as the 1966 Gore Memorial Lecture at Westminster Abbey.[36] This London church has been the site of royal coronations (and often burials)

35. Guder, ed., *Missional Church*, 6.

36. Donald MacKinnon, "*Kenosis* and Establishment," in *The Stripping of the Altars* (New York: Collins, The Fontana Library, 1969), 13-40.

since William the Conqueror on Christmas day in 1066.[37] MacKinnon, at that time Norris-Hulse Professor of Divinity at Cambridge University, made his position clear — ironically in the setting of Westminster Abbey — by favorably quoting "Father R. M. Benson, founder of the Society of St. John the Evangelist, that the conversion of Constantine was the greatest single disaster ever to overtake the Christian church."[38] However, after expressing "heartfelt agreement," he goes on to remark that the advent of the post-Constantinian age offers both unparalleled opportunity and profound testing for the church. *Kenosis,* then, functions for MacKinnon as a key idea "for the renewal of the church's understanding of mission."[39]

To begin with, MacKinnon uses the implications of *kenosis* to juxtapose contemporary dependence on the church as an established institution versus Jesus' own remarkable dependence on his father. Referring not only to the famous passage from Philippians 2 but also to the Fourth Gospel, MacKinnon writes that Jesus depended on an authority "because of and in the context of a supreme humility." That supreme humility is shorthand for the core biblical text on *kenosis:*

> Christ Jesus, who, though he was in the form of God, did not regard equality with God as something to be exploited, but emptied himself, taking the form of a slave, being born in human likeness. And being found in human form, he humbled himself and became obedient to the point of death — even death on a cross (Phil. 2:6-8).

In this text MacKinnon finds a Christological "key" to an adequate theology. Attending to the humility and receptivity of Jesus shows us a way to critique false gods of security and autonomy that we set up to bolster our traditions. This way of Jesus belongs to God, "as he is in himself" for in Jesus we have God's "very self and essence all divine." Thus Jesus' "invitation to the outcast is not adequately seen as a mere parable of the divine invita-

37. The abbey has a wonderfully detailed and designed website: http://www.westminster-abbey.org/our-history (accessed Oct. 11, 2010).

38. MacKinnon, "*Kenosis* and Establishment," 15.

39. There is a long and problematic history of this term both in biblical studies and theology. For the first, my colleague David Frederickson has done very significant work: see his "The Kenosis of Christ in the Politics of Paul," *Journal of Lutheran Ethics* (April 2005): http://www.elca.org/What-We-Believe/Social-Issues/Journal-of-Lutheran-Ethics/Issues/April-2005/The-Kenosis-of-Christ-in-the-Politics-of-Paul.aspx (accessed Oct. 11, 2010). Theologically, Rowan Williams traces some of the important literature in "Incarnation and the Renewal of Community," in *On Christian Theology* (New York: Blackwell, 2000), 225-38.

tion, but rather as its actuality become event."[40] Here, it becomes clear that MacKinnon is taking the notion of *kenosis* and all it represents for Jesus' birth, life, and death on the cross "back into the initiating act of the whole incarnate life." Implications for a theology of the Trinity are clear here, for example distinguishing between the essential and the economic Trinity, but even more so are implications for ecclesiology.[41]

In terms of ecclesiology, relevance of the Christological concept of *kenosis* is arguably difficult to formulate exactly because our vision of the God-human relationship is obscured by the "radically distorted image presented in and by the institution supposed to convey its sense to the world." Such a strong claim naturally leads to criticism of the church's institutional experience, including "even rejection of long tracts of that experience as fundamentally invalid." MacKinnon evokes the typical "establishment" authority of an "English bishop who graduates to the Episcopal bench from the headmastership of an English public school," pointing out that the sort of authority buttressed by hierarchy and position is a kind of authority the "career of the rabbi of Nazareth does not suggest." Among his most pointed examples of this, he takes up the idea of state church chaplaincy to the industry of war. Were establishment to finally pass away, MacKinnon then imagines "a day in which Episcopal lawn sleeves would cease to flutter in the breeze as their wearer bestowed the diocesan benediction upon the latest Polaris submarine. Here we should find sheer gain without any loss at all." The larger issue, then, is "not with Establishment in the narrow sense" but "with the cultivation of the status of invulnerability, issuing in a devotion to the structures that preserve it."[42] The language of cultivation here raises the issue that has been in the foreground, namely, criticism of the malformation of the church, but also implicitly the question of missional imagination and formation. Thus it is not surprising to see MacKinnon suggest that our first duty is to free our imaginations, and the path toward this is, as I said at the beginning, living into the practice of "exposure" or "stripping" — what Rowan Williams, in his development of these ideas, calls "the practice of dispossession."[43]

Before developing MacKinnon's ideas with the help of Williams's

40. MacKinnon, "*Kenosis* and Establishment," 17, 24.

41. A classic text on the relationship of economic and essential Trinity is Karl Rahner, *The Trinity* (New York: Continuum, 1970), 18, 21ff.

42. MacKinnon, "Kenosis and Establishment," 17-18, 32-33.

43. Rowan Williams, *A Ray of Darkness: Sermons and Reflections* (Cambridge, MA: Cowley, 1995), 231.

theology, I want to pause briefly to sort out what we might be after with Williams's use of the term "practice." It is a term — or, better, a concept — that has played a central role in numerous threads of important academic and now also popular books.[44] While the term "practice," or "practices," has given these works a kind of surface family resemblance, they have not always shared the same conceptual underpinning and sometimes have claimed too broad a territory to really be coherent as distinct practices.[45] I have myself drawn on multiple frames in various pieces I have published, from the subtle notion Pierre Bourdieu develops in connection with the idea of *habitus* as a "regulated improvisation," to the more distinct action Alasdair MacIntyre refers to by his definition of practices as a "coherent and complex form of socially established cooperative human activity."[46] While implicit rules for using salad forks and patterns of conversation over dinner point toward Bourdieu's notion of durable, transposable, patterned habits of action, the action of a shared meal as a whole fits more MacIntyre's vision of social practices done for the goods internal to the activity itself. Ted Smith, a theologian at Vanderbilt Divinity School, has articulated the sense in which these two understandings of practice speak "in different registers." MacIntyre's version of practices helps make sense of the *telos* and goods internal to eating meals together as a whole. Bourdieu's version of practices focuses on a smaller scale, helping to elicit the way most meals "are congeries of practices."[47]

What, then, might Williams mean by his phrase "the practice of dispossession" in the context of writing about theology of mission? In his 1991 Berkeley Divinity School lectures on mission and spirituality, Williams remarked that the word "mission" is not found in the New Testament. An

44. Philosophy: McIntyre; social science: Bourdieu; theology: Hauerwas; popular series: Jossey-Bass, Practicing our Faith series; Nelson, Ancient Practices series; Fortress, Christian Explorations of Daily Living series, and so on.

45. Nicholas Healy raises this question with vigor in "Practices and the New Ecclesiology: Misplaced Concreteness?" *International Journal of Systematic Theology* 5, no. 3 (Nov. 2003): 287-308.

46. For Bourdieu, see his *Outline of a Theory of Practice,* 79; for my use of this, see "Baptismal Practices and the Formation of Christians: A Critical Liturgical Ethics," *Worship* 76, no. 1 (Jan. 2002): 62-66; for MacIntyre, see his *After Virtue: A Study in Moral Theory* (Notre Dame, IN: University of Notre Dame Press, 1981), 187. See also Christian Scharen, *Faith as a Way of Life: A Vision for Pastoral Leadership* (Grand Rapids: Eerdmans 2008), 53-54.

47. David D. Daniels III and Ted A. Smith, "History, Practice and Theological Education," in Dorothy Bass and Craig Dykstra, eds., *For Life Abundant: Practical Theology, Theological Education and Christian Ministry* (Grand Rapids: Eerdmans, 2008), 214-40.

awkward beginning place, to be sure, but his point in this observation is that in order to talk about mission and the Christian faith, one must first of all "plot" one's path on the map of the New Testament. Williams remarks that while mission is not a prominent term in the New Testament, Scripture does speak of "sending": a God who sends Jesus and a Jesus who in the Spirit sends us. In one remarkable verse, Jesus' identity is equated with being sent: he is called the *apostolos* in Hebrews 3:1, the one who is sent. This sending is for the sake of the world — and thus, in very specific terms, for the poor, the prisoners, the blind, the oppressed (Luke 4:18). Jesus' "mission," if you will, is not first of all the delivery of a message ("The reign of God is near!") or an effort in persuasion ("Repent!"), but rather the delivery of a person: the very reality of Jesus coming to be in relationship with those to whom he was sent. In Jesus, Williams writes, "mission and person are identical."[48] Von Balthasar observes: "[T]he act of sending grounds the entire earthly existence of Jesus."[49]

This point for Williams is central: "In Jesus person and mission are identical." While humans suffer enmity and violence toward others, Jesus is the "one for others," such that his very being is an expression of unreserved communion. While his crucifixion was a rejection of this divine action in Jesus, to believe in his resurrection is to say that his radical communion is now reality. His resurrection is the reality that he goes before us, and that mission is being sent in his name as part of that reconciling work of new communion. Here, Williams shows, the articulation of Jesus' identity and mission leads us into the presence of the Trinitarian life. "If we want to speak adequately of mission, we have to speak of the Trinity, of God's life as communion." Our experience of Jesus, and of his life of self-giving for the sake of new community, leads us to an understanding of God as three-in-one, communion in essence, but also back to the world through this very same Trinitarian life outpouring as wisdom and word in the power of the Spirit. Thus, as Williams puts it, "mission is a matter of *dispossession*. Jesus is God's giving-away, a holding of nothing back: all the Father has is given to Jesus (John 16:10)."

As if all too aware of the abstract nature of all this reflection, Williams sets forth three implications that would figure in our taking up dispossession as a missional practice. First, he says in no uncertain terms that "there is

---

48. Williams, *A Ray of Darkness*, 221.

49. Hans Urs Von Balthasar, *Theodramatik II: Die Personen des Spiels;* Teil 2: *Die Personen in Christus* (Einsiedeln, 1978), p. 140.

no gap between the gospel and life together." Each congregation may fall short, be subject to division and fear yet by virtue of its very life the church presses against the sources of division and fear. Second, in its call to communion, the church has a very specific responsibility to "the one," recalling Jesus' famous "lost" parables in Luke 15. While it rejoices in those who are already well, of course, the church, like its Lord, is sent out in particular for the sake of the sick, the lost, the hungry, the hurting, and the hopeless. Third, given that the church is, as Williams says, "a flawed and often profoundly unimpressive historical reality," mission involves repentance. Taken together, these three points compel one to recognize that mission is not finally like the instructions one receives for using a new phone or computer. Rather, the practice of dispossession is a way of being Jesus, sent by his Spirit, which in its living opens opportunities for communion that we are not in control of (thinking of congregations wanting members who "will join us"). Mission as dispossession — as outpouring in Jesus' own life in the Spirit — is real gift and hence must be given freely to see what shape communion takes. Finally, Williams intends these three points to be a guard against letting our language about incarnation and Trinity "become a system for our intellectual or institutional possession: it is only plausible or authoritative, only makes sense, within the practice of dispossession, an authentically self-forgetting practice that allows and nourishes the otherness of others."[50]

While it has been implicit up to this point, the practice of dispossession is deeply grounded in the church's sacramental life. Baptism and Eucharist presume our condition "pre-sacramentally," so our speaking is transformed through participation in the sacrament. Williams works out these implications, grounding our practice of dispossession in our participation in the sacraments as the foundation of our life in Christ.[51] In baptism, our very selves are given over and given in return, stripping away our various allegiances in order that this new belonging can take root in us. In the Eucharist our identity and mission are transformed into the unity of Christ's own identity and mission, so that, in the words of Augustine, "it is to what you are that you reply, 'Amen.'"[52] In a beautiful passage, Williams observes:

50. Williams, *A Ray of Darkness*, 222, 225, 229-31.

51. For example, see his "Sacraments of the New Society," in *On Christian Theology* (New York: Blackwell, 2000), 209-21.

52. Augustine, "On the Nature of the Sacrament of the Eucharist," Sermon 272: http://www.earlychurchtexts.com/public/augustine_sermon_272_eucharist.htm (accessed Oct. 11, 2010).

By his surrender "into" the passive forms of food and drink, he makes void and powerless the impending betrayal, and more, makes the betrayers his guests and debtors, making with them the promise of divine fidelity, the covenant, that cannot be negated by their unfaithfulness.[53]

To recall MacKinnon here, the point is that our security, the assurance of the meaning of our identity as persons and as Christians, is not secured by our possession of some earned status but by receptivity, by gift, by the very promise of God for us.

Therefore, we, who become Christ's with and without the apostrophe, as Luther liked to put it, might speak of our formation for mission being rooted in the very actions of Jesus, who, in presiding over our sending by his Spirit, takes us, blesses us, breaks us open, and gives us over to the world's hunger. To return to the discussion of practice(s) above, I might say that what Williams intends with this idea of the "practice of dispossession" is something like what Bourdieu is after in terms of habituated, regulated improvisation that exists as a component part of the Eucharist as an example of the kind of coherent and shared social practices MacIntyre describes. Unlike the Eucharist, the practice of dispossession is transposable from the context of the Eucharist to many everyday settings where the Gospel challenges us to live *in,* or *as,* mission — to and for others. Such specification, I think, helps further clarify what I want to get at with the "practice of dispossession." I now conclude by returning to the congregations I began with, seeking to offer some pastoral provocation for our conversations in this consultation.

"Real Triumphs"

> *The real triumphs of the gospel have not been won when the church is strong in a worldly sense; they have been won when the church is faithful in the midst of weakness, contempt, and rejection.*[54]
>
> Lesslie Newbigin, *The Open Secret*

First, taking our bearings from Newbigin's powerful comment here about the "real triumphs" of the gospel, I have tried in this chapter to portray the

53. Williams, "Sacraments of the New Society," 216.

54. Lesslie Newbigin, *The Open Secret: An Introduction to the Theology of Mission,* rev. ed. (Grand Rapids: Eerdmans, 1995), 62.

faithfulness churches have lived as a missional witness in the face of institutional weakness and external contempt and rejection. These stories of faithful witness can be understood more deeply, I argue, by thinking through the ways they embody the Christological idea of *kenosis,* the self-emptying of Christ, "who humbled himself." The incorporation of a body of believers into this kenotic action gives us the particular practice of dispossession by which we are formed — or better, transformed — in Christ.

Second, I came to this theological framework by listening deeply to particular congregations in context and paying attention to their missional imagination and practice. While my theological reflections are certainly likely to articulate aspects of their work, they do not articulate themselves; it is an effort to show how building from these various responses to secularism leads us to begin, not with a Trinitarian theological perspective, but a Christological one, and a radical one at that. It leads, to be sure, to a robust doctrine of the Trinity, creation, and all the rest (much more than I could elaborate here); but the starting place is closer to the ground than, as Williams cautions, talking abstractly about, for example, Trinity and communion would be. It is very much like the place where Dwight Zscheile ends his chapter: with the radical new monastic communities in the United States and elsewhere, which would fit well as another case study for my argument here.

Finally, the dramatic challenge of the congregational witnesses is irritatingly clear. In what ways can we imagine being open to the "taking, blessing, breaking, and giving" that God in Christ wishes for us? How can we open ourselves to being drawn by Christ's Spirit more deeply into the practice of dispossession in our churches for the sake of those to whom we are given? Can we, in short, imagine posting a sign on our church door that announces: "Welcome: we are a church and therefore are never locked for the sake of you, the one knocking at the door." And could we also, to remember Peter Rollins's parable — and the fact that Christ presides at the table — never lock our hearts?

CHAPTER 6

Ministry in the First Third of Life: Human Development or Missional Formation?

Nancy S. Going

Their stories aren't detailed. And, proportionally speaking, only a few biblical figures are children or adolescents. Yet, look at the similarity in the nature of the stories of those who are there. There are the stories of young Joseph, David, Samuel, Isaiah, Mary, and Jesus in the Temple, to name the most prominent. Scripture contains very little about them or their life situation, yet there is something unique and compelling about their narratives. Their stories are almost exclusively about how God is using them to further God's mission in the world. They are stories of how these young people said, "Yes," and how "being about my Father's business" is the very thing that forms — and even transforms — them.

While the conversation in this book calls the church to become sent communities by focusing on missional spiritual formation, Sunday schools and youth ministries in churches all over the country are still concentrating their energies on issues of classroom discipline or finding the perfectly engaging confirmation curriculum. The very missionality of the church is compromised and even stymied by the approaches that we continue to take in the faith formation of the next generation. However, before God sent a church or a community like Israel, God sent individuals. Just like the youthful examples above, Abraham's mission was foundational to the faith that he developed because it was foundational to his growth as a person. "God did not just use Abraham for the fulfillment of God's purposes. The Lord also transformed Abraham in the process."[1] While we

1. Mark D. Roberts, "Missional and Formational in the Old Testament": http://blog.beliefnet.com/markdroberts/2009/06/index.html (accessed July 20, 2010).

rarely think about biblical figures in terms of their human development, a persistent problem for a missional church lies in our willingness to live in a very cramped view of faith development led by our fondness for a psychologically focused view of human development. Ministry with those in the first third of life has been particularly captive to a fascination with developmental stages, which function quite differently from missional formation, or God shaping humans for God's mission in the world.

It All Depends on Where You Begin

This chapter will argue that ministry with those in the first third of life has embraced a predominantly psychological developmental approach to children and adolescents, and thus that ministry acknowledges only minimally the theological nature of the human life cycle. Consequently, this lens has not only limited our understanding of the first third of life, and the adolescent life phase especially, but it has also shaped and restricted our view of God's missiological action in us and in the world.

Within the years of the first third of life, adolescence is clearly the most studied and chronicled life phase. Because adolescence is the focus of my doctoral work, I will for the remainder of this chapter primarily focus my first-third-of-life conversation on the adolescent life phase, believing that both the issues in our current ecclesiology and the exploration of a missional formational approach will apply to younger children or young adults as well.

While developmental psychology has been very helpful in its capacity to center ministry on the specific needs and capabilities of an age group, the conversation in youth ministry especially engages adolescent development as human development only. Erik Erikson's developmental tasks are what often drive the conversation about ministry with this age group: identity, individuation, identity foreclosure vs. identity moratorium.[2] More recently, Robert Kegan's cognitive developmentalism has provided additional depth to the picture of the stages of life.[3] Spiritual

2. Erik Erikson wrote extensively about adolescence in *Youth, Identity and Crisis* (New York: W. W. Norton, 1964). The notion that there are various identity statuses in adolescence comes from James Marcia, "Development and Validation of Ego Identity Statuses," *Journal of Personality and Social Psychology* 3 (1966): 551-58.

3. Robert Kegan, *In Over Our Heads* (Cambridge, MA: Harvard University Press, 1994). Kegan is well known for his interdisciplinary developmental schema that focuses on

development is generally discussed only as a layer of application of
Erikson's or Kegan's developmental schema, rather than the church
claiming the developmental task in any age as created by God and being
about the mission of God.

Because we have begun by thinking about ministry with adolescents
based on developmental theory, do we see their faith as somehow "less
than" and "not yet," since stage theories necessarily relegate children and
youth to lower levels of cognition? Despite the postmodern questions
about the validity and applicability of developmental stages, those who
work with youth often carry heavy cultural and psychological images of
adolescence and look through those fairly limited — even negative —
lenses at those they serve.[4]

Further, when such stage frameworks are reinforced in the church,
we infuse our already heavily age-segmented ecclesiologies with an underlying belief that inherently limits the church's ability to see young people
as full members of the body of Christ, and even further undercuts a
missiological approach to formation. Does the church, in fact, encourage
approaching youth in the church as a problem because of the way we teach
about adolescence rather than looking not only at adolescents, but also at
adolescence itself, as part of the very mission of God?

Finally, how does a psychological approach to adolescent development limit the concept of formation itself? The Greek word *morphe* means
"form": it can refer to the external shape of something, but also to its essential character.[5] Consequently, are we declaring and teaching the transforming work and person of Jesus Christ as Savior when we continue to
talk about development as a separate biological/psychological process
from spiritual formation? Do we actually claim the biblical assertions:
"For those whom he foreknew he also predestined to be conformed to the
image of his Son"; or "be transformed by the renewing of your minds"; or

---

the individual's ever-growing ability to have a cognitive sense of the "other." In his structure,
therefore, the end goal of development would be a state in which the subject-object distinction comes to an end. He is most famous for noting that many postmodern adults are "in
over their heads," and he says that many American adults are being asked to respond to life
in a way that is actually beyond their cognitive capabilities.

4. These questions about the validity and meaninglessness of developmental stages
for current youth and young adults are the primary thrust of Fredrick Schweitzer, *The Postmodern Life Cycle* (St. Louis: Chalice Press, 2004).

5. Roberts, "Missional and Formational," June 2009: http://blog.beliefnet.com/
markdroberts/2009/06/index.html (accessed July 20, 2010).

"I am in the pain of childbirth until Christ is formed in you"(Rom. 8:29; Rom. 12:2; Gal. 4:19)? The reclamation of the missiological impulse in to-day's church calls for a new exploration of the relationship between forma-tion and mission as an essential playing field of ministry in the first third of life. If so, then it is time to claim those insights for the church by declar-ing that all of the human life cycle cries out to be studied as a theological process.

Human Development as a God Process

My research explores the notion that the various ages of the life cycle could be "signs," as in the Gospel of John, each pointing us to experience unique aspects of God's nature and the way of Jesus.[6] If so, beyond claiming a theological frame for a life phase, the church could also recover develop-ment itself as a process of the mission of God, progressively revealing to us God's nature, mission, and life as we are biologically and psychologically most receptive to comprehending and taking them in.

This is a very different picture of development. Now we see God as the source of development, and a formational process as given by God for the purpose of drawing us nearer to God and moving us into the mission of God. Each time of life provides us with unique learnings about the nature of God to be absorbed and integrated into our very selves and faith, and sup-plying the momentum for psychological growth, that is, transformation.

Coming at the same discussion from the question of mission itself, the 2009 Renovaré Conference offered an entire track of workshops called "Transformational and Missional: The Jesus Way for Church Life and Leadership." Reflecting a new interest in the relationship between mission

6. John Trokan, "Stages of the Marital and Family Life Cycle: Marital Miracles," *Pasto-ral Psychology* 46, no. 4 (March 1998): 281-95. My first exposure to the idea of the life cycle as pointing to God came in this article by Trokan. He uses the frame of the family life cycle from family-systems theory and believes that each stage of life offers varied opportunities for encountering God's revealed presence. He encourages perceiving the growth demanded by each stage in the life cycle, not just as a hurdle to be mastered, but rather as "the work of the Spirit to cultivate love." He asks if the phases of a family's life aren't designed by God to point us to various aspects of God's very nature. "There are those who hope for physical wonder within their life transitions, but fail to perceive the faith-relational invitation of these events and stages." I wondered if that idea could be equally applicable to the human life cycle. One ideological value is the way that such a framework frees us from the greater than/less than and questionable end goals of stage frameworks.

and formation and how that might affect our understanding of Christian discipleship, the series of workshops sought to explore this question: "Is it possible to be missional and not formational?"

> If the church sees itself as missional, in what sense might it also be formational (helping people to become more like Christ)? At first glance, it seems as if missional and formational are apples and oranges. I expect that we'll be able to see, not only that missional and formational go hand in hand, but also how they depend on and fulfill each other. A church that is truly what a church should be will be both missional and formational.[7]

Thus, the issues raised in this chapter point out quite the opposite reality in the church's practice. It appears that the church's approach to children and youth has been waylaid by our fondness for goals other than spiritual formation (such as education or safety) instead of claiming a missional (and thus a formational approach) to ministry with young people.

The Child Is Mission

At the same time, there is something unique about the very nature of the first third of life in and of itself. When exploring Matthew's story of Jesus placing a child in the midst of the disciples, Keith White identifies that action as missiological at its very core: "The placing of a child in the midst of Jesus' disciples is a unique sign or acted parable and represents a surprising new way of understanding the way of the cross and the kingdom of heaven."[8] White says that in Matthew 17:14, Jesus is identifying children as a "key sign" of the kingdom. Placing a child in their midst was not accidental; rather, he chose it to point to the central truth of the kingdom, of God's mission for and in the world.

> Though unremarked by Matthew, children are in a real sense God's language, in and through which he reveals his true nature and therefore the nature of the kingdom. It is not just that children are sign; rather as children qua children they are God's language. The child

---

7. Roberts, "Missional and Formational."
8. Keith White, "He Placed a Little Child in the Midst," in Marcia Bunge, ed., *The Child in the Bible* (Grand Rapids: Eerdmans, 2008), 373-74.

standing by Jesus is the language — not because they are trusted with a message, like the prophets, but because they are the revelation.

While our churches have tended to think of the formation of the next generation in terms of information to be shared or problems to be solved, this passage from Matthew and White's insights about it would seem to suggest something profoundly important about the spiritual formation of children for the larger mission of the church. If children are "sign," then how do we engage them as church members. It will be a "key sign" of the church's willingness to take up the *missio Dei*. How are we to participate in the mission of God in the world when we aren't willing to attend to this key sign in our midst?

A Study of Adolescent Faith

How can we begin to see and appreciate the *missio Dei* that is human formation? What if the faith stories of adolescents could allow the church to see the actual contours and practices of "missional formation"? In order to study and describe it in the adolescent life phase, one would need to listen to young people who are committed Christians. Could adolescents of committed faith further point to a theological framework for development across the life cycle? What if the church were actually to use theology, specific theological themes reflecting various aspects of the nature of God, to teach about the nature of development?

To begin the process of studying adolescent faith, I interviewed young people to listen to the stories of their faith development. However, I also wanted to identify specific theological themes that might be present (e.g., the *missio Dei*) in the natural "faith energy" of adolescents.[9] I chose several themes in Luther's theology as possible tools for the listening process, because of Luther's focus on the work of God in everyday life. Luther focused his writing in a pastoral direction, on the living faith of real people, which I thought might resonate with adolescent thoughts about faith. I chose the following three Lutheran theological themes to ground this look at adolescent development: *simul justus et peccator;* justifying faith as knowing, trusting, and affirming; and the *larvae Dei*, or

---

9. I use the term "faith energy" to describe what these twelve adolescents talked about most frequently and freely.

masks of God. I had a sense that these classic theological themes about the nature of God and humans might just be evident in the expressions of the faith of adolescents.

I built my research on the Exemplary Youth Ministry (EYM) study and interviewed adolescents from churches whose young people scored higher on a Maturing Christian Faith measure.[10] My work consisted of conducting in-depth interviews with twelve adolescents from four EYM churches. In addition, I met with a dozen other students in two focus groups to triangulate the data, and I completed a theme analysis of the data. Although there were wide individual variations in the faith experiences of these twelve disciples, the content of their conversation about faith — their "faith energy" — was remarkably similar. The results of this qualitative study of committed Christian adolescents showed them engaged in absorbing the notion that "faith is a living relationship with Jesus" into their self-understanding. Luther's theme of justifying faith as knowing, trusting, and affirming (all relational attributes, according to Luther, to be further explored in the next section) was the most prominent topic of their conversation. These were clearly the expressions of a newly redefined relationship with God for all twelve of these adolescents. Several said: "When I was younger, I knew *about* God. Now I *know* God because I know what Jesus did for me."

While the theme analysis of the interviews with the twelve students produced ninety-six different themes clustering around nine big ideas, the concept of a newly shaped relationship with Jesus is the single most significant theme to emerge from the interview data. These twelve disciples affirmed this theme as the most important part of what they knew about God, and distinct from how they may have understood God before. This is how some of them talked about it:

Carrie:[11] I was a baby Christian then. Back then, I got the concepts like Jesus died on the cross to save our sins, but that was about it. Now I

10. Roland Martinson, Wes Black, and John Roberto, *The Spirit and Culture of Youth Ministry: Leading Congregations Toward Exemplary Youth Ministry* (St. Paul: EYM Publishing, 2010). The Exemplary Youth Ministry study was done by representatives of seven denominations under the auspices of a Lilly grant and was completed in 2003. It sought to identify the characteristics of congregations whose young people scored higher on levels of mature Christian faith. The complete study results and the book are available at: www.exemplarym.com.

11. Names have been changed to protect anonymity.

understand more about who God is as a person. I've grown more to understand him. I've gotten to know him.

Lindsay: After becoming a part of Trinity, we have our youth classes for the juniors and we'd hear talks from the youth leaders, and you would, like, listen to those, and be like, wow, that really does make sense. And I went to a few Christian camps too. Sixth grade I went to a horseback riding camp, and I really didn't understand the whole relationship thing quite well yet. And in eighth grade, I went through Young Life to a camp for teenagers. It's a group we have in Owatonna, and I went to Castaway, and that was just a really good time to get away from everything in this world and focus on God. It just kind of helped me to figure out what it means to have a relationship with God.

Not Just Any Relationship

While each of the twelve talked about knowing God relationally, they also reflected a remarkably intimate relationship. They said things like, "I am my faith" (Julie), or "I am a Christian" (Mark). Or this insight from Lindsay:

> At first I thought God was just the one who sat above and just watched us, but, like, the whole relationship thing is like having him here with you. He's here to be with you and he's feeling all the emotions that you are at the same time, and he's like your best friend, and he's the person who's going to understand you the best, better than you know yourself. And he's just really important to have as a friend, and he's like your livelihood in a way, because he's the one who can breathe life into you when you don't feel like you have any.

The following is how Princeton Seminary professor Kenda Dean has theorized about the theological nature of what these twelve disciples described:

> Our identities take shape in relationships that mirror back to us "who we are" and the kind of person we are becoming; but not just any relationship will do. Ultimately, identity requires the self-confirming presence of reliable love . . . and when we do find it, this authentic love reorders our view of the world and our place in it.[12]

12. Kenda Dean, *Practicing Passion: Youth and the Quest for a Passionate Church* (Grand Rapids: Eerdmans, 2004), 55-56.

Faith as Transformation

While it would be easy to relegate these young people to a "me and Jesus" kind of Christianity, there was a distinct thread in the conversations that indicates a missional move. Not only did these young people talk about newly reshaped relationships with Jesus, but they also talked about that relationship as transformational in its very essence. They celebrated the ways that faith had driven and focused their growth toward others.

> Ruth: And so, like, when I get back this year, our school is blessed again with an eclectic bunch, and while you wish you wouldn't have some of the diversity, regardless of personality, I am trying to remember that Jesus was the God of the outcast, and it reminds me that I need to try to love this person, and just not hating them would be a step in the right direction, and I've really been trying to work on that in living out my faith.
>
> Eliza: A Christian is to me a person who believes that Christ is the Son of God, and actively tries to become more Christ-like. Being a Christian is unique, because you are not searching for Nirvana or enlightenment, you are searching to become more like Christ. My tendencies are not towards Christ, which makes it a lot harder, but as a Christian you are trying to develop that meekness of spirit and that passion for others that allows you to be there for your brothers, and stand against the grain — all those qualities that Christ possessed.

In contrast to the self-focus of our culturally driven beliefs about adolescent search for identity, our theological frames have long accounted for such development: "A central point of patristic Christology was that God became man, took flesh in order to redeem humanity to a new human nature in Christ."[13] These are the seeds of missional formation.

Adolescence as a Missiological Move

Wasteful love transforms us into bearers of such love for others. . . .
When we realize what God has done, when we discover that Christ has

---

13. George Newlands, "Christology," in Alan Richardson and John Bowden, eds., *Westminster Dictionary of Christian Theology* (Philadelphia: Westminster, 1983), 108.

bound himself to us so radically that nothing can separate us from him, when we gratefully reciprocate by fastening our lives to his life, death, and resurrection in baptism, the Holy Spirit empowers us to consciously participate in the life of God. . . . Mission means participating in the very life of God, taking part in the "to die for" love of Jesus Christ, which is the purpose of the church.[14]

I took a second look at the interviews with these students for expressions of specific Lutheran theological themes. Of the three theological themes I explored, Luther's "justifying faith as knowing, trusting, and affirming" was clearly the unique theological expression that claimed the focus of their adolescent faith and formational energy. Luther wrote that justifying faith has three areas of activity: knowing, trusting, and affirming. By exploring these three aspects of faith, we can further understand the remarkably Christocentric nature of adolescent development. The amount of "faith energy" displayed by these adolescents around these three activities was the central finding in the theme analysis: their faith journey at this point resonates with Luther's notions of what faith is and does.

The reason, Luther says, that people don't believe faith justifies is "because they don't know what faith is."[15] Luther uses the phrase "justifying faith as knowing, trusting and affirming" to describe not *categories or stages* of faith, but rather the kind of fluid relational *movement* of faith that these twelve adolescents were so excited to receive. This phrase of Luther does not automatically translate to missiology; yet we will see in the following words of the twelve committed young Christians how it does identify important aspects of a critical development in faith, one that could actually be fundamental to the theological process that is adolescence.

First, It's About Knowing

A historically significant part of Luther's theological breakthrough came in the way that he approached Jesus Christ. Luther's focus on justifying faith led the way for a discovery of history and the self and provided fresh Christological language:

14. Kenda Dean, *Almost Christian: What the Faith of Our Teenagers Is Telling the American Church* (New York: Oxford University Press, 2010), 88.

15. Alistair E. McGrath, *Reformation Thought: An Introduction* (Cambridge, MA: Blackwell, 2001), 111.

[F]irst of all from the standpoint of life-experience: First Luther's own, and then that of the believer. We know Christ only as we know what he has done for us — hence the work is key to understanding the person. Faith in him is not mere intellectual assent, but the thankful, confident, trusting response of one's whole self to God's life in the midst of our own estrangement and pain.[16]

These adolescents talked about their relationship with Jesus as the significant appreciation to emerge from their varied recent experiences of God. They expressed new understanding of the reality that God loved them and that they now knew Jesus. Their conviction is also apparent in the fifty examples of the theme "God speaks to me." Even though they had all grown up in the church, if they understood and experienced that Jesus had died "for me," it was not real to them prior to this. This is just the kind of personal knowledge of Christ that Luther described.

> Adam: He [the speaker] put it in words that I understood for the first time, and something just clicked, that you have to have a personal relationship with Jesus Christ. I'd never heard that before. I am sure I had heard it, but that was the first time that I heard it and understood it.
>
> Lauren: For me, when I was younger, having God was just an abstract concept, and it wasn't really that real. It was just kind of like how we dream about talking horses or something like that when we were younger. It was just something that just really didn't make sense. And as I said, I wasn't a big fan of going to church, and pretty much the only reason I would go is to socialize with my friends. And then when I moved I realized that I don't have my friends, it's just me alone. I realized that there was just something missing in my heart, and I felt really incomplete. And then I heard about God; well, I had heard about him before, but I heard what he was trying to get me to hear for a really long time. And now it's kind of like he's always there when I am down.

Not only can adolescence be an exploration with this new personal information about God, but for these twelve, that "for me" relationship

16. Luther scholars trace Luther's having been immersed in nominalism as a philosophical frame during his years at Erfurt. Nominalist influences would have encouraged the interest in the particularity of individual faith for Luther. See "Martin Luther," in Leslie Houlen, ed., *Jesus in Thought, History and Culture* (Santa Barbara, CA: ABC CLIO, 2003), 581.

has been incorporated into their self-understanding and shaped (even become) their very identity:

> Travis: I can laugh about it, because it's part of who I am, and faith isn't like separate parts of my life. My life is constantly like, pray at this time, and don't pray at this time. My life is constantly like, "God, what do you want me doing right now?" Everything I think and everything that I do is God centered, as opposed to before, when it was just a part of it — and now it's all of it.

Richard Peace has written at length about this phenomenon. He notes that Christians have often shied away from acknowledging the importance of faith that knows that God has come "for me" as a distinct aspect of the process of faith.[17]

The theme analysis indicates several ways that this new understanding developed: several talked about a gradual opening of their eyes; some experienced a kind of Damascus road experience, either in the context of a church event or a negative life experience. Eleven of the twelve pointed toward an established pattern of personal prayer and engagement with Scripture that appears to have provided additional depth to their connection with God. However, this relationship with God — knowing that Jesus died "for me" — is the lens that these adolescents now use to view themselves and the world. This is a critical part of their functional Christology. "For me" means that "I am" the work of Jesus. Kenda Dean describes it as a critical and definable step in the journey: "But until young people (and the rest of us) have experienced the coherence of the whole design, *until we have experienced God's engulfing presence with us,* the relationship between faith and other aspects of our lives will seem opaque and meaningless."[18]

---

17. Peace describes the "for me" experience as a kind of experience that takes place when a person is confronted with reality as it really is. This is what James Loder would call a "convictional experience." In the moment that a person is caught up in this experience, suddenly she or he "knows." No argument or proofs are necessary to understand that one has encountered God; the experience is self-validating. It is its own proof. Richard Peace, *Conversion in the New Testament: Paul and the Twelve* (Grand Rapids: Eerdmans, 1999), 77.

18. Dean, *Almost Christian,* 162.

Movement from Knowing to Trusting

For Luther, faith is "being prepared to put one's trust in the promises of God, and in the integrity of the God who made those promises."[19] This experience of faith as learning to trust, and focusing considerable energy on the nature of the one in whom trust is placed, was repeated by these students again and again throughout the interviews. The comments that were folded into the theme of "God as immanent" all confirmed a new understanding of the very nature of the one who can be trusted: God was described as "best friend, father, counselor, always there, love." These images were mentioned a total of forty-two times; the interviews reflected an additional twenty-four occasions where these adolescents built conversations around learning to let go and trust this God, who can be trusted.

> N: How do you see that faith in everyday life? Is that something that is a part of every day?
>
> Julie: I don't know, but when something is getting me down, or I am stressed out, I can just be like, "Okay, just chill out, God is with you." You can realize that God is with you and it will all be okay.
>
> N: Can you tell me more about your relationship with God? What's it like?
>
> Amanda: Everyone always says that your parents will always be there for you, but I really have to contradict that. I really don't think that they are always going to be there for you. There are times when my parents aren't there for me, and there's only one person I can go to. It's not my friends, it's not my boyfriend, it's not my family, it's God, and he's the only one who's always going to be there for me, and he's the only one who's going to love me no matter what. Sometimes, it's hard to accept the choice he makes, but then you have to know that he sees the bigger picture of things, no matter what I'm doing.
>
> I've never been one to trust people. I'm so skeptical, beyond your imagination, because of my past. I'm used to people judging me, so I have to judge them before. I've got to stop them. I'm trying to get over that, but it's been very hard for me to learn to trust God, because I've always shut out people. I would never let anyone get close to me, I'm always afraid they are going to hurt me or judge me, so I judge them first, which is very wrong. But learning to trust God, I

19. Peace, *Conversion in the NT,* 88.

think accepting myself was a big part of learning to trust God. And that was the next step in my faith. I had to get over that one boundary; I had to trust God, and I had to give everything to him. I was not giving God everything. I was giving him my prayers, that's about it. If you can give up your biggest fear to God, that's when you really trust him. That's when you really let God take over your life, and that's when he's in charge of everything you do, and that's when you take that step of faith, and you put your most fearful thing in him. That's how it should be.

All of the students applied the commitment to trust God consistently and directly as they faced change and the future. Ruth used it as one more thing that she needed to tell me before her interview ended.

Actually, my favorite passage in the Bible is Psalm 91, that whole thing of God's protection. That is one thing that is constantly coming back to me, that God is always there to protect us. Even when you are in the pit of the viper, he will protect you, and that is one thing that has just pervaded my life and faith — that I really have nothing to fear. God is always there, and he will never fail me even though I fail myself, and I fail him. I really don't have to worry about it. I think it always comes back to the point where I think of the Psalms and know that he's done it before. Even though my life is perfectly unique, it has been sculpted by God, and God knows what's going to happen.

This is not assent to an abstract set of doctrines. Rather, according to Luther, it is like a "wedding ring" pointing to mutual commitment and union between Christ and the believer. It is the response of the whole person of the believer to God, which in turn leads to the real and personal presence of Christ in the believer.[20]

Movement from Trusting to Affirming

But that's not all. Most significantly, the final move in Luther's description of faith is from trusting to affirming. Luther describes affirming as "faith that is not just about believing that something is true. It is being prepared

---

20. Peace, *Conversion in the NT*, 100.

to act on that belief and rely on it."[21] In the interviews with these twelve disciples we can see that adolescence is not so much about the right date for the prom as it is about how these newfound theological insights play out in the way these adolescents live and are able to see the world and its people as the setting for living out their faith.

The twelve talked about some aspect of this in what I identified as the themes of "Faith Is Living It" and "Faith Means Moral Choices," with sixty-one and forty-three comments respectively. They displayed a profound engagement with this newfound piece of a missiological understanding. The following quotations all indicate a critical third aspect of what faith looked like for them, because they so deeply expressed the power and centrality of a "for others" movement in their faith. Amanda said:

> To know that I can influence their future, that I can help them and in-still in them that God loves them, and accepts them — because no one ever instilled that in me — and that God will love them no matter what. They're beautiful, [God] wanted them that way, and if you don't love yourself, then it's putting down God's work. Just being able to help others, and giving, for me, is what I am getting to love.

Amanda believes that she is there for the sake of others, but not just to gently lend a hand or ear to others in some comforting way or another. She sees herself as no less than the vehicle for God's transforming of others. Amanda focused on this outward movement in "living it" and "living for others."

> Childhood faith was knowing I am going to heaven, and being nice to everyone, love your neighbor, and that was it. As a kid, it's hard to understand how to live something. The whole concept of not living for yourself, it's a hard concept; you're kind of learning to be your own person, and living for God is a whole different concept. I think, more or less, childhood faith is living knowing that you are saved. There are some exceptions of people who actually understand the concept of living for God, but middle school, high school, whatever your maturity point is, I guess, it becomes more living it, and it's more acting on it.

Travis articulated the most striking example of missional formation in faith. For him, even beyond a readiness to go against the grain to be a

---

21. McGrath, *Reformation Thought*, 112.

disciple, he is willing to put himself out there and single-handedly minister to his friends. In contrast to many of the twelve, Travis consciously keeps himself squarely in the midst of kids who are not necessarily Christian, friends who are in no way making the same choices that he is. And he very clearly sees this as an important part of his current life's purpose.

> I feel closest to God when I give other people glimpses of him. Jim [his youth minister] is so good at relating to people, and talking to people about faith, and evangelism comes so easy to him. For me, when I try, I say, "God, I don't know the words to say, if you could help me, that would be great." This past summer I was talking to a friend of mine about her drinking and what she thought about it. She said, "I know that senior year is going to be hard, and I know that you feel really strong about it." And she said, "Help me not to drink. I know it's going to be hard because everyone is going to be doing it." She ended up drinking a lot — she has a family history of alcoholism — and she's addicted now pretty bad. When I tell her things like that her mistakes aren't like final, she says, "Travis, you look good to everyone — you don't screw up, and I don't like sending off that image." I just say to her that we're all the same in God's eyes: everyone has sinned, and I'm not perfect and you're not — it's that no one is perfect. Talking through that with other people makes me feel so much stronger about it, and it makes me feel like God is actually talking to me. By me trying to teach her about it, [God is] reminding me and trying to teach me more and more about what I need to be doing, 'cause I get caught in looking down on other people. It's a lot easier for me to stay closer to God when I am talking to other people about it, instead of just holding it in.

Then there was Eliza, who never talked about camps or conferences or special youth events that she may or may not have gone to, but talked at length about the abused kids that she met at a shelter and the impact that she knew she was having on their lives. That experience had shaped her future goals, because she wanted to pursue studying psychology so that she could work with kids like these.

> One area that I possibly want to go into is psychology, working with troubled teens, and I have often been criticized because my relatives compare that to my sister's majors of political science and international business. I've been able to let it roll off my back, and say, you

know, I am not out there to have a great degree or make a great deal of money. I am out there to make a difference.

In addition to shaping her life's purpose, these experiences helped her understand the church.

> I would have to stress, making sure they are keeping an adequate balance between educating Christians and serving. I mean, there are some churches that are so focused on, you have to do all these good deeds, and there are other churches that are focused on feeding you all this stuff, but you don't have to. One of my huge frustrations is that we're becoming so lazy and fat and comfortable with our little faith — and that our country has become so comfortable. But what can we do to grow closer to God and become a stronger instrument for his purpose?

Eliza discussed this further when asked about what practices of the faith are the most important for her.

> Serving is huge for me. Often times I feel that we go to these conferences and we become very fat. God feeds us but . . . we can get so fat and so comfortable with our intake of what the right Christian should be that we don't want to live our faith, and we're not out there trying to make a difference. We're really out there to show others this incredible gift that we've been given. I mean, that's absolutely imperative. I think serving has made one of the biggest impacts on my life.

Another student, Ruth, was also very honest about all the places where she struggles with faith. For her, faith means being called to places and people that she would rather not have to think about. She gave the following remarkable reflection on what it is like living the priorities of the life of faith and at the same time struggling to continue to buy into the purposes of life that her school has held up as priorities for this very bright, achievement-oriented person. When we talked about how the effects of her mission trips played out in her life when she got back, Ruth reflected on the ways that God used those experiences to open her eyes to the needs around her.

> And I would say [God is working on] also a compassionate spirit. In a middle-class life in an affluent city, I would say compassion is touted, but it's pretty easy for it to be lost. My school is very ambitious: every-

one is ambitious, and everyone is working towards getting into the right college and getting the right scholarships and everything, and compassion is seen as, "It's a really good thing if you have time." Compassion is one thing that I think I lack the most often. When you're in Africa and you're caring for AIDS orphans, and you are playing duck-duck-gray-duck with them, you can't help but feel compassion for them. They are watching you eat your lunch, and you know that they will not eat lunch, and they might not eat dinner, they might not eat for a day. So you can't help but feel compassion, and when you come home you try to recognize that everyone has needs. It might not be clothing and shoes, but you are trying to be more Christlike, and you are trying to see those needs and love people for them.

These twelve were able to articulate their new insights about how God had moved them developmentally. Their conversations were full of reflection on their new understanding of this relational God, who had called them to "be" and "do." They weren't clear on the full picture of what that meant for them, but they had fully absorbed that much. When these three moves of justifying faith are viewed all together, one wonders if this new missiological exploration is actually what drives further self-understanding. The twelve disciples went on to discuss the many ways this new knowledge of God has created change in them. For them, "faith unites the believer to Christ; I get what is Christ's."[22]

Implications

In many churches today, ministry with young people is driven by fears of losing youth. However, a greater concern needs to be raised. What if they stay and we never let the unique, uninhibited, unencumbered power of their newly formed or re-formed relationships with Jesus shape and move us? What if the Christocentric nature of this part of their formation is a powerful missiological tool for the whole church, and we never hear it, because it is sitting on the couches in the youth room, much less allow it to be used? The results of this study have real implications for an exploration of the relationship between formation and mission, and they encourage the church to grow in its perception of the nature of youth ministry.

22. McGrath, *Reformation Thought*, 111.

See Human Development as a Theological Process

"In attempting to flesh out the *missio Dei* concept, the following could be said: In the new image mission is not primarily an activity of the church, but an attribute of God."[23] If young people can talk about a relationship with Jesus that shapes their very selves, transforms them, and allows them to move from focus on self to the ability to genuinely care for others, then can we as Christians also claim faith in a Savior who does no less? Can we as Christians talk in very real terms about what it means to see our formation as people as a function of our relationship with our Creator? As Rouse and Van Gelder describe the mission of the church in terms of the *missio Dei,* their reflection on the process of the church living into that mission is remarkably similar to Luther's desire to have the faithful comprehend and take in the notion of faith as something to *be* and *do.* We need to reclaim the developmental ministry with young people as a formational process.

> Based on the clear teaching of Scripture, these questions assume something about God's agency — that God is present and is directly acting in the world. They assume that God's actions through the Spirit can to some extent be discerned in our midst. These basic scriptural commitments require us to focus on the very *identity* of congregations — their nature or essence — as the key to understanding how to help them respond to all the changes taking place in the world around them. The key premise of the missional church is that what a congregation *does* needs to be deeply informed by what a congregation *is* — what God has made and is making it to be.[24]

See Young People as Critical to the Missio Dei

Secondly, the more we continue to minister to children and youth based on stage theories, the more we will continue to relegate adolescents to a "less than" role in the church, thereby naturally limiting our sense of mission. A theologically driven developmental framework allows every portion of the life cycle to be an exploration of the various aspects of the na-

23. David Bosch, *Transforming Mission: Paradigm Shifts in Theology of Mission* (Maryknoll, NY: Orbis, 2008), 390.
24. Rick Rouse and Craig Van Gelder, *A Field Guide for the Missional Congregation: Embarking on a Journey of Transformation* (Minneapolis: Augsburg Fortress, 2008), 26.

ture of God and regards each part of human life and experience as equally valuable for formation.

> [T]his teaching [become humble like this child] seems to stand everything on its head. The disciples have the greatest claim to be insiders of this kingdom: that is why they are talking about their positions within it. They are sure they are in: the main unanswered question concerns their future status. Peter, James, and John are the frontrunners, having been with Jesus on the mountain. But now Jesus introduces a rank outsider, the little child, and indicates that the reality is the very opposite of what the disciples believe to be the case. The outsider is inside; and they, unless they change, are outsiders! The conclusion is that children, whatever the age, are not only active participants in the unfolding story but are also essential for a true reading of the Gospel, understanding the identity and person of Jesus Christ, modeling the way of the cross, and representing the radical nature of ecclesial community.[25]

The exploration of specific God-themes that are "signs" pointing to Jesus in childhood become no less important to the mission of the church than the unique foci of the "faith-energy" of old age. We are all exploring various aspects of the nature and mission of God. We can remind one another what we might have forgotten about how God works. We can encourage ecclesiologies based on the appreciation for the theological strengths of each age, rather than on the limitations of stages.

See the Missio Dei in a Life of Faith

This leads to a critical recognition of the formational nature of our life stories: "[T]o a degree that we are only beginning to realize, our formation as persons and communities, the shaping of our identity and practices, is 'storied.'"[26] There is much that can be learned from the recent discoveries in brain research and the powerful formational impact of experience and reflection on our formation as storied.

---

25. White, "He Placed a Little Child in the Midst," in Bunge, ed., *The Child in the Bible*, 364.

26. Joel Green, "Tell Me a Story," in Bunge, ed., *The Child in the Bible*, 221.

Human beings are always in the process of formation. . . . Though the organization of the brain is hardwired genetically, genes shape only the broad outline of our mental and behavioral functions, with the rest sculpted through our experiences. From birth we are in the process of becoming. Becoming is encoded in our brains by means of synaptic activity. Hence both nature and nurture end up having the same effect, shaping our neuronal interactions in ways that form and reform the developing self. . . . Embodied human life performs, then, like a cultural neuro-hermeneutical system, locating (and thus making sense of) current realities in relation to our grasp of the past and expectations for the future.[27]

Since one of the key moves being encouraged in the movement toward a missional ecclesiology is articulated as "fostering a people development" culture, there is significant conversation about the programmatic focus and expression of church. This has encouraged a move from "church as a place of participation to church as a place of maturation."[28] There is still much work that needs to be done to explore and articulate the relationship between mission and formation. However, it would be a loss both for the church and for Christian people living out the mission of God in the world to continue to focus our time together on anything less. This insight especially calls for new ways of looking at our ministry with those in the first third of life — "until all of us come to the unity of the faith and of the knowledge of the Son of God, to maturity, to the measure of the full stature of Christ" (Eph. 4:13).

27. Green, "Tell Me a Story," 221.
28. Reggie McNeal, *The Missional Renaissance* (San Francisco: Jossey-Bass, 2009), 94.

CHAPTER 7

Congregational Discerning as Divine Action in Conversation

David C. Hahn

Introduction

The triune God calls, gathers, forms, and sends local congregations in the power of the Holy Spirit to participate with God for the sake of the world. But what is the nature of the local congregation's participation, and how can this participation be conceived within the life of a community of faith? This chapter offers a theology of congregational discernment within which a host of theological engagements are at work, and from which a host of congregational possibilities may be formed. Congregational discernment, which I develop in this chapter, focuses on one part of the process known as *attending;* thus I focus on congregational discerning as divine action in conversation.[1] This assumes that the triune God is always and everywhere in a relationship with the church that the Lord Christ called into new life in the power of the Spirit, such that congregational discernment offers the possibility of a liberating participation in God for the life of the world.

This chapter proceeds in three sections. The first section introduces a brief typology of discernment through five movements within the Christian tradition: (1) Scripture, (2) early monasticism, (3) St. Ignatius of Loyola, (4) Quakers and the Clearness Committee, and (5) the emergence of congregational discernment processes. The reason I trace these is to im-

---

1. See Patrick Keifert, *We Are Here Now: A New Missional Era* (Eagle, Idaho: Allelon, 2006); see also Craig Van Gelder, *The Ministry of the Missional Church: A Community Led by the Spirit* (Grand Rapids: Baker Books, 2007).

ply a historical rootedness of discernment in the broader Christian tradition, and to further consider the work of discernment within the congregational context. I will, in the second section, move toward articulating a congregational discernment description. However, the particular kind of discernment I explore in this chapter moves beyond only understanding discernment as an operational technique for congregational decision-making. I want to take a deeper look at what the triune God might also be forming among the gathered discernment circle interpersonally through action in conversation. At this point I introduce a construct of the modern self, known as the "buffered self," as one potential factor impeding the conversational process, which God also might be dismantling among those engaged in the discernment process.[2]

The third section begins to develop the focus of the entire chapter: congregational discernment as divine action in conversation. First, I explore the reason I chose the term *action*. Second, I look at the process of action itself, not as a set of technical fixes or task management toward goal achievement, but rather in light of a kind of communicative agency for forming community. I lean on what the leadership consultant Peter Block says in his book *Community: The Structure of Belonging* to navigate these different approaches for understanding how action can be communicatively productive within organizations in light of the social category of belonging.[3] The remaining portions of the chapter begin to theologically account for these references from Block by suggesting that action, and its ensuing social construction of belonging, is best understood in light of the social Trinity as communicative agency for a congregation's life in the world. I draw on an Eastern Orthodox perspective, that of John Zizioulas, on the social Trinity to highlight that it is here where a person's identity is affirmed in the triune God as defined with respect to another, and where attention to the other offers a participatory, constructive element of the self in community.[4]

The further component of this conversation in action also involves a

2. See Charles Taylor, *A Secular Age* (Cambridge, MA: Belknap Press of Harvard University Press, 2007), and *Sources of the Self: The Making of the Modern Identity* (Cambridge, MA.: Harvard University Press, 1989).

3. Peter Block, *Community: The Structure of Belonging* (San Francisco: Berrett-Koehler Publishers, 2008).

4. John D. Zizioulas, *Communion and Otherness: Further Studies in Personhood and the Church* (New York: T&T Clark, 2006). I am grateful to Dr. Gary Simpson, who helped to further my understanding of the importance of the social Trinity for constructing congregational imagination in light of theologians such as Zizioulas.

posture of embracing the future that is breaking in, and hence becomes an anticipatory posture, through the other. Learning the importance of the exchange of value of listening and speaking, the dialogical process inherent within the social Trinity, is to bear witness to where the Holy Spirit is emerging in the world. This, then, has the possibility of reorienting the communicative process of discernment away from an impersonal, task-oriented management of future activities, and toward an enlarged attention to the Spirit's present forming of congregational life as the very defining act of participatory engagement itself in God's world. This chapter concludes with a gesture toward how one might lead this kind of process of discernment within a congregation.

The question I address here is: What does it mean theologically that the triune God is active in the discerning process? And further, how would such an understanding affect its participants such that the possibility for liberating the self through the anticipated divine action in conversation — through the other — becomes a *socially embodied expression* of God in the world? This offers a potentially different posture that may deepen what it means to participate in the life of God and the world. It also seeks to offer a renewed appreciation for why the Holy Spirit gathers and forms congregations as an anticipating, hopeful, and liberating presence in God's world. I explore a congregation's discernment process as one expression of a congregation's participation in the life of God in the world. The discerning process that I articulate is not an attempt to differentiate this theological proposal from another (new and improved) model, but to theologically describe *how* the process of discerning itself, as divine action in conversation, is an engagement in and a missional equipping of the life of the triune God in the world.

Traditions of Western Christian Discernment in Five Movements: A Brief Survey

The first movement of this chapter is to propose a description of congregational discernment. In order to move toward a proposed description, let us first trace the rich cultural tradition of Western Christian discernment. Amid this historical trajectory of discernment expressions that have developed over the last two thousand years, I highlight five movements here: Scripture, monasticism, St. Ignatius of Loyola, Quakers and the Clearness Committee, and contemporary congregational discernment in the context of the United States.

Discernment in the Scriptural Tradition

Scripture is the primary text in the Christian tradition, where the term "discernment" is used and where the testimony to the practice embedded in a life in God can be discovered. The occurrences in the Old Testament reveal that the term is used as a trait in reference to the character of Joseph when he is selected to be set over Egypt because he is a "discerning and wise" man (Gen. 41:33, 39). The term is also used for making moral decisions or judgments when Solomon is asked "to discern between good and evil" (1 Kings 3:9). In other Old Testament texts, while the term is not used explicitly, practical instances include prophets and priests who are *listening* to God's voice and participating responsively to a life in God, either through call narratives (Gen. 12; Exod. 3; 1 Sam. 3; Isa. 6) or carrying out their ministries, for example, when Moses had to listen to the Lord in order to communicate with Aaron (Exod. 4:15-16).

The New Testament includes direct word occurrences and practical instances. Paul uses the word in Romans 12:2: to "discern the will of God, what is good and acceptable and perfect." In 1 Corinthians, "discernment" is used to recognize the gifts of God's Spirit or the fruits of the Spirit (1 Cor. 2:14-15). John warns the community to "test the spirits to see whether they are from God" (1 John 4:1). The early church's first engagement, according to the book of Acts, is an act of discernment, where Matthias replaces Judas through the drawing of lots (Acts 1:12-26). We learn in Acts 15 about the moral decision made to extend the missionary journey into Gentile territory amid the early transitory ecclesial dynamics between the Jewish laws of circumcision and the Spirit's broadening mission in the world. The report is that it "seemed good to the Holy Spirit and to us" (Acts 15:28).

Discernment in the Monastic Traditions

Beyond the testimony of Scripture, it is important to trace a leading influence that shaped numerous historical and contemporary movements of discernment, that found in the emerging communities of faith known as the "Desert Age."[5] Those communities took up the practice of discernment

---

5. Lutz Kaelber, "Monasticism: Christian Monasticism," in Lindsay Jones, ed., *Encyclopedia of Religion* (Detroit: Macmillan Reference, 2005), 6131-36.

through their monastic beginnings and are associated with the desert fathers and mothers. The period between 200 and 500 CE represented the beginnings of two movements, known as the *anchorites,* those who lived alone, and the *cenobites,* those who lived in community. Athanasius's *Life of Antony,* the portrayal of Anthony of Egypt (251-356 CE), exemplifies the former as one who sought perfection and sanctity through the solitary life. The cenobitic representative, Pachomius of Egypt (290-346 CE), is known for establishing fixed locations and communally operating under a rule, the precursor for the later Western monastic era of the Benedictines.

The Western monastic movement, from 500 to 1200 CE, began most prolifically in the sixth century with Benedict of Nursia (480-587 CE). The cenobite community officially became known as the Order of St. Benedict and in the eighth century adopted the Rule of St. Benedict as its primary form for an ordered Christian life together. This rule offered the structured life that emphasized stability, peacefulness, order, and collective self-sufficiency. The primary routines of the community focused on collective prayer through the practice of *lectio divina,* a contemplative reflection on Scripture texts, private meditation, and work. It served as a fourfold process: (1) *lectio,* (2) *meditatio,* (3) *oratio,* and (4) *contemplatio,* all of which allowed the individual to delve into and rest in an intimate communion with God through Scripture readings and reflection.

The integrative move that coalesced between discernment and monasticism was highly influenced by the fourth-century imperial decree of Constantine to baptize all infants. According to Karlfried Froehlich, the development of the monastic movement was propelled by this colonization of Christianity.[6] For those who desired to take seriously a religious vocation, it was necessary to pursue a way of life within these cenobitic communities. Discernment during these monastic years, therefore, mediated the vocational life in God that was focused within community, where one committed to the community rule of prayer and work. While other revivalist monastic orders emerged during the next several centuries, such as the Cluniac and Cistercian monasticism of the tenth century, as well as the mendicant orders of the Franciscans and Dominicans of the twelfth century, none contributed significant new discernment practices.[7]

---

6. Karlfried Froehlich, "Luther on Vocation," *Lutheran Quarterly* 13 (1999): 197-98.

7. Mendicant literally means "begging," which referred to their reliance on charity for survival, since their monastic expression was lived out more within the public life than the rest of the cloistered, "enclosed" monastic communities.

Discernment in the Tradition of St. Ignatius of Loyola

St. Ignatius of Loyola (1491-1556) has been, classically speaking, the single most influential source on discernment in the Western monastic tradition. Ignatius was aligned with the Franciscan Order, where he uniquely situated his spirituality as an integrative link between discerning a life in the world in light of a life in Jesus Christ.[8] Specifically, Ignatius's *Spiritual Exercises* were a process by which the normative spiritual life was no longer lived merely as an external "rule," but one that attended primarily to internal affairs of an individual. Ignatian discernment happens through a series of personal introspective exercises in which one negotiates Christ's life in light of the tension between sin and grace. Ignatius shifted discernment to a deeper prescriptive process of attending internally in order to form one's life through the life of Jesus Christ himself. Ignatius's *Exercises,* after years of development, have been configured into a four-stage retreat process, divided into four weeks (or eight days as an alternative adaptation). The participants are guided by a retreat master to pursue these spiritual exercises in quiet reflection and prayer.

The first week relates to what is known as the purifying stage, in which one reorients one's life to Jesus Christ in light of one's own brokenness. The aim of this first week's meditations is to confront one's limitations because of sin and root out attachments to creation in which one has failed to effectively move toward one's end, that is, life in God. The second week emphasizes the life and person of Christ. The goal here is to conform one's life to the norm of Christ's life by means of interior reflection on the knowledge and love of the person of Jesus. The third week is concerned with the passion of Christ and the gifts that come because of his suffering in light of one's own sinfulness. The fourth week is focused on the resurrection of Christ. These spiritual exercises are intended to serve as the contemplative space to obtain love.[9]

---

8. The central features of the Franciscan Order, different from the intellectual focus of the Dominicans, was their explicit focus on preaching to the populace, admonishing the laity to repent and seek inner conversion. They left the cloistered life for the busy streets and voluntarily renounced possessions.

9. St. Ignatius of Loyola, *The Spiritual Exercises of St. Ignatius,* ed. Anthony Mottola (Garden City, NY: Image Books, 1964), 14-15.

Discernment in the Quaker Tradition
and the Clearness Committee

In the seventeenth century, separatist English dissenters from the Church of England formed what became known as the Quakers under the leadership of George Fox. Michael Birkel explores what he considers to be two central elements of Quaker spirituality in his book *Silence and Witness: The Quaker Tradition*.[10] The Quakers, or Religious Society of Friends, demonstrate a significant integration of the practice of discernment with respect to cultural issues like social justice in light of a responsive, living, and active faith in the Spirit. In his chapter on discernment, Birkel articulates the fourfold testing process as moral purity (or integrity), patience, resting on convictions of the Holy Spirit's reliability to speak, and unity (or consensus). A Quaker meeting's agenda was determined, not by *Robert's Rules of Order*, but by the Quakers' understanding of the Holy Spirit's ways of engaging through the attending and listening community. Of particular interest in their discernment practices was the emergence of the Clearness Committee. This practice first appeared as a way to assist couples preparing for marriage. It later evolved to include individuals seeking community confirmations in order to discern the Spirit in regard to moral and ethical decisions.

Discernment in Congregational Literature

A few contemporary sources offering insight into an understanding of and engagement with congregational discernment can be found in the missional church literature. The first source is a staple among the missional church conversation, *Missional Church: A Vision for the Sending of the Church in North America*. In her chapter in that book, Inagrace Dietterich suggests that viewing how congregations organize themselves as discerning communities should be reframed: they should be neither hierarchical nor egalitarian communities, but pneumocratic communities. The community's emphasis, she says, shifts from tending to a congregation's own interests or preoccupations to tending to the presence of the Holy Spirit's promptings in its midst.[11] One is left wondering, however, *how* such a

---

10. Michael Lawrence Birkel, *Silence and Witness: The Quaker Tradition* (Maryknoll, NY: Orbis, 2004).

11. Inagrace Dietterich, "Missional Community: Cultivating Communities of the

practice is reflected in congregational life, because Dietterich does not of-
fer a companion process for such rich theological considerations. But
Craig Van Gelder *(The Ministry of the Missional Church)* and Patrick
Keifert *(We Are Here Now)* offer two distinct processes.

Discernment Summary and Observations

Discernment within the *scriptural witness* refers to character traits and
participatory acts of creation through attention to God's presence and
movement in the world. This happens with individuals and missionary
communities; both are accomplished through attentive encounters with
the leading of the Spirit's activity in the world. Discernment is about individual and communal decision-making capacities with respect to leadership and in participation with the Lord's Spirit. It is about testing and
judgments concerning good or evil spirits — and even God's will.

What the monastic traditions have contributed to an understanding
of discernment exists via a structured, ordered life in prayer and work by
means of a "rule" under which the community seeks stability, peace, and
collective self-sufficiency. The monastic traditions established a movement
that was an alternative to the watered-down expressions of faith that resulted from Constantinian Christianity and the state church, and they succeeded in developing sustaining practices for intentional engagement in
Jesus Christ. However, the monastic life did not adequately affirm the ordinary and secular life as a location from which ministry in God could happen. One wonders whether this privileged location of being within a monastic order restricted the life of faith practiced in God through a limited
and narrow understanding of the other. But monasticism can be celebrated for formally developing a discernment tool known as *lectio divina.*
Here the pinnacle of the process is contemplative resting in God's love and
joy, in the rather aloof terms of participation in a God removed from the
world. The resulting goal of this practice is internal cohabitating between
an individual and God.

Both Ignatian and Quaker discernment take into account the individualized notions of revelation in light of the larger community. Ignatian
spirituality emphasizes the individual's own inward journey, focusing on

Holy Spirit," in Darrell Guder, ed., *Missional Church: A Vision for the Sending of the Church in North America* (Grand Rapids: Eerdmans, 1998), 142-82.

vocational calling, sanctity, and perfection through a highly structured guided process through the *Exercises* — as opposed to the free-flowing Quaker process of discernment. Both, however, and in differing degrees, still acknowledge the importance of communal companionship in the midst of individual discernment. Unique to Quaker discernment circles are the more explicit movements toward the world, particularly with regard to taking seriously one's life lived responsibly in relationship to neighbors. This was accomplished in Quaker settings through what became known as Clearness Committees, which showed the Friends' strong emphasis on social justice taking into consideration the Spirit's calling and involvement beyond one's own internal perfection and helpfully acknowledging a larger world within which one is situated with the Spirit.

Reflecting on the Western cultural discernment tradition, one comes to notice a high degree of similarity among the diverse expressions of discernment developed since the fourth century. This similarity exists primarily with respect to the privilege of the individual over the community. Why is this the case? Could it be that the West's adoption of St. Augustine's Trinitarian theology set the trajectory for a specific way of engaging God?[12] Could Augustine's internalized, psychologized notions of the Trinity have fanned the flame for these discernment patterns to have emerged over the past two thousand years in the West? That is not the focus of this chapter, nor is there space here to explore these patterns; I only call attention to them as possible theological trends to consider further. These questions do begin to call into question the importance of and connections to particular understandings of God with respect to practices of God. In light of these concerns, one would find it helpful, when articulating discernment, to explicitly begin with understandings of God and the relationship such an understanding of the triune God has in conjunction with how God is practiced or engaged in and with the world.

In *The Ministry of the Missional Church*, Van Gelder introduces the important hermeneutical turn congregations need to keep in mind in the discernment process.[13] For Van Gelder, the hermeneutical turn is a multi-perspectival, interpretative communal engagement in which each discerning congregant is situated within his or her own formative history and

12. For a detailed argument on these questions and claims, see Catherine Mowry LaCugna, *God for Us: The Trinity and Christian Life* (New York: HarperCollins, 1993), 81, 101ff.

13. Van Gelder, *The Ministry of the Missional Church*, 97ff.

where a tapestry of conclusions may be reached as a result of that. This discernment process seeks to encourage congregations to discover what God is up to in the surrounding congregation's neighborhood. The congregation's mission is organized around the discerned reality for what the triune God is doing in the world.

A second approach is in Keifert's *We Are Here Now.* This congregational-based discernment process has been tested for over twenty years. The four phases that make up this process include *discovering, experimenting, visioning for embodiment,* and *learning and growing.* It is Phase One of the attending process, known as discovering, where Keifert describes the place of Scripture as the formative event in which the congregation can begin to imagine the triune God's life in the world. This becomes the formative initial stage in which congregations move more intentionally into the world with a formed and attentive posture to discover what God is up to, as well as what God is calling out of congregations for participation in God's life in the world.

Toward a Congregational Discernment Description

The focus of this chapter is to suggest that *how* the triune God expresses communion in the world can also be associated within the congregational discernment process. In the survey of traditions of Western Christian discernment above, I offered a brief description of the process of discernment in order to recognize two things. First, any proposed description of congregational discernment must be situated within this historical trajectory: a congregational discernment description needs to appreciate the various pluriform expressions of discernment that have developed within its historically situated existence. Second — and in relation to this pluriformity — it is necessary to recognize and be open to any resulting unique expressions of communal discernment that might be emerging within the congregational settings of the particular U.S. context.[14] One developing dimension of the process of discernment that I am exploring relates to an integrated communal expression and a relatively unusual development

14. This chapter assumes the imaginations of congregational life within the U.S. context. I will not develop the issues surrounding the current context here, but only recognize a multiplicity of contexts that are present, including late modern and postmodern assumptions. For more information, see Guder, ed., *Missional Church.*

within the emerging landscape of the Christian church. This development primarily involves particular Trinitarian assumptions in light of congregational processes.[15]

A further matter in this discussion is the importance of the modern construction of the self, how a particular sense of personhood may impede awareness of and participation in God's life being given in the world. For the many ways that modernity has been critiqued, we can also celebrate that it did offer the importance of both a self in relationship to a world and the self as mediated through one's unique experience. This essay draws attention to one challenging notion of personhood that may impede the process of congregational discernment, and that also may be a place where the Holy Spirit is seeking to liberate a person for a greater awareness of and participation in the life of the triune God in the world. The context of personhood I am looking at relates to the Western landscape and the forming of the buffered self. This exploration is important because the theological work of discernment has direct implications for what the Holy Spirit is present and active in the world doing. It also has specific implications for *how* congregations organize their life in God around the life of the triune God in the world.

Discovering What Is at Stake:
Context as Anthropological Condition

One issue that is at stake in the process of congregational discernment can be traced through Charles Taylor's critique of the sources of the self in modernity.[16] In *A Secular Age,* Taylor suggests that the mechanized world has involved a withdrawal. In the Cartesian formula *Cogito ergo sum,* a radical shift happened with respect to where truth was constituted. The mind within the self became privileged because it was believed this was the only location where doubt itself could not be achieved. Taylor says that what resulted from these Cartesian influences is that the center of being as experience shifted to the privileged place of the mind, even as experiences themselves are generated in other areas of the body. Taste, for example, is not a

---

15. See Patrick Keifert, "The Trinity and Congregational Planning: Between Historical Minimum and Eschatological Maximum," *Word and World* 18, no. 3 (1998); Gary M. Simpson, "No Trinity, No Mission: The Apostolic Difference of Revisioning the Trinity," *Word and World* 18, no. 3 (1998).

16. See Taylor, *Sources of the Self: The Making of the Modern Identity.*

notion that begins in the mind, but the tongue. The privileging of the mind over other external generations of truth, Taylor suggests, is what now determines a modern source of itself. For Taylor, then, this highlights a disconnection between the location of where meaning is constituted in the mind and apart from one's existence as an embodied human in the world.

Taylor calls the process by which the self perpetuates this gap "disengagement." This disengagement comes, he says, from the "role of disengaged thinking in the most prestigious and impressive *epistemic* activity of modern civilization." This disengaged thinking becomes what he calls the "self buffered" from the rest of the world as one lives isolated — in the mind. Taylor says this is an illegitimate explanation of the world, where every experience is filtered through and reduced to the mind, and it remains, he says, one of the strong cultural trends of modernity. He says, "'[E]xperience-far' methods based on the natural sciences risk *distorting* and *missing the point* when applied to the phenomena of psychology, politics, language, historical interpretation, and so on."[17]

After Taylor's sobering description of the modern self, one is left to wonder *how* discerning processes might serve to sustain such an anthropological condition, no matter what traditional discerning model is used in the modern context. What is at stake, then, is the possibility of cultivating a congregational discerning process that does not perpetuate the disengaged, withdrawn, and buffered self. What is at stake is a posture of relationship to one's neighbor as other; it is a turn from self to the other, from which emerges a Spirit-led community for a responsive life to the triune God. What is at stake theologically is God's liberating action through a disoriented self, whereby communities might enter into, share, and celebrate the life of the triune God as gift emerging through the other.

Congregational discerning, therefore, might *not only* serve an instrumental, intermittent practice for the sake of exercising missional tasks for God in the world, though this may be a resulting expression of the fruits cultivated. It is also *not only* a move toward individual efficacy, sanctity, or vocational calling as the primary intent of discernment, as in the earlier traditions of St. Ignatius and the Quaker Clearness Committee. Yet these blessings may result from such activity. Discernment, in this sense, is also *not only* about trait characteristics, or testing the spirits, or ascertaining the will of God, as was seen in the scriptural witness, though they may be discovered — and in a fresh sense — along the way, too.

17. Taylor, *A Secular Age*, 285, 27 (italics added).

Congregational discernment, always and everywhere, involves the participation of the life of God in the world. The question at hand in this chapter is about how congregational discernment can be framed theologically as participating in the life of the triune God in the world, and how a particular way of conceiving this practice might offer the possibility of a liberating expression from the buffered self by a turn to the other. This is the Holy Spirit's being given in conversation, and it is something that has the possibility of offering congregational discernment as an active participation in God.

Congregational Discerning: A Proposal

A proposal toward a congregational discernment process takes into account the modernist anthropological condition and its effects on the discernment process itself. This is important to consider because I am asking a theological question within the categories of selfhood and divine action in conversation. A robust framing of congregational discernment as Spirit-led action in conversation through the other can challenge modernist assumptions. It can do so by suggesting an alternative engagement within which a community is invited to attend by opening up toward God's being given through the other. This creates possibilities for attending to God's future breaking in to be proclaimed. Thus the descriptive proposal that I am considering is that congregational discerning as divine action in conversation has the possibility of liberating the self through the other as a *socially embodied expression* of God in the world. What this entails for congregational discernment is a reorienting posture toward one another that reframes the Holy Spirit's emergence in the world for the life of the congregation, which bears witness to the flourishing life of God in the world.

Congregational Discerning as Divine Action in Conversation

Why "Action"?

First, let me explore here the relational and cultural connotations of a task-oriented word such as "action." On the one hand, the congregational project within the United States is steeped in pragmatism and its values for achievement, success, improvement, and optimism. These values have carried over into an understanding of what it means to *do* ministry and mission. Therefore, I offer the term to help highlight Taylor's suggestion of a "disengaged," withdrawn, and buffered self, while also reconsidering an alternative sense of the word in light of its social construction. Theologically — and relationally — action allows insight into how God is involved in the world: the way God is being given communally through the other in the power of the Holy Spirit is not static but active. Thus, theologically speaking, action can refer to the ongoing creative, redeeming, and sanctifying expressions for how the triune God is sharing God's life in the world.

I will now develop more explicit understandings of the term "action"as it relates theologically to the congregational discerning process, first, with respect to thinking about action in light of a social construction, and, second, with respect to a theological framework of action as receptivity and otherness. I will consider both in light of the Holy Spirit's turning of the buffered self, withdrawal, and disengagement toward the other, where an encounter with the divine action in conversation is opened up to the life of the triune God in the world.

Action as Socially Constituted Construction

Congregational action plans are typically associated with developed strategies and specific action items to address the strategies, including roles and responsibilities for who is attending to the action of each strategy, a concept that is associated with various tasks and duties from to-do lists and committee minutes and is used for the sake of reaching a goal. Ironically, for congregational life, a socially constructed understanding of what constitutes action has become depersonalized to task management and goal accomplishment. It is not that such action is unimportant or unnecessary for the life of a congregation, only that an understanding of what constitutes action is relegated to tasks that do not intentionally attend to the deeper gifts that are socially and theologically present. In fact, the concept of action that I am critiquing here follows Taylor's understanding of the buffered and withdrawn self. Theologically speaking, if action is only about achieving a task, the personal action of the Holy Spirit's participating in the world is unrecognized, uncultivated, and can go unproclaimed in all God's liberating fullness.

Peter Block offers an enlarged horizon for which action is situated socially. While not using an explicitly religious perspective — and, in fact, writing primarily for audiences interested in organizational development — his argument seeks to address the fragments present in organizations by reframing the way an organization thinks about its life in relationship to the categories of community and belonging. The premise of his book *Community* assumes that the answer to the dissolution of all systems of humanity is community, and, as such, his approach is a communicative methodology toward restorative community. His approach intentionally avoids technical fixes that are inherently associated with a problem-solving culture of procedures and destination processes.

Block offers an engagement through conversation as the primary key to restorative community. This assumption, embedded in a social construction, leads him to think more broadly about how action might be understood. While recognizing the usual way action operates within organizations, he wonders, "What qualifies as action?" To this end he offers additional questions that highlight the important condition toward which a socially constructed understanding of action might be engaged. "Would a meeting be worthwhile if we simply strengthened our relationship?" "Would a meeting be worthwhile if we learned something of value?" "What would be the value of only discussing the gifts we wanted to bring to bear on the concern that brought us together?" For Block, what happens when a socially constituted understanding of action is used is that the guided community conversation becomes a generative "exchange of value."[18] This value, expressed as action, is associated dialogically through conversation. In fact, for Block, the shift toward speaking and listening *is* the place of transformation.

Therefore, conversation — with respect to congregational discerning — functions more than as a communicating tool for generating tasks, visions, responsibilities. It is the means for cultivating and creating an experience of shared participation and restorative engagement in the divine. Language becomes more than ideational constructs of the mind; it is also embodied expressions in conversation that open one up to the possibility of the other. Additionally, this situates belonging in community, rather than in the mind, in the way that each becomes present to the other as socially embodied, making space to listen, in order that the other is invited to be called out in free speech. The sense of personhood that Taylor speaks of, as the withdrawn and disengaged self, has the possibility of becoming reengaged and present, not in the mind, but by turning toward the other,

---

18. Block, *Community*, 80-81.

who is being given space to have a voice. The other becomes a legitimate participant, not by how he or she contributes to the functional task and goals of action plans, but by a responsive invitation to express *who the other is* through his or her gifts, dissents, and commitments. The other is being given to the community as divine action in conversation.

Action as Relational Ontology: Person-in-Relation and Otherness

Theologically, what I am speaking of here is the socially constituting nature of the Trinity as person-in-relation *and* as other. This becomes important for what is theologically at stake in congregational discerning. In *Communion and Otherness,* Zizioulas speaks about this structure as a relational ontology wherein the Father, Son, and Holy Spirit are three differentiated persons who are completely other to one another, who are free in relation to one another, but ultimately, who cannot be defined apart from one another.[19] Their divine personhood is identified only with respect to how the one lives in relationship to the other. The Father's love is lived out in the world through the Son, Jesus Christ, in the power of the Spirit. The Son speaks the horrifying, isolating, and empty existence of the consequences of sin from the cross, as the Father and the Spirit make space for the Christ to have his voice. The Father raises the Son in the power of the Holy Spirit, proleptically, inviting the future promises to break into the present. The Holy Spirit continues the creative and sanctifying ministry of the Father's relationship with the Son as lived in the world. Person-in-relation and otherness are active within the three persons, and that constitutes difference in otherness as holy and good.

This differentiation creates a dialogical character within the life of the triune God. It is this dialogical, conversational reality that is relationally conceived and socially constructed, allowing for both listening and voicing of one person for and with the other — as an immanent expression in the triune God. The creation of the world ex nihilo reflects the dialogical, conversational engagement in God and presupposes this underlying theological assumption of person-in-relation that is constitutive for true otherness. The world discerning the triune God comes to receive the other as gift and life, not only threat, and from which the very nature of the triune God acts. Congregational discerning that makes the conversational/dialogical move,

19. Zizioulas, *Communion and Otherness.*

where otherness and person-in-relation are allowed to flow, has the possibility of becoming more fully conscious and actively aware of the power of the triune God as socially engaged in the congregants' midst.

A Divine Structure of Belonging: Inversion and Resonance

This theological conceptuality also suggests a divine structure of belonging. It can be accessed when these expressions — person-in-relation and otherness — are operative within a community of faith. The structure of belonging is the world's attending to inclusion, and thus the proclaiming of God's presence in and for the world, in light of God's triune community. A congregational discernment approach where person-in-relation and otherness is practiced offers the possibility of receiving the divine action present in the world as gift. Notice that it is a move away from an essential or static framing of God's presence, as well as a move away from the withdrawn reduction of God as an idea in the mind to be adopted or convinced of. In addition, action is not understood as a removed pragmatic task apart from a socially constructed understanding of action. Instead, congregational discerning flourishes through an inversion, where the other is given space to speak, and through her or his speech is being given as divine action in conversation for the community.

This inversion is further seen as the work of the Holy Spirit establishing a dialogical environment within the world. Michael Welker suggests that the "Spirit forms a domain of resonance." These domains of resonance, he says, are formed by the Holy Spirit "for the benefit of other persons," and are where the Holy Spirit "effects a domain of liberation and of freedom" within which "people are liberated *for* action" and "acting *for* the benefit of the development of others."[20]

Anticipating Possibilities of God's Future

Congregational discerning as divine action in conversation proclaims the communal activity as a Spirit-led and imbued action, whereby a congregational discerning culture is invited to anticipate the possibility of being created anew by the Spirit. I have used the word "possibility" frequently in

20. Michael Welker, *God the Spirit* (Minneapolis: Fortress, 1994), 296.

this chapter, and it needs to be addressed as a significant piece toward framing a more complete process of congregational discerning.

Peter Block's project toward restorative community through conversation suggests that the sense of possibility plays a specific anticipatory role. Possibility does not function as an optimism that anticipates the accomplishment of a task through a goal. Neither does it operate as a future predictor based on a team's planned hopes for improving the past. These understandings of possibility are oriented toward problem-solving that allows the past dissatisfaction to take a privileged role in the present and for the future. Instead, Block inverts the concept, where he conceives of possibility as an orientation that is presently open to the future breaking in through conversation, where personal intersections are happening, and where imaginative acts are being created.

Block believes the effects of such an orientation free the conversation "to be pulled by a new future." The necessary key to openly accessing the future possibility "is to *postpone* problem solving and stay focused on possibility until it is spoken with *resonance* and passion." The possibility, Block suggests, is further engaged by a declaration of it as a possible event, which then "*works on us* — we do not have to work on it." He continues: "It is a declaration of a future that has the quality of being and aliveness that we choose to live into. It is framed as a declaration of the world that I want to inhabit."[21]

Congregational discerning also offers rich possibilities for imagining the Holy Spirit's action as breaking in from the future. Theologically, this is an understanding of God's future for the world shaped by God the Father, who raised Jesus Christ from the dead by the power of the Holy Spirit. This divine action is conversation breaking in, not by attending to the past to make improvements, nor by making tasks that need to be accomplished to meet future goals, but by reorienting it in light of a new future of resurrected life. What is at stake in the possibility of conversation for congregational discerning is about giving up control and in turn cultivating a posture of openness toward what the Holy Spirit is actively creating in the world — in the community conversation. What is at stake is a liberating posture to what divine action is bringing about in the world. Taylor's construct of the buffered self, withdrawn and disengaged, is challenged in this understanding of anticipated future coming through conversation with the other. It offers the possibility of the congregation occupying a more open posture to the Spirit's activity in the world.

21. Block, *Community,* 124-25 (italics added).

Leading Congregational Discerning
as Divine Action in Conversation

At this point, one can begin to hear critiques being offered about such a proposal for congregational discerning: "What exactly is the content of the conversation in congregational discerning?" "What are the possibilities that will be declared in congregational discerning?" "You mean congregational discerning is about sitting around and just talking, but about what?" "Isn't this merely an ideal configuration that has no payoff in the end?"

These questions are legitimate concerns for the process of congregational discerning. Some of them reveal, however, the consequences of control and certainty that the buffered self needs in order to survive. An open-ended process requires uncertainty, interdependency and anticipation for a future that is not yet fully clear. This is communal life in the divine in the world. What has been offered here is a description of theological suggestions for what congregational discernment might look like in light of a modernist anthropological condition, and for the sake of learning to hear the divine action in *conversation* as the very act itself of attending to the Holy Spirit's presence and activity as gift. This accompanies different congregational discerning models. Here the emphasis recognizes that an additional theological operation is working on the discerning participants themselves through the Holy Spirit's action through the other. The practice of discerning, therefore, is a practice that theologically affirms and proclaims the triune God's socially embodied engagement in the world.

This is not a magnetic program that is intended to grow congregational attendance. It is learning to practice the call of the triune God communally and interpersonally. This process is not one that is attained by achieving desirable goals or seeking practical solutions for improvement, nor is it merely about an ideational construct of or about God that serves to convince others to come to church. It is a present and unfolding engagement of the triune God and the Holy Spirit coming into our midst. Congregational discerning offers the possibility of fuller awareness of God's presence breaking into the world through a conversation with another.

If there is a leadership key through this process that is being proposed, it would be to track the conversation and attend to it again and again, exploring and imagining how the Holy Spirit is present and active through the conversation. Congregations maintain long records of congregational life through minutes, annual reports, policies and procedures, constitutions and by-laws, and baptismal, wedding, and burial records.

Many congregations bifurcate the process of business and spiritual activities, but rarely if ever do they learn to integrate the two, and more rarely understand why it matters. It matters because integration helps keep the focus of the congregation on God's work amid the conversational process as the very forming of a missional community attentive to God's ever-emerging presence through the other. It matters to continue to proclaim the congregational ministry as the primary work of the triune God, rather than a ministry work the congregation does on behalf of God toward the world. It is a work whereby the congregational discernment circle practices the life of listening to learn about, attend to, and assert God's work in the world. What would it look like if, instead of tracking the tasks and activities, minutes were kept in light of a reading of the Holy Spirit's attending of our conversation? How could a new imagination for divine action in conversation enlarge and form a congregation's participation with the triune God's life in the world?

Conclusion

In this chapter I have proposed an alternative way of thinking about the congregational discernment process. The focus, *congregational discerning as divine action in conversation,* has emphasized how a theological understanding of the congregational discernment process invites the possibility of the Holy Spirit's liberating action of the self through the anticipated divine action in conversation with and through the other. The congregational discerning process, attending as such, becomes a socially embodied expression of God in the world. I have also suggested that what is at stake in this engagement of congregational discernment is an attempt to challenge the modernist construction of the buffered self, withdrawn and disengaged, which often goes unrecognized or unchallenged in most congregational discerning processes and other ministry settings. This is the case because congregational discernment typically has functioned instrumentally as a decision-making tool of one kind or another. It does not directly confront the disengaged self as anything to be concerned with, and more often than not, is not attended to with any awareness or competence.

It has not been my intent in this chapter to argue against, or to appear unsupportive of, congregational tasks and necessary decisions that every congregation will make in its life of being faithful to the life of God in the world. It has been suggested that delving more theologically into the practice of discernment might help to cultivate further the divine action in conversation through the world in the congregation itself and to form a congregation's missional capacity. In light of this deep listening to the Holy Spirit, in congregational discernment, action plans, tasks, and decisions may be given new priority for how the instrumental tasks fit into a larger horizon for the divine action that is being cultivated in the congregation.

Lastly, this focus has considered congregational discernment as an action of the Holy Spirit where, through person-in-relation and otherness, the divine structure of belonging invites attending to the gifts of the Spirit active in the conversation. The Holy Spirit brings liberating good news, not merely as something the congregation gives to the world, but even more importantly and primarily, as the gift the Spirit gives to the world through the congregation growing into a fuller expression of participating in the world God loves. The congregational discernment process, as Spirit-imbued community, anticipates possibilities emerging from the future even as the community attends to the gift of divine action in conversation through and with the other.

CHAPTER 8

Missional Spiritual Formation in the Ethiopian Evangelical Church Mekane Yesus (EECMY)

Dinku Bato

Introduction

According to Luke's narrative in the book of Acts, the Spirit moved Philip to draw near to the chariot that carried the Ethiopian eunuch who was reading the book of Isaiah on his way back home from Jerusalem (Acts 8). That same Spirit still initiates and forms missional spirituality in the Ethiopian church — part of the early history of the spread of Christianity — as outreach takes place to hundreds of thousands of people. In this chapter I explore the story of the emergence, growth, and impact of the Ethiopian Evangelical Church Mekane Yesus (EECMY), highlighting the main factors that contributed to the formation of missional spirituality. I emphasize here the dynamic interplay of these factors, including the role of Scripture in missional spiritual formation, charismatic renewal, lay participation in ministry, and experiences of persecution. By way of introduction, this chapter also briefly deals with the role of the Spirit, the creator of the sent-out community of God, in the process of missional spiritual formation.

The prime purpose of the coming of the Spirit of God upon the disciples in the New Testament was to equip them for mission. The Comforter comes not in order to allow people to be comfortable, but to make them missionaries. The Spirit enables Christians to bear faithful witness to Jesus, despite the costly consequences. Jesus looked forward to the age of the church marked by evangelism and the Spirit: "You will receive power when the Holy Spirit has come upon you; and you will be my witnesses . . ." (Acts 1:8). The Spirit is the power of mission. The impressive

166

list of nationalities present on the day of Pentecost in Acts 2:5-11 indicates that representatives from many nations heard the mighty deeds of God being proclaimed in their own languages. Therefore, the Christian Pentecost, as many theologians have observed, was the reversal of the curse of Babel.

Luke shows us that the Christian good news is for the whole world. Ethiopia is one of the few ancient kingdoms mentioned as an example of the gospel being preached to the ends of the earth. Bevans and Schroeder, in concluding their discussion of this missional encounter between Philip and the Ethiopian eunuch, write: "The story ends as Philip is snatched away by the Spirit and the eunuch continues on his way to Ethiopia, the 'ends of the earth,' rejoicing (Acts 8:39)."[1]

A Brief History of Christianity in Ethiopia

Christianity became the official religion of the Kingdom of Axum in about 350 CE,[2] mainly through the work of Frumentius, the son of a Syrian trader and philosopher who later became the first bishop of Axum in 341.[3] The Axumite Church was in close touch from the beginning with the church in Egypt, and when that church severed its relationship with the Orthodox Church during the Monophysite controversy, the Axumite Church followed its lead. From the middle of the seventh century, when the larger part of the Byzantine Empire and the Red Sea coasts came under the domination of Muslim Arabs, its relationship with the Church of Egypt became closer still and has been maintained through varying vicissitudes to this day. Christianity had not spread far beyond the borders of the Kingdom of Axum in northern Ethiopia before it began to decline, but during the historically obscure period from 650 to 1270, it did expand and by some miracle spread southward beyond the limited confines of the Axumite kingdom. This was by a process of assimilation and adaptation to the Judaic

1. Stephen B. Bevans and Roger Schroeder, *Constants in Context: A Theology of Mission for Today* (Maryknoll, NY: Orbis, 2004), 22.

2. Axum (or Aksum) is a city in northern Ethiopia that was the original capital of the kingdom of Axum. Axum was a naval and trading power that ruled the region from c. 100 BCE into the tenth century CE. It was the first center of Ethiopian and sub-Saharan Christianity.

3. Fekadu Gurmessa and Ezekiel Gebissa, *Evangelical Faith Movement in Ethiopia: The Origins and Establishment of the Ethiopian Evangelical Church Mekane Yesus* (Minneapolis: Lutheran University Press, 2009), 26.

tradition, which became an effective medium for the expression of the spiritual aspirations of the Ethiopians.

According to J. Spencer Trimingham's account, Ethiopia steadfastly maintained its faith as a remote outpost of the church, even though it was cut off from relationships with all other churches except that of Egypt. This enforced seclusion led to the development of an indigenous form of Christianity and the integration of the church as the symbol of Ethiopian nationality, enabling it to preserve its faith in the face of many dangers, though at the same time these same factors paralyzed its spiritual life.

Christianity has been the most vital cultural factor in the lives of the Ethiopians. It lies at the root of the social order, with the relationship of the church and state historically being almost feudal. It became the sole depository of traditional learning, maintained village and monastic schools, "and entered fully into the lives of its adherents in the observance of feast and fast from birth to death, but its deeper spiritual life remained petrified and moribund in traditional ceremonies and customs, exercising little influence upon the moral life." Popular observance was, and still is, due in the main to its social significance. Religious satisfaction is gained from emotional absorption in the rites and the possibility of obtaining protection against evil influence, rather than from any real perception of the spiritual significance of the religious acts.[4]

The Emergence of a National Evangelical Church

The seeds that gave rise to the first congregations and ultimately to the formation of a national church were sown in the nineteenth century. This came through the European pietistic movement of the seventeenth century and the effort of Protestant missionaries to revitalize the Ethiopian Orthodox Church (EOC) through dialogue, colportage, and pairing the evangelistic enterprise with artisanship. The tireless, persistent, and sacrificial efforts of European missionaries were thwarted by the fact that they ventured into a religiocultural milieu where the people took enormous pride in their religion. In northern Ethiopia, the missionaries labored diligently amid a society that maintained indigenized Christian beliefs and practices rooted in the early centuries of Christianity. It was a hostile envi-

---

4. J. Spencer Trimingham, *The Christian Church and Missions in Ethiopia (Including Eritrea and the Somalilands)* (New York: World Dominion Press, 1950), 6-7.

ronment where the rulers and church leaders harbored profound suspicion of foreigners. Trimingham has described this as follows:

> When they began their work during the 20th century the aim of most of the missions working in Addis Ababa and Ethiopian Church areas was not to proselytize but to help the church of Ethiopia to regain its prophetic vision. Yet it was inevitable that Ethiopians who came under their influence should adopt a religious outlook and ideas of worship quite different from those of the national Church. This led, at any rate in the case of the Swedish Mission, to a crisis when the Ethiopian Church authorities refused burial to those whom they considered apostate and refused to baptize their children. The natural consequence was the formation of the "Evangelical Church of Ethiopia."[5]

The main work of the European missionaries, as briefly discussed above, was to engage the Orthodox clergy in theological dialogue and to distribute Scripture in northern Ethiopia. This initiated a Bible Readers Movement within the EOC. Many Orthodox clergy read Scripture, embraced the evangelical faith, and dispatched missionaries to western Ethiopia. This later became the epicenter of growth and expansion of evangelistic outreach to the rest of the country, where early Protestant and Catholic mission efforts had not been successful for various political and practical reasons.

The indigenous evangelists who converted to the evangelical faith through contacts with missionaries grew in their faith because of their personal quest for truth and God. Their collective biography gives an amazing texture to the narrative of the expansion of evangelical Christianity and offers an explanation as to why indigenous evangelicals succeeded in winning many converts in southern and western Ethiopia. Without reducing the importance of the many foreign missionaries who have worked in the country, I must emphasize the contribution of indigenous ministers. As Johnny Bakke observes, "Even before foreign missionaries were allowed to enter the country and in periods when missionaries were expelled or confined to their stations, devoted Ethiopians proclaimed the Gospel and directed the work."[6] The post-Italian period has witnessed the emergence of local evangelical leaders who made a determined effort to adopt a com-

5. Trimingham, *The Christian Church and Missions in Ethiopia*, 45-46.
6. Johnny Bakke, *Christian Ministry: Patterns and Functions within the Ethiopian Evangelical Church Mekane Yesus* (Atlantic Highlands, NJ: Humanities Press International, 1987), 232.

mon doctrinal statement, a governing constitution, and a common designation, the Mekane Yesus (Jesus' dwelling place) Church.[7] It became a national evangelical church with all the attributes of independence: self-governance, self-support, and self-propagation.

Organized Outreach

Early translations of Scripture into the vernacular languages were largely done by local persons beginning in the 1830s. The Swedish Evangelical Mission (EFS) began organized efforts to reach the Oromo in 1866. Christian merchants from the Oromo area, in a base in Eritrea, received Bible training and returned as missionaries to Wollaga in western Ethiopia.[8] They were entrusted with former slaves, including EECMY pioneer Onesimos Nesib, who completed a translation of the entire Bible into Oromo in 1899.[9] Ever since, this has been a major influence in the missional spiritual formation that spurred the Oromo people as the first indigenous people group to carry evangelistic outreach into the rest of the country, first to the center and south and later to the north and east. This goes in line with what Krapf imagined almost a century ago: "The light of the Gospel and Science will be kindled first among the [Oromo], and thence proceeds to the Abyssinians, who have nothing but the name of Christ."[10] It is thus not a mere coincidence that the Oromo make up the lion's share of membership and ministry in the EECMY and in Ethiopian evangelical Christianity in general.

7. The post-Italian period followed the end of the Italian imperialistic war in Ethiopia (1935-36). Earlier the Italians had invaded Ethiopa following the European colonial "scramble for Africa," only to be defeated on May 1, 1896. This makes Ethiopia the first and only country in Africa that defeated a European colonial power. The Second Italo-Ethiopian War began in October 1935 and ended in May 1936 — with the defeat of the Italians by the Ethiopians for the second time — and their final expulsion. Ethiopia was the only uncolonized country in Africa.

8. This region has the largest number of Oromo people (the largest people group in Ethiopia), and it is the place where the first EECMY congregation was established to expand to the rest of the country.

9. Lutherans commemorate Onesimos Nesib on June 21 as an Oromo who translated the Bible into the Oromo language. Nesib laid the foundation for evangelical mission in Ethiopia. Gurmessa and Gebissa, *Evangelical Faith Movement in Ethiopia*, 128.

10. Gustav Arén, *Evangelical Pioneers in Ethiopia: Origins of the Evangelical Church Mekane Yesus* (Addis Ababa: Evangelical Church Mekane Yesus, 1978), 69-70.

The German Hermannsburg Mission was next in line to establish a mission station among the Oromo people in 1928 at Aira, in western Wollaga. During the missionaries' absence throughout the years of the Italian invasion, the Oromo church grew under local leadership and evangelized the whole area around Aira. After the Italian occupation, the use of the Oromo Bible in worship and teaching by Ethiopian and German missionaries greatly influenced the establishment of the evangelical church throughout the area.[11]

The Presbyterian Church USA had worked in Sudan for many years and had medical and evangelistic contacts with Nilotic groups (especially the Anuak and Nuer), who inhabited both sides of the Ethiopian border in the west, especially during the 1919 influenza epidemic. In the 1930s, Bethel (Presbyterian) congregations were organized in the western regions of Wollaga, and medical and outreach missions had close fellowship with the Oromo Lutheran believers. The Presbyterian believers organized the Bethel Church in 1947, and that became part of the EECMY in 1973.[12]

Mission initiatives from the Nordic countries expanded significantly from 1948 with the arrival of the Norwegian Lutheran Mission, followed by the Danish Evangelical Mission, and later by Finnish and Icelandic missionaries. The work in the south included hospitals, clinics, schools, Bible schools, and a seminary. The American Lutheran Mission came to Ethiopia in 1957, carrying out medical, educational, and agricultural work, as well as outreach to the northern Afar peoples and neighboring lowlanders.

Thus the EECMY is a church of a diverse evangelical background serving in a multireligious society where the Orthodox tradition dominates. Some of the persons who played a mediating role between the Ethiopian Orthodox Church (EOC) and the evangelical believers brought to the fore some of the issues that were much debated later: the dominant position of the Bible over against martyrologies and saint stories, and a critical view against regarding fasting as a merit. These are some of the essential elements with which to understand the EECMY as an Ethiopian church in the Orthodox setting. The EECMY represents, on the one hand, a continuity of Orthodox traditions with regard to the church year and theological vocabulary. The EECMY also has, like the EOC, an ordained ministry, with most of the clerical titles adopted from the same. On the other hand, the EECMY represents a discontinuity with respect to some of

---

11. Gurmessa and Gebissa, *Evangelical Faith Movement*, 141.

12. Abraham Emmanuel, *Reminiscences of My Life* (Oslo: Lunde Forlag, 1995), 281.

the Orthodox traditions, as mentioned above: martyrologies, saints' stories, and views about fasting. There are also the EECMY features of allowing lay people to preach and the use of local languages in sermons and worship. These two later factors, as I will discuss below in this chapter, are some of the major contributors to the formation of missional spirituality. They particularly promoted the priesthood role of members as advocates of reconciliation and fostered awareness of the significance of different vernaculars as God's special media of evangelization as demonstrated in the Pentecost event.

Partnership for Missional Spiritual Formation

In 1972, the EECMY published a letter entitled "On the Interrelation between the Proclamation of the Gospel and Human Development," which outlined its understanding and commitment regarding holistic ministry — "Serving the Whole Man [Person]." It also challenged donor limitations that sharply separated development from evangelism in favor of the former as a separate entity to which most donor and mission organizations showed lopsided financial support.

Upon EECMY's invitation, the Lutheran World Federation established in 1973 a World Service country program for relief and development work, which continues today as a joint LWF-EECMY program.[13] The Committee of Mutual Christian Responsibility (CMCR), established in 1979, provides an annual forum for the Ethiopian church and its partners to address common concerns in mission at national and global levels. Emphasizing the missional nature of partnership with other churches and mission organizations, the EECMY declares:

> The EECMY and her Cooperating Partners should do everything possible both to prevent one another from weakening and withering away and to help one another to live for Christ. It is a ministry with a cross. The EECMY sees the carrying of the cross as an essential part of this joint ministry. What is more valuable for the Christian churches than joining hands for this most rewarding field of cooperation in ministry and paying the cost of discipleship?[14]

13. The EECMY became a member of the Lutheran World Federation in 1963.
14. EECMY. "Executive Committee Minutes," Addis Ababa, February 1983.

Toward the accomplishment of its mission of "serving the whole person," the EECMY, with active participation of its partners, has established and run several institutions. These include four seminaries, one leadership and management college, and several Bible schools, three senior secondary schools, four junior schools, twenty-seven elementary schools, two schools for the deaf, a school for the mentally challenged, a center for the differently abled, one technical school, and another vocational training workshop. In the social sector, the church runs thirty-eight social institutions: twenty-one hostels, one orphanage, thirteen day-care centers, two vocational training centers, one extended child-support program, two family empowerment programs, and thirty Compassion-assisted child development programs. All these have served one way or another as vehicles of forming missional spirituality among various social and economic classes that include leaders, pastors, the youth, children, and the underprivileged.

From the national interdenominational partnership point of view, the EECMY, during the widespread religious persecution, had taken the precarious initiative of forming the Evangelical Churches Fellowship of Ethiopia so as to challenge the enduring harassment. Many churches were closed down, and pastors and other leaders were imprisoned with the aim of muffling the budding church. With what was left at its disposal, however, the EECMY provided a place of fellowship for other denominations whose worship places were closed and confiscated. This paved the way later on for the establishment of the Evangelical Churches Fellowship of Ethiopia (ECFE), the first of its kind in Africa, which continues to be a platform of organized outreach after serving as one of the strongest survival mechanisms against the crushing fist of the communist regime that ruled the land for just under two decades. The fellowship has also served as a ground for sharing and mutual edification in Christian witness, the cost of discipleship, and spirituality in times of persecution, during which most of the meetings were clandestine and in the form of small groups in houses or in the woods.[15]

Persecution and Growth

The EECMY and the other Protestant evangelical churches of Ethiopia carry a legacy of persecution. From the very beginning in Eritrea, until the

15. Commonly, young Christians in rural Ethiopia during most of the Marxist-Leninist regime (1974-91) used to conduct their Bible studies and prayers in the woods in a group of two (or a maximum of three) to seek cover from the rampant persecution.

fall of the last emperor, there were numerous incidents of persecution all over Ethiopia. Most of these incidents bear witness to harassment and resistance by the Ethiopian Orthodox Church (EOC). The persecution during the Marxist-Leninist regime, under the reign of Mengistu Haile Mariam, far surpasses anything experienced in previous periods — both in extent and cruelty. At least 2,500 church buildings were closed during the persecution by the communist regime, all of them belonging to the non-Orthodox denominations. A large number of church employees and lay members were imprisoned for long periods. Many of them suffered severe torture and harassment. The most serious incident was the assassination of the Rev. Guddinal Tumsas, general secretary of the EECMY.

Nevertheless, the persecution deepened the understanding of the meaning of the suffering of Christ and led to a maturation of faith among the nucleus of the faithful. The closing of the churches and the deep emotional crisis created by revolution, hunger, civil war, and so forth resulted in a tremendous search for spiritual meaning. The witness of the nucleus of the faithful in each congregation who had dared to stand up against the pressure from the government became a powerful demonstration of the depth and preciousness of the evangelical faith. When the people were given freedom to worship, they turned to the churches in great numbers. Looking back at the Mengistu Haile Mariam persecution, the witness of the few during that period may be the single most important reason for the tremendous growth in membership of the EECMY. The experience of persecution left its mark on the theology of the EECMY, a theology of the cross in the tradition of genuine Lutheran theology. This may prove most valuable for the church when faced with the extremes of the charismatic movements' theology of glory.

Membership Growth of the EECMY

The year 1991 was the beginning of a new Ethiopia after the downfall of the Dergue (Marxist) regime. On May 28, 1991, the regime was defeated by the Ethiopian People's Revolutionary Democratic Front (EPRDF). The EPRDF issued a decree of religious freedom, resulting in freedom of worship, the reopening of church buildings and the return of church properties (at least partially) upon the relentless request and diligent follow-up of the church, its synods, parishes, and congregations. Hence the 1990s was a decade in which the EECMY took a big leap forward to revitalize its holistic ministry throughout the country. It was a decade in which:

- Its membership grew by leaps and bounds.
- Its activities were normalized and managed in a planned way.
- It reclaimed some of its main properties that were illegally confiscated by the Dergue (Marxist) regime, including the current Central Office building.
- Growth in outreach programs occurred, and they sent a missionary to Zambia.
- Three new synods and one work area were established.
- The Women's Ministry in the EECMY was upgraded, and the policy decision was made to ordain women as theologians and pastors.
- The church planned a better financial strategy.
- Diverse development and social services programs were designed and implemented.
- The church established a Peace and Justice Commission in order to strengthen its advocacy role and train its members to be more responsible in their role in society.
- The religious leaders were actively engaged in peace and reconciliation work during the Ethio-Eritrean war.
- The church celebrated various anniversaries — both at the national level and in its synods.
- The document "Visions and Challenges of the EECMY" was prepared, and the EECMY developed the Vision/Mission Strategy, which led to the five-year plan (1996-2000).

During this decade the EECMY membership grew year after year for several reasons. First, this time of rest allowed for the planning and execution of evangelistic programs in a peaceful environment. The congregations were able to take care of their members and to open new preaching places. Second, the revival movement had moved members to witness to people. Third, synods were able to advance to new areas and open outreach programs, namely in the Nile Valley, Dawuro, Surma, Hamerbako, Majangir, Somali, and so on. Fourth, former members who had left the church and were working against its interests by siding with the Marxist government confessed their sins and asked the congregations to be pardoned and admitted into membership. The congregations forgave them and, having reinstructed them in the Christian faith, accepted them into membership.[16]

16. Megerssa Gutta, "EECMY's 50 Years Journey in Fulfillment of God's Mission, 50th

In the first years of the twenty-first century, the EECMY member-ship grew by leaps and bounds — an average annual rate of 5.7 percent.[17] The following table shows the yearly growth of the EECMY membership.[18]

Year	Membership
2000	3,359,089
2001	3,599,659
2002	3,888,388
2003	4,033,413
2004	4,164,066
2005	4,323,254
2006	4,665,739
2007	4,869,157
2008	5,012,486
2009	5,279,822

Since 1959 the EECMY as a national church of unified Lutheran and Presbyterian congregations has grown steadily in numbers and in mission and partner relationships. It has over 5.2 million members today,[19] made up of many ethnic and language groups, in 6,644 established congrega-tions and 2,818 preaching places organized under twenty-two synods and one work area. The church has 2,061 pastors and 2,728 evangelists. What is more, in resonance with the principle of the priesthood of all believers, there are more than 300,000 volunteers actively involved in the mission of the church (which I will discuss further below).

The membership increase of nearly one million in the last five years is attributable mainly to growth in families [20] and sustained outreach efforts to new language groups, incorporating Bible translation and training of lo-

---

Jubilee of the Establishment of the Ethiopian Evangelical Church Mekane Yesus (EECMY): Overview of the Major Achievements in the Past 50 years (1959-2009)" (unpublished, 2009), 34-36.

17. Megerssa Gutta, "Reflection Paper on the 1972 EECMY Paper, 'On the Interrela-tion between Proclamation of the Gospel and Human Development,'" 2008.

18. EECMY Central Office, Addis Ababa, Annual Official Statistical Information, Sep-tember 2010.

19. This makes the EECMY the largest Lutheran church in Africa and the second larg-est in the world, following Sweden, which has 6.4 million members.

20. This refers mainly to the increase in family size and, on the other hand, the addition of families into church membership particularly in new outreach areas mentioned below.

cal evangelists as major strategies. It is the work of the Holy Spirit to effect such growth amid the difficulties the church has had to pass through.

Charismatic Renewal for Mission

The time of intense persecution during the revolution witnessed the growth of the charismatic movement in the church, in which many youth and adult members of the church exercised charismatic experiences of the Holy Spirit. These had the characteristic expressions of prophecy and visions, as well as speaking in tongues, while there was a special emphasis on healing and exorcism. According to Johannes Launhardt, "several Christians in the EECMY were involved in a healing ministry, having received a special gift of asking for healing through prayers or of sensing who should be healed that way." The simple preaching of the gospel was very often accompanied by healing, exorcism, or by some other signs that were interpreted and shared with others as demonstrations of divine power, much like the Samaritan woman who encountered Jesus at the well (John 4:1-42). Different kinds of physical healings and exorcisms were reported to have taken place in various EECMY congregations that run these programs once or twice a week apart from Sundays. Members of these congregations revealed that their faith had been strengthened, and this helped them to witness and invite unreached people in their communities.[21]

The charismatic revival can be traced back to 1963, when students in the Mulu Wongel church (later the Ethiopian Full Gospel Church) and of the Mekane Yesus in Addis Ababa made contacts in the common facilities they were using for worship and Bible study programs. The most important development took place, however, in the western periphery of Ethiopia, where the charismatic revival started in Gore, Ilubabor (1970), and in Naqamte, Wallagaa (1972). The great growth of the charismatic movement within the church took place during the 1980s, and by 1991 most of the youth in all synods were influenced. Seminars, consultations, the theological commission of the EECMY, and the executive committee were all involved in the question.[22] As a result, the charismatic revival was gradually

---

21. Johannes Launhardt, *Evangelicals in Addis Ababa (1919-1991): With Special Reference to the Ethiopian Evangelical Church Mekane Yesus and the Addis Ababa Synod* (Piscataway, NJ: Lit Transaction, 2004), 301.

22. The initial period of charismatic renewal in the EECMY was characterized by de-

integrated into parts of the church. Today the church enjoys the blessing of the gifts of the Holy Spirit as it carries out the God-given mission of "serving the whole person," as its motto proclaims.

Missional Spiritual Formation and the Word of God

The evangelical movement in Ethiopia was from its beginning a movement toward reading, preaching, and studying the Bible in the vernacular of the people.[23] This concern also shaped the life and ministry of the EECMY during the time of the Marxist regime of atrocities. The central place in a Sunday service in many EECMY congregations is given to Scripture readings and the sermon based on a biblical text. Often volunteers take over the reading of the Bible and the preaching. Bakke notes:

> As far as the evangelicals in Ethiopia are concerned, theological understanding and authority to preach the word of God have not been the prerogative of the ordained ministers. Some of their most gifted men and women are not counted among the ordained ministers. In view of this, it seems realistic to pursue a practice in which the call, and not the training, qualifies for the different positions. Such a distinction is by no means anything new in a Lutheran context.[24]

Hymns and songs having their origin in Bible passages are sung by a choir or the congregation. The biblical truths are explained in Sunday services and more specifically in confirmation courses, conducted on a congregational level. People who want to take part in Holy Communion and become full members of a congregation have to attend a confirmation class of two hours every week for at least six months. In a confirmation course the basic teachings of the Bible are taught, and the participants are expected to learn at least the Apostles' Creed and the Lord's Prayer by heart.

Christian education does not end when one finishes the confirmation classes; it continues with discipleship class, which extends for three

---

bate between two groups of leaders and pastors: one group supported the movement as God's visitation and the awakening of gifts in the church today, as it was in the early church; however, the other group contested this view based on its cessationist view of charismatic gifts.

23. Arén, *Evangelical Pioneers in Ethiopia*, 184-85.
24. Bakke, *Christian Ministry*, 263.

months every week for two hours. Here communicant members engage in the process of discerning their giftedness and where group members also take active roles as they prepare for voluntary ministry in the church. Once a member begins service in the area of his or her conceived giftedness, he or she would continue to be part of a weekly small-group Bible study, where he or she would be mutually nurtured and edified. This process has helped significantly in the missional spiritual formation of members as they turn out to be active agents of God's mission rather than passive participants in programs and services.

The Bible has been a source of comfort in times of mourning, suffering, and affliction for the evangelical Christians of Ethiopia; people were strengthened and encouraged by reading verses from Scripture in their mother tongue. In times of changing and competing political ideologies, the New Testament provided guidance and a helpful reminder of what is most important for life and death. In his paper entitled "Report on the Church Growth in Ethiopia," the Reverend Gudina Tumsa, the late general secretary of the EECMY, discusses how the departure of missionaries — as a result of the Italian invasion of Ethiopia — goaded a significant number of believers in some parts of the country to take upon themselves the responsibility of reading, preaching, and witnessing for the gospel of the Risen Christ. "There was thus a revival, during the five-year period of occupation by Italy, among the Christians left behind around the mission stations."

He mentions further that many Christian groups that had nowhere to turn for guidance decided to depend on the reading of Scripture. Thus the missionaries, to whom they formerly looked to draw advice, counseling, and assistance, were soon replaced by the Bible. Since the Bible was the only source to turn to, Bible study and reading played a vital role in bringing about a revival among the groups of believers. I should note that these groups of believers had a minimal knowledge of Christian doctrines; one could even say that, in many respects, their knowledge of basic Christian teaching was almost nil. The reading of Scripture, combined with prayer, was the main cause of the revival movement, which sent deep roots in the life of believers left by the missions.[25]

---

25. Gudina Tumsa, *Witness and Discipleship: Leadership of the Church in Multi-Ethnic Ethiopia in a Time of Revolution: The Essential Writings of Gudina Tumsa, General Secretary of the Ethiopian Evangelical Church Mekane Yesus (1929-1979)* (Addis Ababa: Gudina Tumsa Foundation, 2003), 125.

It would be unfair not to mention the role that the translation of the Bible into different vernaculars had in forming missional spirituality. In a land that hosts more than eighty languages, the EECMY has taken upon itself, as a pioneer, the formidable task of translating the Bible. This has offered to these peoples the possibility of becoming Christians without losing their ethnic identity. Instead of being the religion of the rulers, the gospel gave even downtrodden people and despised groups a sense of worth in accordance with God's will for humanity. This has resulted in missional engagements from the very beginning of the task with the EOC priests in north Ethiopia as I have discussed above. As people read and understood the Bible, they were motivated for mission. A case in point is the translation and use of the Oromo Bible, translated by the former slave Oromo Onesimos (Hika) Nesib in 1899: it has had a considerable impact on the Oromo people of western Ethiopia, who have spread the initial indigenous and massive missionary enterprise to the rest of the country.

New Missional Songs

The hymns sung in the Mekane Yesus congregations during the 1940s and 1950s were mostly translations of European hymns with tunes from Sweden or Germany. One of the significant events worth noting is that the revival movements of the early 1960s developed indigenous patterns in which traditional melodies were used in worship and evangelistic outreach, and the people were thus made to feel at home with the message proclaimed to them. Forms of worship and music were made indigenous without the church's working out a specific plan for that.[26]

The congregational choirs, mainly composed of young people, were the ones who made the new choruses known. The text and rhythms were very much liked by the singers and the audience. When the revolution began, all Mekane Yesus congregations in most parts of the country had at least one choir, and some had two or three. Joining a choir was not just a decision of the person concerned, because it was expected that choir members believed in Christ and supported the beliefs expressed in the hymns they sang. Singing in front of a gathering was understood as a Christian witness. When choirs met during the week, they not only practiced the hymns for the next performance, but they stayed together for Bible study

26. Tumsa, *Witness and Discipleship*, 129.

and prayers. Thus choirs became the spearheads of the evangelical churches. They not only sang at their own church, but they traveled — when possible and at their own expense — to other congregations or places to witness to the love and power of Christ.[27]

Missional songs in the EECMY are like wildfires that swiftly spread over a vast area. Their evangelistic themes beg for the attention of the listeners. It is not uncommon, therefore, to hear people giving testimony to how songs touched their lives and led them to Christ or how they were comforted by the message and tunes, and how their burdens were rolled away, much as Luther expressed it: "The devil, the originator of sorrowful anxieties and restless troubles, flees before the sound of music almost as much as before the Word of God. . . ."[28] Mothers sing the songs as they bathe their babies and lull them to sleep, missionally shaping them in this way. The kids, in turn, sing as they play both in the village and at school playgrounds among friends; those friends learn to sing the songs at home, and thus they set everyone's heart aflame.

It is not surprising, then, that the evangelical choirs were a special target of attack by revolutionary political agents during the Marxist regime. Choir members often were the first ones to be repressed or detained. Some cadres even went further and tried to force young Christians to sing hymns praising scientific socialism and to use their guitars for mobilizing the masses to follow the Marxist cause. Out of inner conviction, many refused to do this, choosing instead to be publicly mocked, beaten, or detained.

Usually the songs made a deep impression on the listeners. Their spiritual impact was experienced especially when the power of Jesus Christ was proclaimed. They touched the feelings and emotions of the people. It can be said without exaggeration that the newly composed tunes and the convincing messages of the songs, presented with personal involvement, reached the minds and heart of newcomers more directly than traditional sermons or doctrinal teaching. The testimony of the choirs continues to play an important role in now democratic Ethiopia.[29]

27. Launhardt, *Evangelicals in Addis Ababa*, 296.
28. http://www.goodreads.com/author/quotes/29874.Martin_Luther (accessed Sept. 25, 2010).
29. Launhardt, *Evangelicals in Addis Ababa*, 297.

Diaconia and Missional Motivation

The accounts in the Gospels often tell us how Jesus was moved by compassion as he saw, for instance, the people like sheep without a shepherd (Mark 6:30-34), or wept over Jerusalem for not knowing the things that would make for its peace (Luke 19:42). A growing realization of immediate spiritual, physical, social, economic, and political needs of their surrounding communities is a strong factor in instigating missional communities to respond with missional compassion. The diverse and deplorable socioeconomic and political conditions the Ethiopian people have been through under different political economic systems, ranging from feudalistic to Marxist, constitute a burden that the church bears and shares with the people. For people who are tormented by the spirit of fear, there is a hunger to accept the new religion of love and justice. Although this fear and oppression did not directly and automatically lead the masses to the church, it did create fertile soil in which to sow the seeds of the gospel, to proclaim the risen Christ, who frees men and women from fear. The church shares the joy of the liberating gospel with those in the darkness of fear and oppression, as in D. T. Niles's metaphor of "one beggar telling another beggar where to find bread."[30]

From the perspective of physical and economic needs, the church lives predominantly amidst people coping with devastating poverty. According to the CIA World Fact Book of February 2010, 38.7 percent of the Ethiopian population lives below the poverty line.[31] Drought, famine, war, and the government policy on land use have produced millions of suffering people, and the churches are not willing to overlook them. That the Mekane Yesus Church responded without hesitation, using its international connections for the benefit of Ethiopian citizens, was a result of its understanding of humanity and the declared policy of an integral human development, which it practices by serving the whole person.

Yet the EECMY could not hold its peace in the face of what it saw as the need to criticize Western churches and their missions for splitting the task of the church into evangelism and development — thus distorting the vocation to serve the whole person. It pointed out, in its famous letter of

---

30. Richard Stoll Armstrong, *Faithful Witnesses, Participant's Book* (Philadelphia: Geneva Press, 1987), 66.

31. https://www.cia.gov/library/publications/the-world-factbook/fields/2046.html (accessed Sept. 2, 2010).

1972, that evangelism and development are not two separate activities, but are united as one.[32] To strip development activities of their evangelistic aspect means to accept the idea that humanity can be treated in parts. The preaching of the gospel does not leave people in the same situation as before; in fact, it leads to improved living conditions. But true development takes place only when people are renewed in their inner humanity. This can only happen when their material and spiritual needs are both satisfied.

Educational and health services within the country remain at low levels compared to the growing needs. The church, with its motto of "serving the whole person," gave diaconal responses toward the alleviation of calamities through a variety of approaches, including emergency relief; establishment and operation of several schools; a literacy campaign; hostels; child day-care centers; sponsorship programs; a family reunification program; health services; programs for mentally challenged children; soil and water conservation and development; and the Integrated Rural Development Project. These all demonstrate missional compassion for the suffering world.[33]

Ministry, Mission, and the Priesthood of All Believers

Laypeople have played a decisive and increasing role in the Mekane Yesus congregations. The ground for participation of all in ministry of the EECMY was strongly tied with the understanding of the concept and practice of the priesthood of all believers, where every baptized member is understood as a missionary (1 Peter 2:5). Baptism, beyond its sacramental significance, entails the initiation of the recipient into Christian mission, a call to live as an ambassador for Christ reconciling the world with God. In line with this, men and women of all ages in the church are trained and equipped for their service in weekend courses, evening classes, and programs such as the Theological Education by Extension and the Mobile Bible School. The majority of members, attendants, and volunteer ministers

32. EECMY, 1974. The EECMY letter, signed on May 9, 1972, was hailed by the Lutheran World Federation (LWF) for raising a central question about the identity of the church and the nature of its service to the whole human being. It provided a particular impetus for the LWF Identity Study, which was launched in 1974. It prompted immediate LWF action and resulted in the LWF-sponsored Consultation on Proclamation and Human Development held in Nairobi in 1974.

33. Launhardt, *Evangelicals in Addis Ababa*, 293.

(75 percent of the church membership) are composed of young people who indefatigably discharge their ministerial commitments in different capacities according to their respective giftedness.

The revival movements during the early 1960s and during the era of the Marxist regime were started by laypeople, and they still continue to have their roots in the same. EECMY congregations do not allow professional pastors and evangelists to monopolize the ministry of preaching and teaching. Lay preachers and teachers have equal access to the pulpit, and there is not too much difference between preaching in churches and personal witness in ordinary life. It may be said that the professional ministry is playing its role in nurture, but the high rate of growth of evangelical churches in Ethiopia comes through the regular witness of lay Christians in daily life. It is true that the biblical knowledge of lay Christians is in many places rather minimal; yet, despite that, there is a general feeling of urgency to reach those who have not had the opportunity to hear the gospel of the risen Christ.

Conclusion

Emmanuel Gebresellassie, a longtime laborer in the effort to establish a national evangelical church, and the first president of the EECMY, had the following to say on the occasion of the founding of the church as a national body: "What we have been speaking and done today might appear ordinary to us; but time and history will reveal the greatness of this day and our accomplishment." Fifty-one years have passed since Emmanuel Gebresellassie uttered those words. As Gurmessa and Gebissa observed, the church has proved itself an instrument in God's hands over these decades in the areas of preaching the gospel and promoting social development.[34]

One of the common ways God works, as clearly demonstrated in the Scripture narratives, is using simple means and humble beginnings. The story of the Ethiopian Evangelical Church Mekane Yesus is a contemporary illustration of this statement. What began with a few native evangelists and foreign missionaries has multiplied to impact the spiritual and socioeconomic lives of millions of people in Ethiopia. One may wonder about the real force working in this growth, change, and transformation. As depicted in Gebresellassie's inaugural speech above, the credit goes to

---

34. Gurmessa and Gebissa, *Evangelical Faith Movement in Ethiopia,* 254.

God, who enabled and equipped his people, through various means, to do the work of evangelists who were continually shaped and guided by Scripture and the sacraments. The multifaceted ministry of the gospel (leading, preaching, teaching, singing, witnessing, healing, praying, comforting, etc.) is carried out by volunteer members who are bestowed with the gifts of the Spirit, who both edifies and beatifies the church as a community of God's sent people.

The rocky and thorny road the church has trod has been one of enormous sacrifices, which demanded the lives of many faithful women and men of God who boldly demonstrated their allegiance in the face of severe persecution and suffering. This has significantly shaped the missional spirituality of their contemporaries and left a legacy of readiness to embrace suffering and death for the sake of the kingdom, which effectively demonstrates Tertullian's famous observation that "the blood of the martyrs is the seed of the church."

CHAPTER 9

A Baptismal Example:
Communal Prayer and the Missional Church

Dirk G. Lange

I. Questioning a Few Assumptions

It might not come as a surprise if I, as a Luther scholar, ask the following question: What is God doing in this liturgical event? I know the classic definition of *leitourgia* (work of the people); but my question revolves around God's action. What is God up to in the liturgy? What is the Holy Spirit doing? This question is one of agency and has played a significant role in rethinking God's action, not only in worship but also in the entire mission of the church. Craig Van Gelder and Dwight Zscheile have observed in *The Missional Church in Perspective* that missional literature has known "significant ambiguity" when it comes to the question of agency. How is the triune God directly involved in the church's sending? They point out that the answer given to this question of agency will also determine the theological framework through which we conceive of God's mission. They very helpfully set out the different theological and biblical assumptions underlying various approaches to the question of agency.[1]

In both the church and the academy there is a renewed interest in redefining what God's mission is in the world and how this impacts our understanding of church. The contours and history of this interest have been amply discussed. A major part of redefining *missio Dei* has concentrated on a retrieval of the action and character of the Trinity and how the church

---

1. Van Gelder and Zscheile, *The Missional Church in Perspective: Mapping Trends and Shaping the Conversation* (Grand Rapids: Baker Academic, 2011).

community reflects this action. (Not only has missional literature helped to reintroduce the Trinity to theological thinking; it has also awakened renewed interest in ecclesiology.) What are the components of this retrieval? Perhaps too simply summarized, Trinitarian models for understanding a missional church revolve, primarily, around two metaphors. Whether it be the Western model of the economic Trinity (God sending the Son to accomplish redemption and, with the Spirit, gathering a community, the church, together for God's mission) or the Eastern paradigm emphasizing the perichoretic nature of the Trinity (humanity as social reality and the church as social community called and sent into mission), the terms of God's action or the descriptors of God's interrelationships (in God's self and with the world) become the basis for understanding how the church, the gathered community of faith, is present in and relates to the world.[2] A representation of God's being (as Trinity) gives us a language for understanding God's action. God, as three persons, is understood as the one who "calls," "gathers," and "sends" — metaphoric actions that find, of course, their basis in Scripture.

The church as the gathered community, gathered by the Spirit and sent out into God's mission, is "elected" to service. It is the community of the redeemed in Jesus Christ. It is the community formed by the Holy Spirit. Even if the church is no longer understood to be the unique place of God's action in the world (God, of course, acts outside the church, in the world, often independently of the church), it is still the place where the Holy Spirit works — gathering, molding, forming, sending. The church is privileged in that it is a workshop of the Holy Spirit and the liturgy is perhaps one of the main tools in that workshop.

I believe, however, that it can be helpful to question this language of call — perhaps even the whole notion of gathering and sending. What lies hidden in such a language or conception of community and mission? On the one hand, it can encourage a potentially dangerous appropriation of "election" and turn it into privilege. Even when the frontiers are blurred between the inside (church) and the outside (world), those on the "inside," the "baptized," as they are sometimes called, can claim and become too secure in their "privilege" as the ones called. Their focus is then on having been chosen rather than on what is to be done. Unfortunately, there are

---

2. For an excellent and fuller discussion of these models and their implications, see Craig Van Gelder, ed., *The Missional Church in Context: Helping Congregations Develop Contextual Ministry* (Grand Rapids: Eerdmans, 2007), 27ff.

too many examples of parishes that have become islands to the world around them, living their faith witness more to each other than toward the unknown neighbor.

Second, I want to ask whether "being chosen" or "called" does not, in fact, run contrary to the witness of Jesus Christ. Of course, that does sound preposterous. Even Jesus calls the disciples to follow. However, when "call" slips into the language of privilege (when congregations seem to be smug in their position or standing within society) then we are, in fact, far from what Jesus was doing when he called someone. Yes, Jesus calls disciples, but this call is not a privilege; it is a cross.

Can God's action/mission be described in yet other terms? How can we better describe the language of "call" as an evangelical action? I propose to explore, not the characteristic of God's being or any other metaphoric representation we might construe for the Trinity, but rather a simple activity, a practice that Christians engage in because God commands it: the activity of prayer, and particularly communal prayer. What can this practice — as an activity where the Holy Spirit promises to be present — reveal to us about the Spirit's ongoing work?

In order to explore the Holy Spirit's agency through communal prayer, I will turn to an insight that Dietrich Bonhoeffer develops. Contrary to the world, which looks to God to solve its problems (or expects God to solve them!); contrary to a popular "religiosity," which looks to God only when distress, disaster, despair, and so forth threaten, and God is expected to use God's power; contrary, I might add, to a God of eternal substance known as power, realized act — contrary to this "God of the gaps" — Bonhoeffer chooses to point us to the powerlessness of God. For Bonhoeffer, this is, in fact, one of the characteristics of Scripture: it "directs [us] to God's powerlessness and suffering."[3]

It is in God's powerlessness and suffering, Bonhoeffer believes, that we can find a starting point for a "secular interpretation" of God and God's revelation in the world.[4] Why is a secular interpretation important for Bonhoeffer? In part, I believe, Bonhoeffer is searching for a theological framework that is not confined to a metaphysical discussion of God's nature or being but finds God's agency active in the world — through sur-

---

3. Dietrich Bonhoeffer, *Letters*, 16 July 1944, cited in Larry Rasmussen, *Dietrich Bonhoeffer: Reality and Resistance* (Nashville: Abingdon, 1972), 83.
4. Bonhoeffer, *Letters and Papers from Prison*, ed. Eberhard Bethge (New York: Macmillan, 1972), 360-61.

prising means. Bonhoeffer, of course, found himself as a church leader and theologian in opposition to the church, living a life of resistance, living outside the classic theological framework, on the margins. He discovered that the question "Who is Christ for us today?" can only be asked, not from a place of privilege, but from the edge, the outskirts, from outside the city walls. God's revealing voice was to be heard in the street, in the often religionless realities that define people's lives.

God's powerlessness and suffering, witnessed in Scripture, is also embodied in the life of communities of faith. In so many ways, perhaps in the church's core expressions, it is engaged in powerless means and suffering. Communities of faith are precisely defined through things (or marks) that are powerless and entail suffering. Deep in the tradition from which Bonhoeffer draws much of his theological thinking, Martin Luther already described the marks of a community of faith or, as they have come to be known, "marks of the church." There are seven marks, which Luther enumerates slightly differently throughout his life. In a later list (1539), he defines these marks as the Word preached, baptism, the sacrament of the altar or Holy Communion, the office of the keys (confession and forgiveness), ministry, prayer and thanksgiving, and the cross. (Note how fundamentally liturgical these marks are!) Of course, these marks (or practices) can be conceived as utterly "religious," as something that represents the church. But what does it mean when I equate these "marks" with powerlessness?

These seven things are not designated so much as "marks" but as realities through which we would recognize a gathered people as church. Now there are obvious problems with defining the church through "marks," because a "mark" would suggest something substantive, something we could hold on to, a kind of check-off list that the faithful could use to make sure that they're "in," that they are still the privileged. Luther himself continually writes about these "things," these marks as holy possessions! But if they are possessions, then are we not back to a language of privilege? Isn't there the risk that for those who possess these things, these marks are once again blissfully secure in their privilege? We all know that the Word can be more about ourselves and, for example, a purpose-driven life. We all know that baptism can be practiced simply as a culturally sanctioned christening. We know that the sacrament of the altar can be celebrated, but the altar can have rails put all around it and be made more into what makes us feel good about ourselves. We know that the office of the keys (confession and forgiveness) can be used to control the conscience of people. We know that ministry can merely be a form of hierarchical organization, control, and exclusion. We know that prayer and thanksgiving can be mere babble. We know that the cross can be simply an image we put in our churches or use as a necklace.

Luther is obviously aware of these dangers. Even if Luther uses the language of possession, he never says that a community actually possesses these liturgical marks. In fact, these so-called marks really cannot be represented. They defy representation when by representation we understand something conventional, something that never closes the gap between itself and what it intends to represent. This failure to possess is particularly important as we reflect on Bonhoeffer's insistence on the powerlessness of God: the "holy possession" of these marks is a rather curious possession. Here is how Luther defines this kind of possession:

> [T]his holy possession is the true holy possession, the true ointment that anoints unto life eternal, even though you cannot have a papal crown or a bishop's hat, but must die bare and naked, just like children (in fact, all of us), who are baptized naked and without any adornment.[5]

Already in his exposition of the first mark (preaching the Word), Luther suggests that this possession is really not possessing anything. It is being bare and naked like children in the font. These marks attest to the Spirit's activity in our lives. The "possessing yet not possessing" characteristic is further accentuated, of course, by the last of the marks by which a community is recognized as an assembly of God — the holy possession of the cross. The cross is never something of our own choosing or something that we could posses. It is radical gift.

Another way Luther speaks about these curious possessions or marks is to emphasize their unquantifiable nature. These are living things, living in a community, and as living things they cannot be simply "represented" or codified. The Word, Luther writes, is preached, professed, believed and lived.[6] But none of these are our works; they are not things "we do" but things the Holy Spirit does to us and through us. It is in this living (and dying) that a community is recognized as belonging to God.

As I have noted above, what is striking about these possessions, of course, is that the community cannot truly possess them. These liturgical marks point to and engage a community in God's own powerlessness and

5. *Luther's Works* (LW) 41:149.
6. LW 41:149.

suffering. These are not weapons. They are not programs to defeat the enemy or tools used to conquer the world. They are, however, like a language that breaks open a community toward this powerlessness and thereby (and perhaps paradoxically) toward a secular interpretation, a secular response to this question: *Who is Christ for us today?* Why this particular emphasis on a secular response or interpretation? Precisely because the other, the one on the so-called outside — the world itself — is not an enemy or adversary or, less dramatically, a subject to be converted, tamed, brought into the sacred. In fact, the incarnation continually reminds us of the contrary: God comes into the world, in flesh and blood. The manger is not a sanctuary but a place of work and daily life. God is already active, continually creating, in the secular.

This is surprising, but it is perhaps even more surprising that we are directed toward the secular in the midst of what is inherently religious — liturgical even — for example, in a sacrament. A secular response begins in the powerlessness of baptism, in the powerlessness of resistance to the dominant culture, for instance, in the powerlessness of a few women and men opposing the Nazi war machine. The starting point of a response is not up in heaven. It is not somewhere up above the high altar in our sanctuaries. It is not in any fundamentalist reading of Scripture (which itself becomes a sort of power used to impose Scripture on others). It is not in any privilege we might have as the baptized. The starting point is found in the powerlessness of these marks, in the powerlessness of the sacraments. This powerlessness points us to the modality of God's presence in the world; it points us toward the places of vulnerability. It points us to the street, to the unexplainable, unjust, and often useless suffering of our neighbor.

The "who is Christ?" question, the ontological question about God's being, becomes a "where" question.[7] Where is Christ, God, the Holy Spirit in this world? And if God is in the street and not above our high altars or in our lovely sanctuaries, then as a liturgical theologian, I want to ask with Bonhoeffer (in his *Letters and Papers from Prison*), "What do a church, a community, a sermon, a liturgy, a Christian life mean in a religionless world?" This becomes for us a question of relevance. Does God's action (the work of the Holy Spirit) in the liturgy engage us in the street? Or how is baptism serving our neighbor? What do these marks, these curious holy possessions, mean for the world and for our life in the midst of the world? In what ways does the liturgy connect with the street and the street with the liturgy?

7. See Rasmussen, *Dietrich Bonhoeffer: Reality and Resistance*, 8off.

II. A Liturgical Event

I wish to speak of a liturgical event, actually one specific event, one histori-cal liturgical moment. And I want to ask what might be called a pneumatological question: not what that event was, but what the event be-comes, and especially what it becomes for us. My reasoning for this kind of question is simple: if we can speak about an event as if we know what hap-pened, then we have confined that event to its place; we control it and make sure it cannot become something for us. But there is something in every event that remains unknowable, something that continually comes back, even to haunt us.[8] The wind blows where it wills. So perhaps I could also ask, What is it that haunts us in this particular liturgical event that continually returns to happen for us? In order to get at this question, I started by questioning a traditional framing of the question (part I). In this section I will more closely analyze the event itself. And part three will return to the beginning and further question the framing, as if to say that any framing, theological or otherwise, is dependent on — even dictated by — the event itself.

The liturgical event I wish to engage is also a singular historical event. It occurred in Dietrich Bonhoeffer's homeland, though more than forty years after his death. The fact that it happened in the former East Germany is not incidental; it is significant. The church leaders who facili-tated this event were directly or indirectly students of Bonhoeffer. They were intensely concerned about witnessing to Christ in a communist state, about defining the church in a religionless context. They were continually asking themselves the question, *Who is Christ for us today?*

Many will remember the autumn of 1989 in eastern Europe, particu-larly in East Germany. The collapse of communist Europe had already be-gun earlier that year in Poland; but it took a visible form in East Germany — the former German Democratic Republic — with hundreds of thou-sands of people demonstrating in the streets. The entire order of a tightly controlled system was disrupted. Dresden and Leipzig were two of the cit-ies that witnessed particularly strong disruptions.

What was striking was the fact that these manifestations in Leipzig and other cities started in churches — with evening prayer. Throughout the 1980s there were many clandestine (and not so clandestine) groups

---

8. Dirk G. Lange, *Trauma Recalled: Liturgy, Disruption, Theology* (Minneapolis: For-tress, 2009), 141.

meeting in apartments and occasionally in churches. These groups were small, sometimes only four or five, sometimes a few more. They gathered for prayer and for discussion. They gathered to have a space in which to be silent, to sing, to hope. These groups, protected by the church, also attracted many who were not church members, even atheists. These groups were numerous.

As I mentioned, the groups gathered primarily for prayer, for what we would call daily, public (though not always public!) prayer. The young people would pray for those who died in the fight against tyranny and those who were imprisoned. They opened the floor so that people could share their own alienation and exclusion, and they would remember the promise of the coming kingdom. At the end of each prayer they would light a candle. Lighting candles as a sign of hope and communion is an ancient tradition in the church, stemming from the celebration of the Easter vigil, when, in the darkest part of the night, the paschal candle is lit and then subsequently all the candles in the church and those held by the assembly. (The community of Taizé, with its own practice of lighting the vigil candles every Saturday evening, had popularized this activity.) But lighting candles or a fire is also an ancient human tradition that crosses religious boundaries and touches the depth of people's hearts. It was an ecumenical symbol, where "ecumenical" means the whole gathered household (and not just a few privileged Christians).

Throughout the 1980s these prayers grew in both number and size. They became more organized, and one particular group became known as *Friedensgebete* (prayers for peace). They became more and more difficult to control, until they finally erupted in the streets in 1989, especially in Leipzig, in what came to be known as the *Montagsdemonstrationen*. The daily public prayer at the Nikolai Church in Leipzig was one of the main gathering places, though not the only one in Leipzig. In the summer of 1989 there were already 7,000 people attending, then 20,000, then 70,000, then 300,000, then over half a million people. Obviously, the church could not contain them and they poured out into the streets. I should really say that they processed out into the streets with their candles in hand. They were like a liturgical procession moving with solemnity, not toward some high altar, some mythical center of meaning, but moving sometimes with song, sometimes silently, always with determination, into the world. They processed out into the street, holding their candles. The openness of this communal prayer, taking the risk of walking out into the street, brought many other people into the street. Those praying listened and met the aspiration from the street. They went out like disciples into the darkness of their world. They went out with their own fear, their own anxiety and darkness, for they did not know what would greet them in the streets. Many were remembering Tiananmen Square in China from earlier that year; but they went out with prayer. They went out with their candles lit.

The candle became a gospel paradigm, not a religious paradigm. Through daily public prayer the young people rediscovered a paradigm that we could perhaps call *via lucis* (a way of light). The metaphor of light — light in the darkness, light as hope, light as way — became for these young people, believers and nonbelievers alike, a symbol, a language, for their own resistance to all that was dark and oppressive, all that was centralizing and stifling in the communist regime.

The candle became a special symbol: it crossed boundaries between the religious and the religionless. It represented not only hope but, most importantly, peace. It was a sign of peaceful manifestation, peaceful resistance: when you set out in procession with lighted candles to face the soldiers, you have no hands for weapons. One hand holds the candle and the other shields the candle's flame from the wind. It was this peaceful procession, streaming forth from the churches, gathering the people, this liturgical procession that brought down an oppressive political, economic, social system.

This story, this single deed, this liturgical event stimulates a question: What constitutes such an event? Indeed, what constitutes this profoundly liturgical event? In a way, there was nothing new here. There was nothing miraculous. This was not an experiment in a new church growth model or the enactment of a newly invigorated spirituality. This was only the faithfulness of a daily, public prayer — faithfulness, for some, to their baptism. So what constitutes this liturgical event? Can this event tell us something about how we are to live and especially how we are to witness in the world? And how might this event inform the church regarding how it lives missionally (that is, participates in God's mission) in the world?

In this event, there is most certainly a liturgical disruption. Already the act of coming to these clandestine prayers in the late 1970s and early '80s was a disruption, a dangerous rupture of one's daily life routine. It could have meant imprisonment. It could have meant — and often did mean — reprisals at work, loss of benefits, and so on. But in order to answer the question *Who is Christ for us today?* these young people did not claim their baptism as a right, as a privilege, but responded to the challenge of their calling. Daily they entered into the waters to be drowned, to

become again like Jesus — powerless. Daily they took the risk of living unrehearsed characters — improvising, if you will, on stage. And what was
their weapon? Or perhaps one might better ask, What was their script?
Prayer! A simple daily, but public prayer. And suddenly the unbaptized
also began coming to this prayer and to this forum. The Holy Spirit's work
was not to be seen in any "claim" or special calling that these young people
demonstrated, but precisely in the unrehearsed, unknowing participation
in a work that could not be defined or even understood in its happening.
Isn't the gospel always the surprise of the unrehearsed?

This liturgical manifestation did not mean just personal disruption;
it also brought with it institutional disruption. It broke open the doors of
the church, when church leaders realized that the doors of the church had
to be open. They knew that the doors had to be open to even those who
might betray them. They allowed the small gatherings to happen in church
sanctuaries and basements. Despite their agreement with state authorities
to curb political sermons and activities, they still opened up churches for a
public prayer that gave space to secular society to express itself. The concerns and anguish, the issues of secular life, were welcomed into the
church. Of course, as the prayers grew in size and the discussions became
more and more political, there was fear; but there was also a deep realization that the gospel calls us to keep the doors open "for coming in and going out."

These small groups of Christians were a form of *ekklesia* (the assembly, or gathering), of "those who are called forth, not regarding ourselves
from a religious point of view as specially favored, but rather as belonging
wholly to the world." They listened to the voice, the call of Jesus; but the
cry of Jesus was to be heard in their neighbor, in the "other," regardless of
his or her political or religious orientation. Christ became not an object of
adoration or of praise but a Christ disseminated in the world. Bonhoeffer
asked, "What is the place of worship and prayer in a religionless situation?"[9] Part of the answer, I would like to say, is this prayer in the heart of
society, in the heart of the world; this prayer with open doors; this prayer
as welcome and resistance, even spiritual resistance; this prayer as liturgical procession that flows out into the streets.

It was this prayer, this liturgical resistance, that brought about an
equally important and even wider systemic disruption. The liturgical event
disrupted the foundations, the laws, the values of an entire society. And the

9. Bonhoeffer, *Letters and Papers from Prison*, 280-81.

ultimate disruption came with the rupture in the Berlin Wall and its collapse. What began as a liturgical resistance in prayer — a baptismal disruption — climaxed in the rupture of an entire political-cultural system.

III. Rethinking Baptism

Disruption, displacement through a simple, repeated liturgical event: in this case, through daily public prayer. That prayer provided a room, a welcome, and a space for disruption. I want to say that daily public prayer offered a space where believers could rehearse and improvise their baptismal identity as belonging to the world. Improvisation was a key characteristic of this identity. Though these young people and their pastors simply used what the tradition gave them (communal prayer), they adapted the form to their specific, often crisis-filled, situation. In its most basic form, communal prayer consists of psalmody and intercessory prayer. The singing and meditation on the Psalms constitutes in itself the proclamation of the Word. This singing was often followed by a Scripture reading (though perhaps not always) and then by intense prayer for the needs of the world, figuratively opening up the gathered assembly to the outside world.

The prayers in Leipzig varied from place to place, but generally they consisted of a short reading; then announcements by individuals of things that had happened over the past week in the city (though these announcements were more like short readings in themselves — "testimonies," we might call them — very specifically relating to events of the week); then a short homily and intercessory prayer. Songs were sung throughout: often the same songs were used from week to week as if to help aid the participation of all those seeking but not yet versed in Christian hymnody. They used many songs from Taizé and other songs in foreign languages, as if to bring the whole world into a place that was literally walled off from the world.

Daily public prayer was lived out by these Christians as an unexpected baptismal improvisation or discipline.[10] They did not know what would happen, or what would be said (particularly in the time for "announcements").

Dietrich Bonhoeffer did not speak specifically about a baptismal dis-

---

10. For use of this phrase, see Glenn L. Borreson, "Bonhoeffer on Baptism: Discipline for the Sake of the Gospel," *Word and World* 1, no. 1 (1981): 20-31.

cipline, but he did speak about a secret discipline alive within the gathered assembly. How this secret discipline is to be defined remains a subject of debate, but I would like to propose that it is closely related to baptism. In baptism, as Bonhoeffer points out, we have made a break from the world, and this break is absolute. But this break has nothing esoteric about it: we are not initiated into a secret society. Rather, as we have just seen, this break immediately pushes us back toward the world. We become part of a community that receives the "cross" as gift, a community that follows Jesus publicly.[11] In Luther's enumeration of the marks of the church (see above), the seventh is the "holy possession of the cross." There are not many "societies" that promise their new recruits a cross. There are not many "societies" that are asked to "endure every misfortune and persecution . . . inward sadness, timidity, fear, outward poverty, contempt, illness, and weakness, in order to become like their head, Christ."[12] This suffering — and here lies the main point — is not just personal misfortune or suffering that befalls an individual in life; it is a public suffering because of one's adherence to the Word of God, which contradicts the values, goals, and privileges of society.

Bonhoeffer can call this public discipline of the community "secret" because the world does not recognize the source of the discipline: the world does not recognize the cross. Christians are "in" the world but not "of" the world. The world does not recognize the marks and power of the cross living in the community. The world is looking for "possessions," whereas this community is "possessed." Often the community of the faithful is labeled weak, insignificant, pacifist, perhaps even unpatriotic. No one, for example, cared about or paid attention to these little prayer groups gathering in East Germany during the 1950s, '60s, '70s, and '80s. The immediate and obvious explanation of the fall of the Berlin Wall, according to our more sophisticated Western intelligence, was American military superiority. That does not recognize the witness to the gospel. The words of Psalm 33:17-19 — "The war horse is a vain hope for victory, and by its great might it cannot save. Truly the eye of the Lord is on those who fear him, on those who hope in his steadfast love, to deliver their soul from death, and to keep them alive in famine" — take on a truly specific meaning.

In *Letters and Papers from Prison*, Bonhoeffer clearly declares that the discipline of the Christian life is "living unreservedly in life's duties, problems, successes and failures, experiences, and perplexities. In so doing we

11. Bonhoeffer, *Discipleship* (Minneapolis: Fortress, 2003), 208, 210.
12. LW 41:161.

throw ourselves completely into the arms of God, taking seriously, not our own sufferings, but those of God in the world. . . ."[13] Though it may be described as a secret discipline, though it is often unrecognized, baptism does pull us out of the world only to throw us back into the world in order to find God suffering in our neighbor — unrecognized by the world. Baptism understood as communion in the suffering and death of Christ means also a communion in the suffering and death of the world, our neighbor, the "other."

Please note this important Lutheran move and its implications. It is, I might say, counterintuitive, even countercultural. Baptism is not just a cute little ceremony celebrated on a Sunday morning and saved in our family photo album. Baptism is not for us to keep as a secret, nor to hide under a bushel. But this is nothing new. We all know that we are called to live our faith in the world. The question is how we are to do that. And it is in answering this question that we discover in baptism a reorientation of our understanding of call and sending. Baptism sets us on a road where we hear God's voice in the wound of Jesus — where, in the wound of the other, our neighbor, we hear Jesus calling. Baptism sets us out on a road on which we encounter God in the street waiting for us. Baptism is, to repeat, not a privilege but a stepping into God's own powerlessness and suffering.

Baptism is this immersion in the life of Jesus Christ, which means it is an immersion into both his death and life, which means it is an immersion into both the suffering and the hope of the world. We may go so far as to say this: when we are baptized and made into children of God, when we are baptized and made into a new people, when we are baptized and become part of the communion of saints, that communion is defined by a communion in the suffering of our neighbor. The suffering of the world becomes our suffering and demands our response, demands, as Bonhoeffer puts it, "obedience" or discipleship — not to some imagined authority or law but to the cry from the street. Baptism is this radical reorientation of life. It is also a radical reorientation of our life in community and as community in the world.

In this reorientation, resistance is simply lived as faith: faith not in our own capacities (for our human nature would never take the risk of death), but faith given by the one who took the risk of death and defeated death. This resistance is, at its heart, living out the baptismal promise, living an unrehearsed role. Just like those young people in East Germany, we

---

13. Bonhoeffer, *Letters and Papers from Prison*, 370.

do not know where this role — this promise — will take us. We do not know whom we will meet and what the welcome will be like.

Jesus sends the seventy out without possessions and to greet the unexpected with peace. "Go on your way. See, I am sending you out like lambs into the midst of wolves. Carry no purse, no bag, no sandals; and greet no one on the road. Whatever house you enter, first say, 'Peace to this house!' And if anyone is there who shares in peace, your peace will rest on that person; but if not, it will return to you" (Luke 10:3-6). Living out a baptismal discipline is never claiming a possession or living out a privilege. It is being continually immersed in the unexpected; it is being dispossessed.

But why speak about baptism? What does it have to do with daily communal prayer? Martin Luther already made a connection between daily public prayer and baptism. He does not speak about a "break," as Bonhoeffer does, nor does he use the word "disruption," as I have done; but listen to his definition of daily public prayer from the *Large Catechism:*

> Nothing is so powerfully effective against the devil, the world, the flesh, and all evil thoughts as to occupy one's self with God's Word, to speak about it and meditate upon it, in the way that Psalm 1:2 calls those blessed who "meditate on God's law day and night." Without doubt, you will offer up no more powerful incense or savor against the devil than to occupy yourself with God's commandments and words and to speak, sing, or think about them. Indeed, this is the true holy water and sign that drives away the devil and puts him to flight.[14]

The definition of daily prayer here is large: it is meditation on the Word, and it is occupying oneself with the commandments, speaking, singing, and meditating on them. Luther uses the metaphor of baptism to describe daily prayer. Daily prayer — this "holy water and sign" — drives the devil away, drives the darkness away, breaks the gates of hell, opens the gates of trust. Daily prayer is a sign of our baptism. It is not a second baptism; rather, it is a continual remembrance of the rupture and displacement that baptism already effected in our lives. It is living into this rupture, this displacement.

This prayer does not have as its goal a centered, balanced life, a sanctified life or growth in spiritual perfection. It does not fit into the mold of what today we might call spirituality, as if we were to be "saved" through

---

14. Robert Kolb and Timothy Wengert, eds., *The Book of Concord*, "The Large Catechism" (preface) (Minneapolis: Fortress, 2000), 381.

such a practice. Daily prayer, for Luther, is more down to earth — literally. Daily prayer, communal and individual, "remembers" the paschal mystery just as the young people in East Germany remembered this mystery: engaging this prayer, praising God's name, lamenting God's absence. I believe that living out daily public prayer as these young Christians did was a visible manifestation of their baptismal vocation. They were literally practicing their baptism.[15] The world certainly did not recognize it, and perhaps these young people did not recognize it either. But at the heart of their practice, and in that faithfulness, the Spirit acts. The devil flees, and the powers of oppression are brought down.

Daily public prayer defeats the devil, Luther said. And today we can say along with him, "Daily public prayer defeats evil in its many manifestations." Daily public prayer defeated the oppressive, stifling, despotic regimes in Eastern Europe. And Luther calls us — though I should perhaps say, even more importantly, our baptism calls us — to this continual practice of daily prayer in our society today — for spiritual renewal and nourishment, to be sure, but more as witnessing to the cross present in our world today.

What does this mean for the life of the church? How does this impact or help us rethink God's agency in the world? Or, what does this liturgical event, this particular baptismal practice, tell us about a missional theology and a missional church? How do we make this liturgical event our own?

First, I believe, it places worship at the heart of the life of baptized people. Communal prayer is a characteristic, one of the defining marks, of a Christian community. It is not something we do because we want to be spiritually enriched; we come together to prayer (and we pray privately, on our own) because that is simply what Christians do! It is a fundamental trait: it is in the DNA of any Christian community. In interviews that I conducted with many participants in these prayers, both young people and pastors, I heard over and over again that they came together because they understood themselves to be resistance fighters, even though the word "resistance" *(Widerstand)* was not part of their vocabulary.[16] They came together to pray because praying together is part of our calling, part of our life together as Christians.

Second, when engaging in communal prayer, a community discovers

---

15. Luther, "The Large Catechism," 461.

16. See my forthcoming work on a theology of communal prayer based on my work in East Germany.

that, rather than retreating from the world, they actually become more engaged in the world. Communal prayer drives the community into the street. This already happens figuratively when, as we pray for the needs of the world, we are really opening the windows and doors of our buildings to the cry of the neighbor.

But perhaps most significantly, and related to both of the above comments, this prayer is one way in which — or through which — God is continually inserting a community into God's plan, into God's own life, God's own powerlessness and suffering. It is not our action plan, not our "possession," for it is a "holy" possession — God's language given to us. Daily public prayer conforms us to the cruciform Christ, with all that that implies (death and resurrection).

A missional church steps into the triune God's mission in all creation, but this mission is characterized (perhaps first) by God's own vulnerability. This vulnerability is lived in the community by an extreme attentiveness to context and margins. And this attentiveness to the need around us, to the cry of our culture, is lived as improvisation, our continually responding to what is unexpected. The marks of the church, those liturgical things such as baptism and communion, preaching and praying, those things are lived — the Word itself is lived — not as privileged possessions but as continual improvisations embodying in our communities that powerlessness of God that defeats evil. That powerlessness, that vulnerability is critical, so that when the world sees the light of the resurrection, when walls crumble and people are freed, it is not human beings or power that is praised, but God. And through this praise, they too, churched or unchurched, participate in God's continual mission in the world.